APPLES, APPLES, APPLES

Apples, Apples, Apples

Judith Comfort and Katherine Chute

1986
Doubleday Canada Limited, Toronto, Ontario
Doubleday & Company, Inc., Garden City, New York

Library of Congress Catalog Card Number: 86–6236
Copyright © 1986 by Judith Comfort and Katherine Chute
All rights reserved
First edition

Interior design by The Dragon's Eye Press
Typesetting by Compeer Typographic Services Limited
Printed and bound in Canada by Gagne Printing

Canadian Cataloguing in Publication Data

Comfort, Judith.
  Apples, apples, apples — an apple cookbook

Includes index.
ISBN 0-385-25055-X

1. Cookery (Apples).   I. Chute, Kathy.
II. Title

TX813.A6C66 1986   641.6'411   C86-094035-7

Library of Congress Cataloging in Publication Data

Comfort, Judith.
  Apples, apples, apples.

1. Cookery (apples).   I. Chute, Kathy.   II. Title.
TX813.A6C66 1986   641.6'411   86-6236
ISBN 0-385-25055-X

For John, Andrea, and Matthew with love

K.C.

For Jean, David, and Cherie

J.C.

And for people who care for our future by planting historic apple trees of the past

Contents

Preface

The apple trees we grew up with were crayon drawings — green smudges of leaves with red circles of fruit on brown, post-like trunks. Real backyard apple trees, the kind you climbed, lazed in, and took for granted belonged to children in the poems we read by Robert Frost and Dylan Thomas.

Kathy grew up with the jungle in her backyard. Avocados and cashews thrived. Whenever a recipe called for apples, her mother substituted mangoes. In my backyard in western Canada, the frost went so deep and stayed so long, that only hardy crabapples survived. For both of us, every apple was a precious individual.

We were grown before we saw apple orchards in the spring — acres of fragrant pinky-white blossoms. We were grown before we saw bending apple tree limbs, heavy with fruit. We could hardly believe how crunchy the apples were fresh off the tree; how ambrosial the just-pressed cider. As adults we planted our own apple trees in our own backyards. And it was with special appreciation that we approached this project.

Studying the differences in apple varieties was fascinating. We drove to the orchards of the Annapolis Valley in Nova Scotia. Here, the river has carved a rich agricultural flood plain. The North and South Mountains rise up on either side of the valley and provide the perfect slope for apple trees.

We bought dozens of varieties of apples, carefully placing samples in paper bags marked with their names. One Sunday morning, we had a family taste test. We lined up all the apples on the kitchen table. Our two small girls, Anna and Ruthie, scientifically compared the colours and shapes. We went through the grand ritual of cutting off small pieces and passing them around. Everyone expressed their opinion. We nibbled on Golden Delicious, Northern Spy, and a cross between the two, Spigold. We decided it looked like the Spy, but tasted more like the Delicious.

We compared Nova Scotia Red Delicious with British Columbia Red Delicious (much, much bigger!). We blindfolded each other to see if we could tell the difference between the Golden and Red Delicious (we couldn't). After far too many apples, we abandoned the Great Apple Test in favor of a sunny Sunday walk. On our return, we made another scientific discovery. Amongst the abandoned apple remnants we found varieties which had turned brown (the apples with the yellowish flesh). Others, like the Cortland, remained relatively unchanged.

Our curiosity was piqued by this first test and we wanted to taste as many varieties as possible. Considering the thousands of varieties grown in North America, not to mention those imported from around the world, this was a formidable task. So we gathered samples from as far afield as we could. One friend, visiting California at Christmas, smuggled us home a Newtown Pippin. It didn't taste like anything grown in Nova Scotia. It was a memorably tart apple that reminded us of pineapple.

In writing this book we worked our way, literally, through bushels of apples. Andrea, our fourteen-year-old, peeled most of them and analyzed the results with teenage taste buds. We took perfect, beautiful, red fruit and reduced it to mush. We bombarded it with spices, squished it into juice and fermented it into vinegar. We did so not because we felt there was anything upon which to improve; nothing beats a good fresh apple. But pie is just as good, in its own way. We feel the same way about the other two hundred or more other apple combinations in this book.

We collected recipes from many cultures and tried every one of them out in our own kitchens. Of course we have our favorites. Matthew, who is five, has made his mother promise she will make the chocolate-chip applesauce cake for his next birthday, and for every other birthday, ever after. And the apple cordial has become a New Year's Eve tradition. We hope that you too will find, in this book, some of your favorite apple recipes.

Judith Comfort   Katherine Chute
Port Medway, Nova Scotia   Milton, Nova Scotia
June 1986

Acknowledgments

We would like to thank the following people and institutions whose help and encouragement were instrumental in preparing this book:

Jerry Miner, Librarian at the Kentville Research Station Library; Bill Craig, Tree Fruit Specialist at the Kentville Research Station; Jean Comfort in Pennsylvania; Carlotta and David Smith in Bowen Island, B.C.; Judith Emerson of Emerson Nursery, Portland, Oregon; David Putt, of Jack Putt Orchards, Argenta, B.C.; Mary Nell Towner, and her Mom in California; Mr. Kale at Farmer's Dairy, Bedford, N.S; Ellen Folvik; Gail Hamlin; Mrs. Alice White; Sandy Brown; Honey Macumber; Phyllis Emerson; Lance Woolaver; Food Advisory Services, Canada Department of Agriculture; Home Economics Division, Nova Scotia Department of Agriculture and Marketing; Wendy Elliott, Alan Comfort, and Steven Slipp of Customs House (for planting an apple seed of an idea); thanks also to all the people who answered the question, "What's your favorite apple, and why?"; and, finally, special thanks to Philippa Campsie for her long-distance patience and to Denise Schon for her vote of confidence.

CHAPTER ONE

All Kinds of Apples

Thousands of varieties of apples were grown in North America at the turn of the century. About fifty types are still being grown commercially, but chances are, when you go to your local store to buy apples, you will find Red Delicious, Golden Delicious, McIntosh, or Granny Smith apples. These are some of the few varieties that have survived the fierce competition in the modern business of agriculture. Why?

THEY GROW WELL. They are resistant to diseases and invasions of insects, and respond well to chemicals. The trees are sturdy and can be pruned by modern mechanical methods. Importantly, they bear fruit every year in great abundance.

THEY STORE WELL. The apples you buy in May have been off the tree for at least four months. Relatively thick skins and dry flesh enables them to last longer. Also, they respond well to coatings and wax sprays which prolong their shelf life, and also the chemicals used in oxygen-reduced storage places.

THEY SHIP WELL. They don't bruise easily. Those Golden Delicious you find in the corner store in New Brunswick, Alaska, and Florida are also shipped to Saudi Arabia and Hong Kong. The Red Delicious always *look* shiny, red, and tasty.

These apples have risen to the top of the marketplace because they provide the greatest number of reasonably tasty, attractive apples for the greatest number of people at the best price.

APPLE VARIETIES

Local and Old-Fashioned Varieties

There are other apples commonly available in certain regions at specific times of year. If you live in Nova Scotia or California, your favorite pie apple is probably a Gravenstein. Right off the tree, it is a wonderful crisp, juicy, sour apple. But it colors best in the cool climate that only Nova Scotia can provide. It turns bland and mealy, however, a month off the tree. Most Pennsylvanians have never tasted a Gravenstein, but love Staymans for eating and cooking.

Whether Nova Scotians will ever be able to buy Staymans or Pennsylvanians be able to buy Gravensteins depends on the farmer's ability to market the fruit, and the development of new strains of these old favorites which will make them more adaptable to different climates.

So what of the non-commercially-viable (but ambrosia-flavored, old-fashioned) varieties (the Red Astrachan, the Esopus Spitzenburg, the Bough Sweet)? They are still grown, and with a little effort, you can still buy them.

Early apples like the Transparent, which are sweet, but bruise easily because they are full of water, cannot be found in large supermarkets, fifty miles away from the orchard. Stores find it difficult to handle small quantities of little-known varieties. But travel to an apple growing area, in season! Basketfuls of Transparents will be found at roadside stands, at farmers' markets, and in local stores. Better still, pick your own, and enjoy the azure blue sky, as well as the crunchiest apples you've ever tasted.

Variations on a Theme

Apples are living things. All trees of one variety have been cloned from the wood of a single original tree. But like identical twins raised by different adoptive parents, other factors affect their growth and eventually their fruit.

Consider one tree in one orchard. The first year it bears fruit, it is young and healthy, and the fruit is of a good quality. The second year, there is a frost during blossoming and half the flowers are damaged (result: fewer but larger apples). Next year there are downpours during the blossoming and the bees cannot pollinate (result: fewer apples). Another season is marked by a lack of rain (smaller, drier, fruit) and an early frost so that apples are hastily picked before optimum ripening (result: hard bland-flavored apples). By this time the tree is older and the soil around it is depleted of nutrients but the orchardist possibly cannot afford to fertilize (result: unhealthy tree, susceptible to insects and fungi; fruit with a different flavor).

Now take a wood graft (scion) off that tree. Transport it one thousand miles to a different orchard with different roots, soil, sun, temperatures, and insect predators. See how the size, flavor, and texture of the fruit differs. Modern British Columbia McIntoshes may be twice the size of the fruit borne on the original tree discovered in Dundas, Ontario, in 1796.

If you are lucky enough to pick your own apples, do a little taste test. Take a bite out of the apples of half-a-dozen trees of the same variety. You will be surprised at the difference from tree to tree.

New Varieties

No matter how good it may taste, an apple is useless unless it can be grown economically. The problem today is one of scale. Years ago, apples that tasted good, bore fruit every other year or so, and were relatively free of insects were naturally selected and planted in a lot of backyards. Today, however, very few people grow their own fruit. Large orchard owners cannot afford to plant trees that take over ten years to bear fruit or, because of size, are difficult to pick or prune.

Most recent varieties have been developed to help commercial orchardists grow and sell more apples. The trend is to plant smaller trees and to plant them more densely. The struggle among apple breeders is to develop strains that fill in the time gap between the summer and more numerous fall apples to satisfy that interim market. They have been working on earlier and earlier strains, usually by crossing fall apples with early summer varieties (McIntosh × Yellow Transparent = Milton). They also breed for hardier strains of popular varieties which can withstand colder climates and plant diseases.

Sensitive to market studies showing people prefer red apples over green, yellow, orange, and striped types, nurseries have been developing apple strains of red, redder, reddest. Unfortunately this often coincides with apple flavor that is bland, blander, and blandest.

Seeds and Clones

In the old days, a person would pick an apple off their favorite tree, eat it, take the seed, and plant it. Fertilized through open pollination, the new mongrel tree would have only half the genetic makeup of the original apple tree. Some of the surprise results of this essentially hit-and-miss method were superior apples. But many were tasteless, useless apples. A more scientific method involves carefully fertilizing the flowers of the favorite tree with the pollen of another noted variety. The Empire is a cross between a McIntosh and a Red Delicious. Either way, it takes years before the tree grows up and bears fruit, before you know if the cross was worthwhile.

Single branches of apple trees sometimes show slight variations from the rest of the tree. The branch may have more fruit closer together, or fruit that is more uniformly shaped or deeply colored. It may be free of insects while the rest of the tree is infested. These living sports or mutations (which occur as living wood or leaf buds) are removed, and grafted onto their own roots. They develop into separate trees with their own special qualities.

COMPARING APPLES AND APPLES: HOW DO VARIETIES DIFFER?

SEASON: Apple trees flower (March to June) and bear ripe fruit (July to November) at different times.

FLAVOR (taste and fragrance): Some apples taste and smell like wine, others like wet paper.

TEXTURE: Flesh textures vary from hard, crisp, and juicy to soft, mealy and dry. The skins may be thick, thin, shiny or rough.

COLOR: Apples are red, green, and yellow with infinite combinations of these colors in stripes and blushes.

SIZE: Some small apples are less than 2 inches (50 mm) in diameter, others are over 3 inches (85 mm).

SHAPE: Apples may be round, flat, conical, or oblong-shaped, but are usually a combination. They may be smooth and symmetrical or pitted, bumpy, and lopsided.

KEEPING QUALITY: Some apples keep in the fridge only one week; others are still good to eat after seven months.

Season

EARLY SUMMER (JULY/AUGUST) APPLES are typically pale colored (green, yellow, or pink), watery, and mild-flavored. They bruise easily and can be stored in the fridge for a week or two before their flavor fades and they become soft.

MIDDLE SEASON, SUMMER (AUGUST/EARLY SEPTEMBER) APPLES are more intensely colored and flavored. They store nicely for a month or two at best.

LATE FALL, WINTER (LATE SEPTEMBER/DECEMBER) APPLES stay on the trees through the cold fall nights and this coincides with stronger flavor, more intense coloring, thicker skins, drier flesh, and better keeping qualities. Kept at moist temperatures just above the freezing point, these will last for many months.

Approximate Order of Ripening

The order of ripening will vary slightly depending on the climate, geography, and strain of the variety planted.

Early Apples

Transparent, Lodi, Quinte, Vista Bella, Julyred, Melba, Puritan, Red Astrachan, Mantet, Jersey Mac, Tydeman's Red, State Fair, Redfree, Hazen, Beacon, Burgundy, Blaze, Niagara, Murray, Akane, Early Cortland, Paulared, Summer Treat, Gala, Gravenstein, Wealthy, Mollie's Delicious, Barry, Ozark Gold, Hawaii Gold Jonamac, Novamac, Prima, Lobo

Mid-Season Apples

McIntosh, Britegold, Jonafree, Spartan, Cortland, Macoun, Sweet Sixteen, Liberty, Sir Prize, Red Delicious, Empire, Jonathan, Rhode Island Greening, Honeygold, Fameuse, Twenty Ounce, Priscilla, Macfree, Moira

Late Season Apples

Northwestern Greening, Gloster, Cox's Orange Pippin, King, Roxbury Russet, Jonagold, Golden Delicious, Keepsake, Spigold, Melrose, Idared, Winter Banana, Seek-No-Further, Tolman Sweet, Hubbardston Nonsuch, Baldwin, Regent, Nova, Easygro, Priam, York, Northern Spy, Esopus, Spitzenburg, Wagener, Golden Russet, Mutsu, Stayman, Rome, Winesap, Newtown, Pippin, Jerseyred, Granny Smith

---

Flavor and Texture: Apple Taste and Your Taste in Apples

You can read whole books on the history and cultivation of apple trees. Field books give you elaborate physical descriptions of apples: the shape, size, color, details of the eye (flower end), and cavity (stalk end). When it comes to telling you what an apple tastes like, however, these sources are usually reduced to vague generalizations like "fine rich flavor, crisp, firm, sweet, aromatic, juicy." Even cookbooks are at a loss to describe this very common, but descriptively elusive, fruit.

Not that people haven't tried. Food scientists have chemically analyzed apples. They can tell one variety from another by the percentage of alcohols, esters, carbonyls, ethers, and lactones. Food chemists at one Canadian Agricultural Research Station have even managed to capture and patent the essence of fresh apple aroma. They crush a vat of apples into a hundred gallons of sauce and juice and separate the essential odors. They condense and concentrate this until they have less than an ounce of odorless dry granules. This appley flavor is sold and later found in everything from bubble gum to shampoo.

A whole fresh apple, though, is a magical combination of flavors, smells, and textures that vastly outstrips the sum of its analyzed parts. An apple is a living thing that cannot be recreated in the lab, and why an individual likes the taste of one variety and not that of another is a mystery. Psychologists and nutritionists may have theories. They say people in general prefer redder, sweeter apples. How do you explain, then, the runaway success of the Granny Smith—a sour green but outstandingly crisp and juicy apple? It doesn't really matter. Your own senses should be the only judge. Buy and eat what you like.

Apple Flavors
You may find this list helpful in selecting one type of apple over another.

SWEET APPLES (THOSE WITH AN ABSENCE OF TARTNESS): Baldwin, Ben Davis, Red Delicious, Rome Beauty, most summer apples (especially sweet varieties).

MEDIUM TART APPLES: Cortland, Cox's Orange Pippin, Fameuse, Golden Russet, McIntosh, Ribston Pippin, Roxbury Russet, Stayman Winesap, Wayne, Winesap, York Imperial.

HIGHLY TART APPLES: Gravenstein, Jonathan, Northern Spy, Rhode Island Greening, Newtown Pippin, Wealthy, Esopus Spitzenburg, Wayne.

AROMATIC APPLES: McIntosh, Gravenstein, Ribston Pippin, Golden Russet, Cox's Orange Pippin, Delicious, Fameuse, Golden Delicious, Roxbury Russet, Wealthy, Northern Spy, Winter Banana.

ASTRINGENT APPLES: (Astringent apples contain tannin which puckers up your mouth like strong tea. It gives wine or cider a full, round body.): Crabapples, Lindel, Newtown Pippin, Red Astrachan.

Color

As consumers, we have come to associate redness with sweetness and ripeness in fruits and vegetables. What can be better than a warm sun-ripened tomato right off the vine? Perfectly ripe apples, however, may be green, red, or yellow, or any combination of these colors. Ruby red apples don't necessarily taste any better than grass green ones. Underripe or unhealthy apples may also be green, so sometimes it is hard to know what you are buying. If we get to know what color is expected in certain varieties, then we will be better judges in the grocery store.

For a number of reasons, heat during the growing season brings out color. If it has been a cold season, you may find apples greener than is usual. The contrast between warm days and cool nights is another factor. That's why Gravensteins color so beautifully in Nova Scotia, but not in Ontario where nights are substantially warmer. If the tree is overfed with nitrogen, most of the food energy goes into the production of leaves, and the fruit may be softer and greener.

Apples color according to where they hang on the tree and how much sunlight penetrates the tree. Apples are blushed on the sunny-side out. The best, reddest apples always seem to be just beyond our fingertips on the uppermost, most exposed branches!

Size

Apples come in a variety of sizes, but are commonly grouped into the following three categories: small (1¾ to 2⅛ inches or 45 to 54 mm); medium (2⅜ to 2¾ inches or 60 to 69 mm); and large (2⅞ to 3¼ inches or 75 to 84 mm).

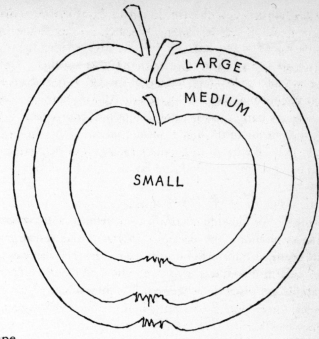

LARGE

MEDIUM

SMALL

Shape

Round

Flat

Conical

Oblong

Keeping Quality

As an apple ripens on and, later, off the tree, it is preparing to provide its seeds with a growing medium for the next season — a thick cellulose mat full of plant food (chemical energy). Ripening involves two basic chemical processes. We welcome these natural processes for they change hard, sour, inedible lumps into choice food for us.

Near the outside of the apple, sugar combines with the oxygen in the air. It breaks down to produce carbon dioxide, water, and chemical energy. This is called respiration. Apples dry out as they ripen.

On the inside of the apple, sugar breaks down without oxygen to produce carbon dioxide, alcohol, and chemical energy. This is anaerobic respiration. The alcohol combines with the acid in the apple to produce esters which give off powerful odors. Apples become more aromatic as they ripen. The acid flavor is changed and so apples get progressively sweeter as they ripen.

Characteristics of the Natural Ripening Process

Unripe	Ripe	Overripe
dense/hard	crunchy/crisp/softer	chewy/mealy
green	light green/yellow/red	dull/fading to brown
sour	sour/sweet	sweet/bland
astringent skin	sweet, aromatic skin	chemical/tasteless skin
little odor	perfume/aromatic	perfume/aromatic
dense/moist	juicy	dry
high pectin	less pectin	cellulose (woody texture)
starch	sugar	more sugar

You Be the Judge: Take an apple in hand . . .

1. What does it look like? Is the skin red, green, or yellow, or a combination, striped or blushed? Is it shiny, dull, or russeted? Is it small, medium, or large; lopsided, conical, flat, spherical, or oblong?
2. How does it feel in your hand? Is the skin greasy, smooth, rough, heavy, light, or pitted? Squeeze the apple. Is it hard and firm, or soft and punky?
3. Cut it open. What color is the flesh? Is it white, cream, tinged green, tinged pink, or yellowish? Does it turn brown quickly?
4. What does it smell like? Does it have no odor at all, or a heavy perfume noticeable even across the room?
5. What does it taste like? Is it generally tart, sweet, or bland?

Here is a mini dictionary of words to help you describe the aroma and taste of apples: sweet, sharp, bitter, ethereal, alcoholic, mild, pleasant, powerful, fruity-winey, penetrating, fatty, grassy-green, intense, caramel-like, brandylike, pungent, pearlike, rumlike, bananalike, pineapplelike, winelike, coffee-like, woody, warm, herbaceous, oily, peachlike, aniselike.

6. Is there an aftertaste? How would you describe it?
7. What is the texture like? Is it firm, crisp, mealy, coarse, fine, soft, granular, smooth, or delicate?

BASIC APPLES AND THEIR DESCENDANTS

Six common varieties provide much of the breeding stock for hundreds of varieties. You've probably tasted most of them: Golden Delicious, Jonathan, McIntosh, Northern Spy, Red Delicious, and Rome Beauty. As an example, it's not hard to imagine what a Spigold (a cross between a Northern Spy and a Golden Delicious) is like. It looks like a Spy and is juicy and crisp like a Spy, but has a flavor more closely approximating a Golden Delicious.

When "?" appears in the list of descendants, it means that the tree was open-pollinated and the other parent is unknown, or that it was a complex scientific cross.

Golden Delicious

The Golden Delicious is a sunshine yellow apple with a dry skin and creamy sweet flesh. It has a distinctive aromatic flavor that is actually enhanced by cooking. It takes a while to fall or break apart in cooking and so is good to use in recipes where you would like apple pieces to hold their shape. Although similar to a Red Delicious in name and flavor, it is not genetically related. It was discovered in Clay County, West Virginia, in 1890 and is thought to have grown from a seed which was a cross between a Golden Reinette and a Grimes Golden (discovered in 1804, in Brook County, West Virginia). Over thirty mutations of Golden Delicious have been developed, mostly to improve the skin texture (non-russeting types) and storing quality (they tend to shrivel).

Descendants

Variety	Golden Delicious crossed with:
Criterion	? (possibly Red Delicious or Winter Banana)
Gala (*See* World Varieties)	Kidd's Orange Red
Jonagold	Jonathan
Developed in 1943 in Geneva, N.Y., this red-on-yellow apple tastes more like a Jonathan.	
Mollie's Delicious	(Golden Delicious × Edgewood) × (Red Gravenstein × Close)
Mutsu (Crispin) (*See* World Varieties)	Indo
Ozark Gold (*See* Red Delicious)	
Sinta	Grimes Golden
Spencer	McIntosh
Spigold	Red Spy
Introduced in 1962 in Geneva, N.Y.	
Summerred	McIntosh (open-pollinated)

Delicious (or Red Delicious)

From a tree discovered growing in Peru, Iowa, in 1870, has come the best-known apple in the world. Brilliant marketing at the turn of the century ensured the popularity of this glossy, red apple with the distinctive five-pointed elongated shape. At its best, it has a special, sweet (never sour) perfumelike flavor. Because of its tough skin, it never shrivels and has a lengthy shelf life. Although fresh Delicious may be crisp, juicy, and "delicious," many apples past their prime are sold, giving Delicious a reputation for mealiness and blandness. Over one hundred mutant variations have been developed, mostly to produce larger and (is it possible?) redder apples.

Descendants

Variety	Delicious crossed with:
Empire	McIntosh
(*See* McIntosh)	
Gloster	Glocken × Richared
Hazen	Duchess × Starking (Delicious mutation)
Holly	Jonathan
Jonadel	Jonathan
Lindel	Linda
Melrose	Jonathan

Developed in Wooster, Ohio, around 1937, Melrose is sweet but zippier than the Delicious. It resembles a Jonathan, stores very well, and is the official state apple of Ohio.

Ozark Gold	Golden Delicious × (Red Delicious × Conrad)
Priscilla	?
Ruby	Rome × Starking (Delicious mutation)

Jonathan

A redder version of its probable parent the Esopus Spitzenburg, the
Jonathan was discovered in 1826 in Woodstock, Ulster County, New
York. It is a good all-purpose crimson apple with a sweet, some say
spicy, flavor. It is not as widely grown as it once was, however, as it
does not adapt to modern storage and transportation methods as
well as other varieties. Jonathan has been bred extensively. You will
be able to find a few of these varieties locally.

Descendants

Variety	Jonathan crossed with:
Akane	Worcester Pearmain
Holiday	Macoun (McIntosh × Jersey Black)
Idared	Wagener

> This bright, solid, red apple is now being grown extensively, probably
> because of its excellent keeping ability. Developed in Moscow, Idaho,
> around 1935, its fresh tart flavor mellows in storage and takes on an
> almost winelike taste.

Jonagold (*See* Golden Delicious)	Golden Delicious
Jonagram	Ingram
Jonamac	McIntosh
Melrose (*See* Red Delicious)	Red Delicious
Monroe	Rome Beauty
Spijon	Red Spy × Monroe (Jonathan × Rome Beauty)
Webster	(Ben Davis × Jonathan) × (Ben Davis × Jonathan)

McIntosh

Probably the best-tasting commercially viable apple grown, it was discovered by John McIntosh growing on his farm near Dundela, Dundas County, Ontario, in 1796. It may have been a chance seedling of a Fameuse. It is a juicy, aromatic, sweet apple with a sharp edge, tough skin, and very white flesh.

It seems that more new varieties have come from McIntosh crosses than any other apple. A major motivation has been to develop McIntosh-like apples that ripen earlier than the parent. Other strains have been developed to suit particular growing conditions. You will find some of these growing locally. They all share qualities of the McIntosh, but it is doubtful that any have the all-over quality of the McIntosh. The Macoun and Cortland come closest to approximating the superb balance of sweet and sour in the McIntosh. The Early McIntosh *looks* like a McIntosh but ripens early and is blander in flavor like its other parent, the Transparent. However it does fill the need for a McIntosh before the real thing ripens later in the fall.

Descendants

Variety	McIntosh crossed with:
Bancroft	Forest
Barry	Cox Orange
Cortland	Ben Davis

  Large, juicy, aromatic apple with a sweet/sour refreshing flavor. Texture becomes coarse as it ripens, but flavor is retained. Very white flesh does not turn brown quickly, so it is excellent in salads. Introduced in 1898 in Geneva, New York. Early Cortland is a cross between a Cortland and a Lodi.

Early McIntosh	Yellow Transparent
Empire	Red Delicious

  Tastes and looks more like a small Red Delicious than a McIntosh. If you like Red Delicious, this is an interesting blend. Introduced in Geneva, New York, in 1966, it is a solid dark red color with a heavy waxy bloom.

Edgar	Forest
Greendale	Lodi
Hume	?

Jonamac	Jonathan
Joyce	?
Jubilee	Grimes Golden
Kendall	Zusoff
Kyokko	Ralls Janet
Lobo	?

Developed in Ottawa, Ontario, in 1930, it ripens a bit earlier than a McIntosh, but is inferior in storing ability.

Macoun	Jersey Black

Pronounced "McGowan," it is a black-red, sweet, aromatic apple. It is very hard and crisp like a McIntosh but has a shorter season.

Melba (and Red Melba)	?

Developed in Ottawa, Ontario, around 1924.

Merton Charm	Cox Orange
Michaelmas Red	Worcester Permain
Milton	Yellow Transparent
Newtosh	Yellow Newtown
Niagara	Carlton
Ogden	Zusoff
Onondaga	Ben Davis
Otsego	Ben Davis
Patricia	?
Puritan	Red Astrachan

Early yellow-pink apple with the characteristic juiciness of the McIntosh but the tang of a Red Astrachan.

Redhook	Carlton
Scotia	?
Spartan	Yellow Newtown

Dark purple-red apple with the aromatic, white, juicy flesh of a McIntosh and the sharp refreshing tang of a Newtown. Developed in Summerland, British Columbia, around 1926.

Spencer	Golden Delicious
Summerred	(Golden Delicious) and ?
Sweet McIntosh	Lawver
Tydeman's Red	Worcester Pearmain

An early, red summer apple developed in England in 1929.

Northern Spy

You will find this apple in the late fall as it is one of the last to ripen. An old favorite, it has yellowish, aromatic flesh, which holds its shape and flavor in cooking. This yellow-green and red-splashed apple was discovered near Rochester, New York, around 1800, and is believed to be a descendant of a Wagener. Redder strains of Spys are said to be inferior in flavor.

Descendants

Variety	Northern Spy crossed with:
Keepsake	? (scientific cross)
Ontario	Wagener
Oswego	Sutton
Quebec Belle	? (perhaps Red Delicious)
Sandow	?
Schoharie	Ralls
Spigold	Golden Delicious (Red Spy)
(*See* Golden Delicious)	
Spijon	Monroe (Rome × Jonathan)
Sweet Sixteen	? (scientific cross)
Tioga	Sutton
Wayne	N.W. Greening

A cross made at the New York Agriculture Station in 1962, this crimson red apple makes superior sauce and cider.

Rome Beauty

Perfectly round and red, with the look of a storybook apple, the Rome Beauty was not named after the ancient city, but rather after Rome Township, Ohio, where it was discovered in 1816. Although it is not one of the best flavored apples around, the hardy trees produce quantities of large attractive fruit, especially in American orchards of the middle latitudes.

The Gallia Beauty is a root sprout of a Rome Beauty. It has been used to develop new varieties.

Descendants

Crosses have been made in an attempt to cross this Beauty with less attractive apples with more flavor. Unfortunately the children can also inherit the taste of the Rome and the looks of the uglier parent.

Variety	Rome Beauty crossed with:
Anderson	?
Ben Hur	Ben Davis
Crandall	Jonathan
Ensee	?
Miller Giant	?
Monroe	Jonathan
Roanoke	Schoharie (Spy × Ralls)
Warder	?

Gallia Beauty Descendants

Variety	Gallia Beauty crossed with:
Downing	Kirtland
Jerseyred	White Winter Pearmain
Ruby	Starking (Red Delicious)

LOCAL AND OLD-FASHIONED APPLE VARIETIES

We wish we could say that we've tasted every single apple available in North America. Unfortunately, many of them are available only in little pockets of the country, out of the mainstream market. Searching them all out would make for a wonderful fall excursion. There are over forty varieties listed, but because there are thousands grown, we are sorry if we have left out your favorite local apple.

Baldwin

The Baldwin is a good, all-purpose, keeping apple that was once widely cultivated, but has been pushed out by other varieties. Discovered in Wilmington, Massachusetts, around 1740, it remained popular until the rise of the hardier, tastier McIntosh. It is now grown largely for its historical value.

Ben Davis

At the turn of the century, when the Baldwin was in its heyday in the north, the Ben Davis was receiving similar popularity in the south. Discovered in North Carolina in the 1700s, it was a productive "keeper," but of questionable culinary merit. Its best contribution to apple history is in its genes. Crossed with a McIntosh, its famous progeny is the Cortland.

Bishop's Pippin

See Yellow Belleflower.

Black Gilliflower (Sheepnose)

This unusual old eighteenth-century, conical-shaped, purplish-black apple was appropriately named.

Blacktwig

Once very popular in the south, this yellow/red apple originated in Tennessee in the early 1800s.

Chenango Strawberry

The strawberrylike aroma of this old variety from Chenango County, New York, is said to fill the room.

Close

This very early, pale green/red apple was developed in Arlington, Virginia, around 1925. Its value lies in its timing, for its flavor is inferior to that of later apples. Thinning and stop-drop sprays are highly recommended and used on this variety.

Duchess of Oldenburg

Imported into England from Russia around 1805, this apple came to the United States in 1835 when it was imported by the Massachusetts Horticultural Society, at the same time as the Alexander, Red Astrachan, and Tetovsky. Considered too tart for eating raw by most, it makes good pies. It is an early fall apple which does not keep well.

Esopus Spitzenburg

A superb eating and also cooking apple, the Esopus Spitzenburg has fallen by the wayside probably because of difficulties associated with growing the tree on a commercial scale. Discovered near Esopus, New York, it was already well known in the nineteenth century. It was Thomas Jefferson's favorite apple. The Jonathan apple is a descendant. Idagold is a cross between a Wagener and an Esopus Spitzenburg.

Fameuse (Snow)

Still commercially grown and enjoyed in Quebec and New England, this small, pretty, delicious apple (with snow-white flesh) was either brought to Quebec from France in the 1600s, or was a North American seedling that was taken back to France at that time. It is believed to be an ancestor of the McIntosh.

Granny Smith

See World Varieties.

Gravenstein

This superior tasting apple is difficult to grow commercially, as it ripens over an extended period of time and does not color or store well. There are two stories about its history. One claims that the Gravenstein was discovered growing in a garden at the Castle Graefenstein in Schleswig-Holstein before 1800. Another says it came from scions imported from Italy to Graasten Castle, South Jutland. This old-fashioned apple is green-yellow with red splashes. Redder mutations have been developed.

Grimes Golden

Before the Golden Delicious stole the show, this was the favorite golden yellow apple. Grimes Golden originated in West Virginia before 1800. It produces excellent fruit, but cultivation and storage problems have made it less commercially viable. Some people speculate that it is in fact an ancestor of the Golden Delicious.

Haralson

This hardy variety was developed in Minnesota in 1923 from a Malinda seed. The fruit is medium-size and tart.

Honeygold

Introduced in Minnesota in 1969 from a cross between Golden Delicious and Haralson, it is a medium, yellow apple.

Jerseymac

This McIntosh-type hybrid apple (Julyred × ? scientific cross) was introduced in New Jersey in 1971, where it is widely planted. It has good color and flavor for an early apple.

Lady

The size of crabapples but with the fine flavor of larger apples, these dainty apples are grown primarily for decoration. Traditionally they are pinned to boxwood or grapevine wreaths and garlands at Christmas time. They are known in Europe as Api, where they have been cultivated for over 400 years.

Lodi

This precociously early apple is typical of early varieties. Pale green/yellow, it is watery, not highly flavored, and will keep only a few weeks. It is a cross between a White Transparent and Montgomery and was bred in Geneva, New York, in 1911.

Maiden's Blush

One of the more accurately named varieties, these pastel yellow apples have blushing red cheeks. An old-fashioned variety dating back to New Jersey in the early 1800s, this apple is supposed to be excellent for drying.

Mantet

Developed in Manitoba from the seed of the Russian apple, Tetovsky, it is hardier than an Astrachan. Its firm fruit ripens just after the Astrachan. State Fair is a cross between Mantet and Oriole.

Newtown Pippin/Yellow Newtown/Albermarle Pippin

Newtown Pippins are good, old-fashioned, crisp, sour, green-yellow apples. Discovered growing in Newtown, Long Island, around 1750, they have become the darling of the west coast. They are grown in British Columbia, Washington, Oregon, and California. They are traditionally a cooking apple, but the flavor of a Pippin is reminiscent of pineapple and is worthwhile eating raw. The Newtown Pippin has been crossed with the McIntosh to produce the Spartan and the Newtosh.

Northwestern Greening

Although the fruit of the Northwestern is not as good as the Rhode Island Greening, it nonetheless has a contribution to make since it is hardy in the north, produces a reliable crop, and keeps well. It originated in Waupaca County, Wisconsin, before 1870.

Orenco

This beautiful, solid bright red apple originated in Orenco, Oregon, around 1920.

Paulared

This chance seedling was found growing in Sparta, Michigan, and was introduced in 1967. It is a very red, very popular summer/early fall apple.

Red Astrachan

This fiery red apple originated in Russia, traveled to Sweden, England, and finally to Massachusetts around 1835. A tart, mouth-puckering summer apple with no keeping ability, it is highly astringent and therefore makes excellent jelly and marmalade. It also makes a good drying apple as it retains its flavor after processing.

Rhode Island Greening (also known as Greening)

A well-known, old-fashioned variety, the Rhode Island Greening is many people's idea of a cooking apple. Picked green, it certainly does have the ability to pucker up your mouth. A little riper and more yellow, it makes a perfectly adequate eating apple. This green apple was grown by a Mr. Green behind his tavern in Green's End, Rhode Island, in the 1700s. What else could they call it?

Russets (Golden and Roxbury)

Most apples have small patches of russet (dull, rough, brownish patches) on them, but the homely Golden Russet is practically all russet. What it loses in appearance, it makes up for in flavor; the yellow flesh is undeniably sweet and fragrant. It makes fabulous perfumed syrupy cider. These small apples keep beautifully in plain cold storage, and were grown for export to Europe until the advent of controlled atmosphere storage. Golden Russets are an old English variety. The Roxbury Russet originated in Roxbury, Massachusetts, around 1635.

Smokehouse

Popular in Pennsylvania Dutch country, the original tree sprang up beside a little wooden structure used for smoking hams, in Lancaster County, Pennsylvania, in the early 1800s.

Stayman (Stayman Winesap)

See Winesap.

Summer Rambo

One of the first apples planted in the new world, this apple is believed to have originated in sixteenth-century France where it was known as the *Rambour Franc*. An early yellow and red-splashed apple, it is extremely juicy.

Swaar

This historic variety was grown by Dutch settlers on the Hudson near Esopus, New York. *Swaar* means "heavy" in Dutch, and this is a very hard, solid, rich-flavored yellow apple which is also a good keeper.

Sweet Varieties

These old-fashioned apples lack any hint of tartness! They are delicious, but you probably will have to travel right to the orchard to get them.

Pound Sweet (Pumpkin Sweet)
This very large fall green apple tends to get waterlogged or translucent. It is unclear whether the name "pumpkin" refers to its size
or its flavor.

Sweet Bough or Bough Sweet
This large green/yellow summer apple was known before 1817.

Tolman Sweet
This large round green fall apple has a suture line from top to bottom.

Tompkins King (King or King of Tompkins County)

Tompkins King are fine-flavored, extremely large red and yellow
apples. Because the trees are not as hardy or productive as other
varieties, they are not grown to any great extent commercially. The
original tree grew in Warren County, New Jersey, but was brought
to Tompkins County, New York, where it was named in 1804.

Transparent: Yellow/White

In a search for hardy varieties, the Yellow Transparent was imported
into the United States from Russia in 1870. It is an early, juicy, yellow
apple. The White Transparent may be a chance seedling of the
Yellow.

Wagener

This very old variety was originally grown in Penn Yann, New York,
around 1790. It is thought to be a parent of the Northern Spy.

Wealthy

It takes a special kind of apple tree to survive the cold and wind of
the prairies. The Wealthy grew up from a Cherry Crabapple seed
planted in Excelsior, Minnesota, around 1855. An experiment was
conducted in which thousands of seeds were systematically planted

over a ten-year period. Most were killed off by the harsh winters.
The Wealthy survived and deserves our respect for its tenacity!

Winesap

Winesaps were cultivated in New Jersey prior to 1800. They have
continued to be widely grown throughout the centuries because
they are good, all-purpose keeping apples. Appropriately named,
they have a certain winelike, almost bitter aftertaste. Over thirty
Winesap strains have been developed.

Descendants

Variety	Winesap crossed with:
Golden Winesap	?
Shenandoah	Opalescent
Stayman	?

    The Stayman grew up from a Winesap seed in Leavenworth, Kansas, in
1866. Because of its superior flavor, it is widely grown in the United
States in spite of the fact that its skin tends to crack and it colors poorly
in certain seasons. It is a well-liked, all-purpose apple.

Turley	? (or may be a Stayman seedling)

Winter Banana

This Cass County, Indiana, native is a clear waxy yellow with a
pink blush. It was raised in 1876 and is a late apple. It is a moot point
whether its name is an accurate description of its flavor.

Wolf River

Wolf River apples are prized for apple doll heads, as they can achieve
tremendous size and have rather dry flesh. Like the Bramley's
Seedling, a British variety, one grapefruit-sized apple is said to
singlehandedly make up into an apple pie. They originated near
Wolf River, Fremont County, Wisconsin, around 1870.

Yellow Belleflower

Originating in Burlington County, New Jersey, in the early 1800s, this yellow, aromatic, conical apple is similar—but some say superior in flavor—to the Golden Delicious. It stores well and its flavor actually improves with aging. It is also known as Bishop's Pippin.

York Imperial (York)

This flat-topped, lopsided old favorite was first discovered near York, Pennsylvania, in the early 1800s. It was called the "Imperial of Keepers" as it would keep well, even after a frost. Because the firm, yellowish flesh holds its shape in cooking, it is an important apple for commercial processing. With a flat top and a small core it also provides processors with a minimum of waste.

DISEASE-RESISTANT VARIETIES

Agricultural research stations have been working to develop varieties that are immune to apple scab fungus and other diseases such as cedar apple rust, powdery mildew, and fire blight. Although these apples may not be as flavorful as some of the more popular types, some people will consider this a worthwhile trade-off for the absence of fungicides on the fruit. They are not resistant to insects, however, and probably will be sprayed with insecticides. Disease-resistant varieties are the result of complex crosses between well-known varieties and more sturdy varieties including wild crabapples.

Britegold
Freedom
Jonafree
Liberty (some Macoun background)
Macfree (some McIntosh, Rome, Jonathan background)
Moira
Murray

Nova Easygro (some Spartan background)
Novamac
Priam
Prima
Priscilla
Redfree
Sir Prize

WORLD VARIETIES

The world is small when it comes to apple varieties. Tomorrow you may find some of these unusual-sounding varieties in the produce department of your supermarket. After all, who could have predicted the worldwide success of those two unrelated Delicious brothers: Red and Golden (from Iowa and West Virginia respectively); or of that sour green lady from Down Under, Granny Smith.

Bramley's Seedling

These very large green/yellow apples are juicy, sour, and Great Britain's favorite cooking apple. High in vitamin C, it originated around 1810 in Nottinghamshire, England.

Belle de Boskoop

Popular in Germany, Belgium, and its native Holland (seedling 1856), this large, round, lopsided apple is a russet variety with creamy, acid, aromatic flesh.

Calville Blanche

A favorite of the French since the time of Louis XIII, who grew it in his garden, it is a large, pale-yellow ribbed apple. Some describe its spicy flavor as bananalike. Others say it is pineapplelike. It also has a reputation for having more vitamin C in it than an orange.

Cleopatra

Although this apple originated in New Jersey in the early 1800s, it is now commercially grown in Australia and New Zealand. It is a mild juicy green/yellow apple.

Cox's Orange Pippin

Considered the finest-flavored of all the English apples, over half the apples sold in Great Britain are Cox's Orange Pippin. Whether they are called "orange" because of their distinctive orange-red cast or because some people liken this rich, aromatic, almost nutty-flavored apple to the more tropical fruit, is uncertain. It grew from the seed of a Ribston Pippin around 1825 at Colnbrook Lawn, Slough, Buckinghamshire, England. The tree is susceptible to scab and mildew and dislikes damp, cold soil. It is not widely grown in North America.

Democrat

This Australian variety was discovered in Tasmania around 1900. It is a good keeper which is sweet and juicy, but rather bland-flavored.

Discovery

Although a relatively new "discovery" (1949), this early apple is gaining popularity in England. It is said to be a descendant of a Worcester Pearmain. The medium-sized fruit is red with juicy, chewy flesh and has a long shelf life.

Gala

A major variety in New Zealand and dating from 1934, Gala is a cross between a Golden Delicious and a Kidd's Orange Red (which is a cross between a Cox's Orange Pippin and a Red Delicious). With this genealogy, it has to be a sweet, aromatic apple. It has just started to take off in North America, so you may be able to buy this nectarine-colored apple in a few years.

Granny Smith

This grass green, sour, crisp, refreshing apple originated in Australia, where it is still widely grown. We welcome it, especially in the spring when we have had our fill of mealy local varieties. It is imported also from New Zealand, France, South Africa, and Argentina. It requires 190 days to mature and so is not widely grown in North America — yet. As it has become one of our favorite apples, pomologists are struggling to develop mutations which will respond to our local growing conditions. Granny Smith apples keep up to seven months in common refrigeration.

Laxton's Superb

This russet-type apple, introduced in 1897 and popular in England and the Netherlands, is a cross between a Cox's Orange Pippin and a Wyken Pippin. It is larger and not as fragrant as the Cox's Orange.

Mutsu (Crispin)

A cross between a Golden Delicious and an Indo, the Mutsu was introduced at Kuroishi, Aomori Prefecture, Japan, in 1930. This yellow apple has provided the Golden Delicious with some stiff competition. Mutsu has coarser flesh than the Golden Delicious but has a stronger tree, larger fruit, and better keeping ability (not shriveling in storage).

Reinette du Canada

Despite its name, this large russet-type apple is a European apple. It originated in Normandy, France in the 1700s. Although it may have been taken to Quebec, it made its way back home to France again. It is commercially grown in France, Switzerland, and Austria.

Sturmer Pippin

A cross between a Ribston Pippin and a Nonpareil, introduced in Sturmer, Suffolk, England, in 1831, this late apple is commercially grown in Australia and New Zealand where the season is long enough for it to mature. A green/yellow apple with a brown flush, it is said to have an aromatic flavor.

Worcester Pearmain

This mid-season apple is popular in England where it was developed near Worcester around 1870 (the seedling of a Devonshire Quarrenden). It does not store well and so must be eaten in season for optimum flavor. The flesh is said to have a faint strawberry flavor.

THE NATURAL HISTORY OF APPLES

Left to their own devices, apple trees would still be growing wild in the Caucasus Mountains of Asia. Hundreds of living and silvery dead shoots would stream skyward, untrimmed by human hands. They would probably look like the wild apple trees that grow in our neighborhoods, the branches a mirror image of the roots. The fruit would be small, sour, and hard, and largely untouched by anyone except hungry wild animals.

But people have been trimming apple trees for at least 5,000 years. They discovered that cutting out branches and thinning out fruit encouraged the tree to produce larger apples. Most important was the discovery that putting an apple in a hole in the ground produced a whole new tree. Better still, the black shiny seeds worked, too. Before leaving their homelands, people would pick apples off their favorite trees and take the seeds with them. They would plant the apple seeds almost as soon as they arrived in new lands in the hope that one out of a dozen trees might bear fruit similar to the favorite old-country variety.

As early as ancient Greek times, it was discovered that living twigs of one apple tree could be grafted onto another tree. This technique would produce fruit exactly like the mother tree. The hit-and-miss method of propagation by seeds could be eliminated. Farmers planted whole fields of trees that were almost exactly the same. The days of trees as one of a kind were gone, and groups of trees were given names reflecting the real or imagined virtues of the fruit.

The trees that produced delicious fruit, however, were not necessarily the hardiest. They were susceptible to an onslaught of fungi and insects. A major discovery was that certain chemicals, sprayed on the trees, the leaves, and the fruit eliminated or reduced many of the problems. A farmer who could produce quantities of blemish-free apples economically had a distinct advantage over his neighbors. This logic has molded the twentieth-century North American apple industry. Today chemicals are used at literally every stage of apple development.

Fungicide sprays may be used up to ten times in a season for apple scab fungus (this spray may also include chemicals to control mildew). Trees are sprayed when the green tips appear on the buds, through the pre-pink stage, when the flower buds are exposed, to the pink stage (just before the blossoms open), followed by cover sprays right through the summer, when the fruit is hanging from the trees.

Insecticide sprays are used for two dozen insects that attack apples including the tent caterpillar, wintermoth, green fruitworm, codling moth, and apple maggot. These sprays may be combined with fungicide sprays.

Herbicide sprays are used to kill the weeds between the apple trees. Weeding is especially important with dwarf trees.

Chemical thinners are used to thin out 75 percent of the blossoms (potential fruit). This improves the growth, color, quality, and rate of maturity of the remaining fruit. The chemicals used to thin blossoms are growth regulators: organic compounds that promote, inhibit, or otherwise modify plant growth processes. They thin the blossoms either by caustically burning the flower parts or by temporarily upsetting the natural hormone balance of the tree. Problems associated with thinning sprays include: damage to leaves, overthinning (through errors in mixing the concentrate), and the killing of pollinating insects and other beneficial insects.

Preharvest or stop-drop sprays are hormonal sprays used to reduce the natural tendency of the trees to drop fruit before normal harvest time. They also usually increase the amount of red on apples. Problems associated with stop-drop include hastened maturity, which can affect the flavor, texture, and storage life of apples.

Flower and fruit bud initiation growth control sprays are used to encourage young trees to start bearing fruit sooner than they would naturally. This provides orchardists with a quicker return on their money.

Chemical pruning is achieved with growth regulators which are added to latex paint and applied to large cuts in trees. It suppresses the growth of new sprouts on and around the cuts. Experiments are being done using these chemicals to train young trees to develop ideal trunk and limb formations or to widen their branch angles.

Hormone sprays are being used on an experimental basis for other purposes. Frost-damaged fruit buds can be coaxed into producing fruit in spite of the damage. The resulting fruit has fewer seeds than normal. Because consumers seem to prefer Red Delicious apples with the stereotypic elongated, pointy shapes, hormone sprays are being used to encourage the trees to bear more conical, oblong-shaped fruit. Some sprays have also been used to reduce russetting, or rough brown patches on apples.

Dips. Apples in controlled atmosphere storage in contact with carbon dioxide have a tendency to get brown patches called scald. As a preventative measure, they are dipped in or sprayed with chemicals and fungicides. Problems related to the use of these chemicals include apples that are paler than normal (especially Golden Delicious) or bitter in flavor. It is not recommended that pomace (apple pulp) treated with CA chemicals be fed to animals as this may lead to residues above the zero tolerances allowed for meat and milk.

Coatings. Apples are dipped in waxes to reduce evaporation from the skin (withering), to reduce bruising, and to make them more attractive. Some fruit coatings are natural vegetable oil emulsions. Others are paraffin-, petroleum-, and shellac-based.

The catch-22 is that as consumers we have come to expect that every apple we buy will be as red, succulent, and perfect as Snow White's apple. But if we take away our farmers' chemicals, they will grow us fruit that is very different. Are we willing to buy apples that are smaller, less perfect, and probably more expensive? Are we willing to do without CA storage and without apples three or four months of the year? Modern orchardists aim for 95 percent blemish-free fruit. Organic farmers produce about 20 percent. But many of those apples go into sauce and juice and vinegar, where the appearance does not matter anyway.

The answer we expect is one of compromise. After all, apples were grown for thousands of years without the help of modern chemicals. The apple industry has thrived in spite of the banning of DDT, routinely used in orchards in this century. The fungicides and insecticides seem to be more vital than the herbicides, hormonal growth regulators, dips, and coatings. Chemicals can be used conservatively. Labor-intensive mowing and thinning seems a lot safer. Snow White's apple may have been beautiful, but it was also poison.

CHAPTER TWO

Cooking With Apples

APPLES AND . . .

Some foods just seem to go together, like peaches and cream. Whether stewed together for hours or sitting next to each other on a plate, they bring out the best in each other. Apples go with a lot of things. Consider these classic combinations:

- Crisp red fall apples with wedges of aged cheddar cheese and hot biscuits;
- Juicy pork chops sautéed with onions and a splash of pink applesauce;
- A mug of fresh-pressed amber cider next to a smoked ham on rye;
- Just out of the oven: apples soft and warm inside topped with a buttery crust of cinnamon and brown sugar.

There must be scientific reasons why these are such successful combinations. Eating salty ham makes us thirsty, and dewy, sweet cider is the perfect antidote. Acids are necessary to digest fats, and so a tangy applesauce makes a pork chop go down with pleasurable ease. Why we feel such natural affinity for these sweet, watery things is a mystery that doesn't really need an explanation. The important thing to know is that apples, butter, and cinnamon sugar make magic together.

Qualities of Apples

Quality	Use in cooking
sweet	a natural in sweet dishes: desserts, pies, cakes a foil to strong flavors: cabbage, turnip
sour	contrast to fatty foods: pork, goose, duck
juicy	contrast to salty foods: salt herring, bacon, sauerkraut adds moisture to dry foods: applesauce cake, oatmeal
aromatic	livens up bland flavors: potatoes, mild cheese, noodles, rice combines with spices for enhanced flavors: cinnamon

Qualities of Apples (continued)

Quality	Use in cooking
starchy/bland	base for sharper flavors and spices: cranberries, strawberries, raisins, mincemeat
crunchy	textural contrast: salads and cooked foods
thickening	natural pectin is used to thicken without adding flavor: jams, jellies adds body to braises and glazes: poultry

EATING VERSUS COOKING APPLES

Somewhere back in cookbook history a differentiation was made between "cooking" and "eating" or "dessert" apples. A cooking apple is basically a sour apple. An eating apple is a sweeter apple. But what about those of us who love to put our teeth into those small, green apples that are so sour they make you blink? Some bland, mealy apples are recommended as eating apples merely by a process of elimination—they are tasteless when cooked without lemon, vanilla, or cinnamon. The Rome Beauty, which is a shiny red lovely thing to look at, is almost tasteless. Its outstanding quality is its high fiber content. It will withstand high temperatures without losing its shape, unlike its more juicy, tasty cousins. So it is often recommended as the best baking apple.

A perfect eating apple is a consummate blend of sweetness, tartness, astringency, and crunchiness. But according to whose standards? Some apples fall (or disintegrate) into sauce almost immediately. Others turn slightly rubbery before cooking down. Do you like your applesauce chunky like mashed potatoes, soft and frothy like snow, or baby-food smooth? Do you like the pieces in your apple pie to be thin, soft, and melting together? Or do you prefer large, half-cooked, semi-crunchy separate slices?

Because taste is so subjective, and because varieties vary so much from place to place, we have deliberately not recommended specific apple varieties for individual recipes. We encourage you to learn as much as you can about the apples available to you, to experiment, and decide for yourself.

STORING APPLES

Apples are self-sufficient storehouses in themselves. Their popularity throughout the ages has had a lot to do with their ability to be saved for later, unlike more fragile fruits such as grapes or strawberries. Before modern times, a person who prudently chose his varieties and had a cool, damp spot to keep them could eat apples half the year or more.

When we bring apples home from the store, they go into the fruit bowl on the kitchen table, if we plan on eating them soon, or in the fridge if they are to last longer. We know that cold temperatures slow down the ripening of apples. Dampness stops them from shriveling.

Generally speaking, apples ripen 10 times faster at room temperature than at freezing (32°F/0°C), and 5 times faster at 40°F (4°C) than at freezing (32°F/0°C).

Whether in large commercial sheds or a cold room in your basement, the best temperature for storing apples is just above freezing (33°F/1°C) with a humidity of 85 to 90 percent or more. (Ideal temperature may vary slightly from variety to variety; ask your agricultural representative for more detail.)

The late fall apples are traditionally the keepers—the apples stashed away for later. If you would like to buy an inexpensive bushel of apples in the fall to save, ask your local apple grower which variety he would recommend, or try these varieties: Cortland, Empire, Idared, Jonathan, McIntosh, Macoun, Mutsu, Northern Spy, Rhode Island Greening, Red Delicious, Rome Beauty, Stayman, or Winesap.

To store apples at home:

- Choose a spot away from other fruits and vegetables, as odors get transferred from one to the other.
- Choose apples that are ripe but still hard. Underripe and overripe apples will not last as long. Smaller apples of each variety are usually firmer, have better flavor and color, and store better than larger ones. If you pick the apples yourself, take care to leave the stems intact (removing the stems may let bacteria in, which causes rotting).

- Avoid any fruit that is bruised. Use windfalls to make sauce rather than storing them.
- Chill apples as soon as possible. The longer they sit at room temperature, the shorter will be their storage life. Do not wash them.
- Store in shallow trays or baskets of cardboard or wood. Place half a bushel or less in each container to avoid bruising bottom layers. Ideally, apples are individually wrapped in clean dry paper, straw, or leaves. Non-individually wrapped apples will also last, but chances of contamination from one bad apple to another is greater.
- Wrap and insulate containers with straw or leaves. You may wish to place an outer wrap of plastic, which keeps in the moisture, but cut holes in it to allow ripening gases to escape.
- Check periodically, removing the ripest apples, and any that are starting to spoil.

Expected Storage Period for a Few Common Varieties

Variety	Storage Period (in months):
Cortland	3–4
Empire	3–4
Golden Delicious	4–5
Idared	4–5
McIntosh	2–4
Northern Spy	4–5
Red Delicious	4–5
Spartan	3–4

Controlled Atmosphere (CA) Storage

A new storage technique, used since the 1950s, combines airtight refrigeration at 32°F (0°C) with an atmosphere that is reduced in oxygen and with increased carbon dioxide levels. The apples' ability for respiration is reduced by the lack of oxygen and so the ripening process is slowed down. This storage method can extend apple sales into the next fresh season with obvious advantages to the grower and the consumer. There are variables involved, however, that complicate the process. Timing and balance are of the essence. Apples put in storage must be of excellent quality to begin with and of a certain maturity. CA storage prolongs youth, but when the apples are removed months later, they begin to age rapidly and must be sold quickly. Certain varieties store better than others. Some develop a discoloration or "scald" and are dipped in a chemical solution to prevent this.

In studying CA-stored apples, scientists have pointed out that although respiration may be slowed down, anaerobic respiration (which works without oxygen), continues. Sometimes there is an increased production of alcohol which may taint the flavor of the apple. Another study showed that while the physical appearance and texture of CA apples may resemble perfectly ripened apples, the flavor may be that of an overripe apple. Too often, consumers are faced with products that look good but taste insipid, or even bad. Let's hope the simple apple does not come to this.

Low Oxygen Controlled Atmosphere Storage

This storage method, which allows even less oxygen into the storage atmosphere, is still at the experimental stage. Potential problems include internal and external damage to fruit through low-oxygen injury and alcohol off-flavors.

APPLE TOOLS AND METHODS

Tools for Peeling and Coring

Peeling
Apple peel contains vitamins, aroma, fiber, and color that you may want in your cooked products. We have specified in the recipes where we have left them on. However, because of the many chemical residues that may be lingering on the surface of apples, we highly recommend that you generously scrub, rinse, and towel dry them; or you may wish to remove the peels entirely. Because cut apples

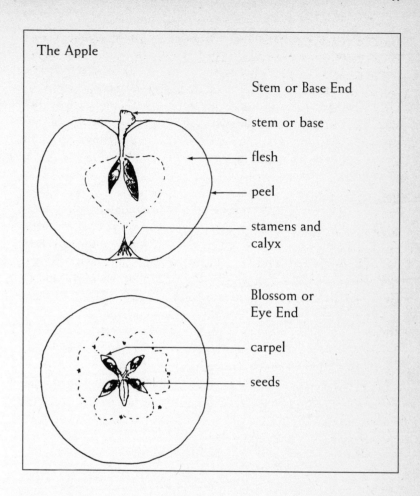

The Apple

Stem or Base End

stem or base

flesh

peel

stamens and
calyx

Blossom or
Eye End

carpel

seeds

turn brown, we recommend that you dip or sprinkle them with lemon, orange, or pineapple juice to prevent darkening.

With a paring knife. The idea is to strip off the outside colored layer of the apple, while leaving the flesh intact.

METHOD ONE: Place the apple, blossom end down, on a cutting surface. Cut it right through from top to bottom into two pieces. Cut each of these pieces lengthwise, in two, so that you have four wedges. Holding a wedge in one hand and knife in the other, carefully slice off the peel. Repeat with the three other wedges.

METHOD TWO: Holding apple in one hand, and knife in other, cut a

shallow strip of peel, ½ inch (1 cm) wide, at top stem end. Cut in a
spiral pattern around and down the apple from top to bottom.
Pressing with your thumb helps prevent you from cutting too deeply.
Continue cutting in this spiral manner until all peel is removed.
Half, quarter, and core, or cut off pieces of peeled apple to the desired
size, according to the requirements of your recipe. Be careful not
to cut too deeply into the core. Discard core and peelings, or, if you
have enough, make applesauce.

With a metal commercial hand peeler. These peelers are made with stainless or carbon steel blades and plastic, wood, or metal handles. They
work like small paring knives that shave off material to a very shallow depth, ensuring little waste. Some are swivel mounted. They
have sharpened points for twisting out the core and any blemishes.
Follow Method Two, following the circular contours of the apple.
Cut in quarters and core with the point or a knife.

With an old-fashioned, patented, mechanical peeling machine. These peelers have a handcranked shaft on which you spear your apple. A
small blade on a spring-loaded arm rubs up against the apple, peeling it in one ribbonlike strip from top to bottom. They work best
with firm, crisp apples.

Coring apple quarters and halves

The idea is to remove the woody, inedible casing that holds the
seeds.

Quarters. With apple wedge point side up, remove core by making a
semicircular slice with knife (or remove core with a melon baller.)

Halves. Insert knife or peeler point into the side of the core. Twist
with even pressure and lift up. Melon ballers remove cores easily,
leaving smooth spherical indentations which are attractive in fancy
dishes.

With a commercial apple corer. The size of a hand peeler, the cylindrical
blade works like a gouge, and will remove a core to a depth of about 3
inches (7.6 cm).

With a commercial apple corer/cutter. This corer/cutter is a small hand tool shaped like a wagon wheel with blades for spokes. The cutter is pressed down on a whole (peeled or unpeeled apple), dividing it into wedges and a cylindrical core.

Coring a whole unpeeled apple
Slice ½ inch (13 mm) off the top stem end of apple. Set aside.

With a paring knife. Cut a cylindrical shaped piece one inch (2.5 cm) in diameter (less for smaller apples) through the center of the apple to within ½ inch (13 mm) of the bottom. Remove and discard core.

With a melon baller or scoop. With cup side of baller into the top center of apple, twist and gouge out a sphere of apple. Repeat a few times gouging deeper into apple until core is removed. Take care to not cut into bottom of apple, leaving ½ inch (13 mm) of flesh.

Tools for Making Applesauce

Applesauce is basically cooked apples broken down into very small pieces. Some apples fall apart when cooked and a simple fork will mash or whip them just fine, especially where you prefer a chunky, textured sauce.

When there is a little more resistance you may wish to attack the cooked apple with a masher which is usually called a potato masher, of wood or metal. The wooden masher is a cup-shaped, flat-bottomed mallet with a handle. The sauce is achieved by pounding the daylights out of the cooked fruit. The metal masher is similar to the wooden one, except instead of a heavy head, it has a perforated metal disk. Pressure is applied by grasping and pushing down on the handle. The apple particles break up and ooze through the holes.

There are several designs for hand presses or metal ricers, which force cooked fruit or vegetables to be extruded through small holes so that they resemble rice. The cooked apples are placed in the perforated cup of the ricer. A plunger is placed on top and two handles are squeezed together. The applesauce oozes out. This process also sieves out peel, core, and seeds, and so this is a handy tool for making quantities of sauce without peeling.

Simple kitchen sieves of any size may be used. Cooked apples are placed in the cup-shaped, flexible, metal-mesh sieve. Puréed sauce is made by rubbing the fruit with a slightly rounded hand tool, such as a spoon, against the wire mesh. This method is tedious so you may want to use it only for making small quantities and for special formulations, such as baby or invalid food, where an exceptionally fine grain is desired.

A ricer specifically designed for making sauce is an applesauce cone. It is worth its weight in gold at harvest time if you have to deal with bushels of apples. Warm cooked apples are placed in the perforated cone (approximately 8 inches [20 cm] wide at the top and 9 inches [23 cm] tall). This sits in a three-legged stand, over a bowl. A cone-shaped wooden pestle with a point that fits the bottom of the metal cone, and a round knobby top, is pushed through the apples to the bottom. Circular motions of the pestle around the top edge of the cone force the apples through the holes. This is a highly efficient method for making sauce. No pulp is wasted in peeling or coring. You'll be surprised at how little bulk is left after processing. A rubber spatula is a handy tool to use with this cone. The old-fashioned cones with pointed bottoms and pointed pestles are more efficient than the newer, more squared-off ones. Try to pick one up at an auction or at a secondhand store.

Food mills are mechanical sieves. The sieve is a rigid metal bowl with perforations only on the bottom and a handle. When the centrally mounted semi-circular blade is turned with an attached crank, the blade revolves, forcing the food through the sieve.

Tools for Making Cider

Electric juicers are of two types. Small kitchen appliances shred the apple pulp and separate it from the juice by centrifugal motion. These are excellent for making small quantities of fresh cider. Large appliances work more like traditional cider presses. They chop, shred, or grind the apples, and then squeeze out the juice. There are also juice extracting attachments that can be purchased to fit onto food processors and other general kitchen machines.

Cider presses are expensive unless you have access to large quantities of cheap apples. They are large enough to be kept in the back shed and brought out only at harvest time. Often they are set up right in the orchard. Apples are collected and put through a hand-cranked, sharp-bladed grinder into a heavy iron-hooped wooden basket. A screw press is turned down on the freshly ground pomace. Gallons of liquid apple gush down the wooden trough into a bucket.

A NOTE ABOUT MICROWAVES

Our recipes were tested in a 700-watt microwave oven. To use these recipes with an oven with less wattage, cooking times may have to be increased slightly.

Power setting terminology is not standard among manufacturers, but most ovens operate at percentages of power ranging from 10 to 100 percent. Maximum power means 100 percent, medium-high means 80 percent, medium means 70 percent, medium-low 50 percent, low means 30 percent, and warm means 10 percent. Check your owner's manual to determine the equivalent terminology for your micro- wave oven.

Waxed paper or microproof plastic wrap can be used to cover food while cooking.

APPLE BASICS: CIDER, HARD CIDER, JUICE, BRANDY, APPLEJACK, VINEGAR, APPLESAUCE, APPLE PECTIN

Apple Cider

(The extracted liquid of fresh apples, also called sweet cider.)

Ripe apples are stored for a week to ten days (called sweating) to mellow and soften the apples. They get sweeter and easier to grind. Then they are washed and ground to a fine pulp to break down the cells that contain the delicious sap. This ground pulp is called "pomace." It is pressed with a ratchet, hydraulic, or screw press and the apple liquid or "must" gushes out.

Buy apple cider at a farmers' market or health food store. This fresh-squeezed cider bears little resemblance to its cooked, canned, clarified cousin, commercial apple juice. It is pinkish or greenish, but as soon as it hits the air, almost instantly oxidizes into its characteristic brown color. It is pulpy and thick and the very juicy essence of apples. It can be refrigerated at 32° to 36°F (0° to 2°C) for a week or two. After this, bubbles form around the edges, and it

starts to turn. Alcohol is forming and it will have a tangy taste. This
is a very simple way, though, to make a little hard cider in your own
kitchen. Simply leave the cider to its own devices and you will get a
slightly alcoholic beverage. Leave it longer, and eventually it will
turn to vinegar.

You can pasteurize cider by cooking it at 170°F (76.6°C) for 10
minutes. This kills the yeasts and bacteria that turn the cider. You
may can this juice, but the flavor is different from the fresh product.
Apple cider freezes beautifully. The defrosted product does not taste
very different from the fresh one. Make sure to leave an ample
headspace (1 inch [2.5 cm]), because the cider, which is largely water,
expands when frozen.

This method of making a small amount of apple cider at home is
only practical when you have loads of windfalls, or another plenti-
ful supply of cheap apples. Scrub and core (but do not peel) apples.
Grate or grind by hand, or process with a blender or food processor
to a fine pulp. Place the ground pulp in a damp jelly bag or in three
or four thicknesses of cheesecloth, over a colander. Squeeze by hand
and allow it to drip through. Chill and enjoy! Any remaining pulp
can be cooked with cider to make applesauce or apple butter.

Hard Cider

(Fermented apple cider with an alcohol content between 2 and
7 percent; also known as cider.)

Traditionally hard cider was made by pouring fresh cider into oak
barrels, which were put in a cold basement and left until the cider
was properly aged. Sugar in the form of raisins, honey, molasses, or
boiled cider concentrate was occasionally added to raise the alcohol content.

Modern cidermakers, especially the commercial ones, in search
of a uniform end product, tend to take a more scientific approach.
They use many of the innovations of winemakers: glass carboys,
hydrometers, thermometers, titration equipment, fermentation locks,
and filters. They may add sugar, honey, yeast, sulfur dioxide, tan-
nic acid, calcium carbonate, pectic enzymes, and carbon dioxide.
Commercial fermentation generally takes five or six weeks. For
sweeter cider, the fermentation process is stopped early, before all

the sugar is converted to alcohol. Drier cider is naturally allowed to work for a longer time. The cider is then bottled and aged for at least six months.

Excellent, completely natural cider, *sans* additives, can be made, but only if serious attention is given to keeping all work spaces and equipment scrupulously clean and free of contaminating bacteria. Only choice apples should be used and the fermentation process must be extremely slow and carefully timed. This kind of cider must also be approached scientifically.

Properly aged hard cider is transparent and ranges in color from champagne to amber. Some ciders are naturally or artificially carbonated. Good cider has a distinctive apple fragrance and experts can tell the variety of apple from which it was made.

Dry ciders are served at room temperature. Sweet ciders are chilled. Mulled cider is served at just below the boiling point.

Apple Juice

(Processed, pasteurized apple cider.)

Commercial juice is cooked, centrifugally spun for clarification, strained and canned. Enzymes to aid extraction, and ascorbic acid may be added to it. Completely filtered juice is sparkling clear. Cloudy juice has pulp solids left in it. Hermetically sealed bottles or vacuum packed cans have a shelf life of a year or more.

Some juice is sealed in paper aseptic packages instead of cans or bottles. The freshly made juice is heated to 180°F (82°C) for 16 to 30 seconds. For this reason, it seems to have a fresher flavor than canned juice. After being cooled to room temperature, it is poured into sterilized paper containers and sealed. Packaged juice also has a shelf life of one year.

Apple juice is sometimes sold blended with other fruit juices such as cranberry and blueberry. Carbonated apple juice is also sold. Apple juice concentrate is also readily available. It is a syrupy liquid produced by evaporating water from apple juice, resulting in a stronger flavored product. Sold frozen, water is added to reconstitute it back into juice.

Apple Brandy

(An alcoholic beverage made by distilling hard cider. The fermented cider is heated, vaporized, and then condensed back to liquid form.)

Calvados is apple brandy from Normandy, France. French law guarantees that the word "Calvados" is used only on apple brandy produced in a particular area of France. *Appellation d'origine contrôlée* means "controlled place of origin."

There are two categories of Calvados. *Calvados appellation régle-mentée* is distilled once in ordinary column-type stills and has a strong apple flavor. *Calvados Pays d'Auge* is distilled twice in copper pot stills and is smoother, more subtle, and refined.

Calvados improves with age in oak puncheons. Ideally it is stored for years at 55°F (12.7°C). By regulation, the cider must be fermented for at least one month, distilled to a strength of 75 percent alcohol, and sold at between 40 percent and 50 percent alcohol.

Although bottled brandy is blended, there are standards which tell you the age of the youngest batch in the blend.

Vieux (old) or Réserve has been aged at least three years. V.O. or Vieille Réserve has been aged more than four years but may contain brandy ten to fifteen years old. V.S.O.P. or Grande Réserve has been aged at least five years but may contain brandy twenty years old. Extra, Hors d'Age, or Age Inconnu has been aged more than five and a half years but may contain brandy up to twenty-five years old.

Apple brandy is served in a snifter at room temperature or over ice cubes. It can also be combined with fresh apple juice or hard cider.

Applejack, Applejohn, Jersey Lightning

(An alcoholic beverage traditionally made by freezing hard cider.)

The water freezes before the alcohol and is removed, leaving the more potent "jack." This process is repeated until the end product is highly concentrated. The volume of the cider is reduced to one-quarter or less of its original size. Generally, the colder the weather, the more potent the applejack. Ordinary home freezers set at about

0°F to −5°F (−18° to −21°C) will produce applejack about 15 percent alcohol by volume.

North American apple brandy is also sometimes called applejack. It is not usually a pure apple distillate. Often blended with grain alcohol, it is lighter flavored than the French apple brandy. Presumably this is done because grains are less expensive to grow and distill than apples.

Apple Cider Vinegar

(A sour, full-bodied amber liquid or vinegar made by the acetic fermentation of hard cider. It is usually 50 to 60 percent acetic acid.)

The sugar in unpasteurized apple cider, left in the open air and with the help of yeast, changes to alcohol. Left for a few months, this fermented hard cider is attacked by acetic bacteria, which oxidize the alcohol and transform it into acetic acid or vinegar.

If you would like to try to make some simply strain hard cider into a glass jar, crock or wooden container, not more than three quarters full. Cover it with something that will breathe (cloth), but keep dirt out. Place it in a dark, cool place for about four months. If it tastes strong enough, strain it into clean bottles and save it. The stringy gelatinous layer that forms on the top of the vinegar is the "mother" and it can be saved to speed up the process of your next batch of apple cider vinegar. If you are in a hurry, this mother can be purchased at wine supply stores. For a continuous supply, leave a small amount of vinegar as well as the mother in your container. Replace the removed vinegar with an equal amount of new hard cider, and let nature create a whole new batch for you.

Commercially prepared apple cider vinegar is often produced by a much faster process. In this quick method, fermented cider is circulated through vats of porous material containing strong cider vinegar. It is then sprayed through the air, and the drops oxidize quickly. Cider can be transformed into cider vinegar in less than seventy-two hours in this way.

Applesauce

(A relish or dessert made of apples stewed to a pulp. It is often sweetened with sugar, honey, maple syrup, corn syrup, or fruit conserves.)

BASIC CHUNKY APPLESAUCE

3 cups (750 ml) sliced, cored, peeled apples
¼ cup (50 ml) water, apple juice, or cider
    White sugar or honey

1. Place apple slices in a medium saucepan. Add water; cover and cook over medium-low heat for 15 minutes or until apples are tender.
2. Stir vigorously with a fork and sweeten to taste with sugar or honey. Chill, or serve warm.
Yields about 1½ cups (375 ml)

BASIC SIEVED APPLESAUCE

10 to 12 medium apples
½ to ¾ cup (125 to 175 ml) water, cider, or apple juice
    White or brown sugar

1. Wash apples and remove blossom end and stems. Cut apples into eighths. Do not core.
2. Place in a large heavy bottomed saucepan. Add water, cider, or apple juice. Place over medium heat and cook, covered, for 25 minutes or until apples are very tender. Stir several times during cooking.
3. Remove from heat and cool to lukewarm. Press apples through a sieve or put through a food mill or applesauce cone. Sweeten to taste with sugar.
Yields approximately 4 cups (1 l)

VARIATION: FRENCH APPLESAUCE

Proceed as above but do not add sugar. Serve hot applesauce sweetened to taste with apricot jam or sieve a thick layer of icing sugar over top.

CIDER APPLESAUCE

The apples are peeled for this chunky applesauce. Use the peelings to make Apple Peeling Jelly (see page 240).

20 apples
1½ cups (375 ml) sweet cider

½ cup (125 ml) brown sugar
2 tsp (10 ml) cinnamon
½ tsp (2 ml) freshly ground nutmeg

1. Wash apples. Cut out stem and blossom ends. Peel, quarter, and core apples. Cut apples into chunks. Place in a large saucepan and add the cider.
2. Simmer, partially covered, over low heat for 40 minutes, stirring every 5 minutes to prevent sticking.
3. Stir in sugar, cinnamon, and nutmeg. Continue to cook for 5 minutes, stirring to break up the apples.
Yields 7 to 8 cups (1.75 to 2 l)

CRANBERRY HONEY APPLESAUCE

Cranberries add color and tang to this sauce.

6 cups (1.5 l) sliced, cored, peeled
  apples
1 cup (250 ml) fresh or frozen
  cranberries

½ cup (125 ml) honey
½ tsp (2 ml) cinnamon
¼ tsp (1 ml) cloves

1. Combine apples, cranberries, and honey in a saucepan. Slowly bring to a boil. Cover; reduce heat to low and cook for 20 minutes. Stir several times during cooking period.
2. Press through a sieve or leave chunky. Stir in spices. Serve warm or cold.
Yields 4 cups (1 l)

FRESH BLENDER APPLESAUCE

8   apples
1   cup (250 ml) apple juice, cider,
    or water

2   tbsp (25 ml) fresh lemon juice
    Honey or white sugar

1. Peel, quarter, and core apples.
2. Process half of apple quarters in a blender or food processor
with half of apple juice, cider or water, and lemon juice until smooth.
Repeat with remaining apples. Return processed applesauce to
blender or food processor container and add honey or sugar. Process
briefly until honey or sugar dissolves.
3. Serve immediately or chill.
Yields 6 cups (1.5 l)

MICROWAVE APPLESAUCE

6   cups (1.5 l) sliced, cored, peeled
    apples
1/3 cup (75 ml) water, apple juice,
    or cider

1   tbsp (15 ml) fresh lemon juice
    (optional)
    Sugar or honey

1. In a 2-quart (2-l) microproof casserole, mix apples, water, apple
juice or cider, and lemon juice, if desired. Cover with lid or a sheet
of waxed paper. Cook for 10 minutes on maximum power, or until
apples are tender.
2. Stir in sugar or honey. Beat until smooth or leave chunky.
Yields 3 cups (750 ml)

Apple Pectin

(The water-soluble substance in apples that binds adjacent cell walls
and yields a gel which is the basis of fruit jellies.)

As the apple ripens, this pectin gradually changes to cellulose. Thus
an underripe apple has more pectin in it.

Apples, crabapples, citrus fruit, concord grapes, cranberries, red
currants, gooseberries, sour plums, and quinces are naturally high
in pectin. Fruits naturally lower in pectin (especially when ripe)
include: apricots, blackberries, blueberries, cherries, elderberries,
figs, grapes, guavas, melons, mulberries, nectarines, peaches, pears,
pineapples, sweet plums, raspberries, strawberries, and rhubarb.

Thickening up a batch of blueberry jam may be as simple as
throwing a whole green sour apple in with the bubbling blueberries,
or making a jam of half apples, half blueberries. If you are looking
for the stronger blueberry aroma, however, you will not want to
cut it with blander flavored apples. You can use commercial pectin
(in liquid or powdered form), but this calls for a considerable amount
of sugar which also overpowers the delicate flavor of the berries.
Another alternative is to supplement the blueberries with homemade
apple pectin jelly stock. This stock can also be made from other
high-pectin fruits, but their flavors are stronger than that of apples.

APPLE PECTIN JELLY STOCK

10 lb (4.5 kg) whole apples or crabapples
2.5 qt (2.5 l) water

1. Wash and coarsely chop apples.
2. Place apples (including peels and cores) and water in a large
enamelled or stainless steel Dutch oven or preserving kettle. Bring
to a boil. Cover and reduce heat. Simmer for 15 to 20 minutes until
apples are fork tender.
3. Pour apples and water into a jelly bag. Allow to drip over a bowl
for 4 to 6 hours. Do not squeeze pulp.

4. Pour dripped juices back into Dutch oven or kettle. Bring to a boil and cook, uncovered, for 15 to 20 minutes until thick and syrupy and volume is reduced by half. Strain.

5. Combine with fruit juices to make jelly using approximately equal amounts of juice and pectin jelly. To store for future use, bring pectin jelly to a boil. Pour into sterile jars, seal, and process in a boiling hot water bath for 15 minutes. Pectin jelly may also be frozen.
Yields 4 pints (2 l)

CHAPTER THREE

Apples for Breakfast, Brunch, and Lunch

Beverages

APPLE-BANANA BREAKFAST SHAKE

A nutritious way to start the day.

1 banana
1 cup (250 ml) fresh orange juice
1½ cups (375 ml) diced, peeled
    apple

1 cup (250 ml) cold milk
1 egg
1 to 2 tbsp (15 to 25 ml) liquid
    honey

1. Process all ingredients in a blender or food processor until smooth. Serve immediately.
Serves 3 to 4

APPLE-YOGURT BREAKFAST SHAKE

Add a few fresh or frozen strawberries for color.

1 apple
½ banana
½ cup (125 ml) plain yogurt

1 egg
1 tbsp (15 ml) liquid honey
    Freshly grated nutmeg

1. Peel, core, and quarter apple.
2. Process apple, banana, yogurt, egg, and honey in a blender or food processor until smooth.
3. Pour into a glass and sprinkle with nutmeg.
Serves 1

APPLE LASSI

In this version of the East Indian beverage, applesauce and yogurt or buttermilk are blended to make a tart breakfast drink.

1 cup (250 ml) plain yogurt or
    buttermilk
½ cup (125 ml) cold, sweetened
    applesauce

Liquid honey
Freshly grated nutmeg

1. Process yogurt or buttermilk and applesauce in a blender or food processor until smooth.

2. Taste and add honey if needed, it will depend on the sweetness of the applesauce. Pour into glasses and sprinkle each serving with nutmeg.

Serves 2

APPLE JUICE BREAKFAST DRINK

A fast, nutritious breakfast drink.

¾ cup (175 ml) apple juice
¼ cup (50 ml) milk
1 egg

1 tsp (5 ml) honey or white sugar
   (optional)
¼ tsp (1 ml) cinnamon
⅛ tsp (½ ml) nutmeg

1. Process all ingredients in a blender or food processor until smooth. Serve immediately.

1 large serving or 2 small servings

Cereals

CREAM OF WHEAT CEREAL IN APPLE JUICE

This cereal tastes and smells like apple pie. Vary by using Cranberry Apple Juice (see page 128).

3¼ cups (800 ml) apple juice
¾ cup (175 ml) quick-cooking wheat cereal (Cream of Wheat)
   Dash salt
1 tsp (5 ml) cinnamon

1. In a medium saucepan, bring apple juice to a boil. Sprinkle in cereal, salt, and cinnamon.

2. Reduce heat and stir until mixture thickens. Remove from heat, cover, and let sit for 5 minutes.
3. Serve with brown sugar, and milk or cream.
Serves 6

OATMEAL WITH APPLES AND NUTS

Toasted nuts and raw apples add crunch to everyday cereal.

3 cups (750 ml) water	2 apples
1½ cups (375 ml) quick-cooking rolled oats	4 tbsp (60 ml) chopped toasted walnuts or almonds
¼ tsp (1 ml) cinnamon	2 tbsp (25 ml) brown sugar

1. Bring water to a boil in a medium saucepan. Slowly add oats and cinnamon, stirring constantly. Cook, stirring occasionally, for 1 minute. Cover and remove from heat. Let stand about 3 minutes.
2. Quarter, core, and chop apples. Stir apples, brown sugar, and walnuts or almonds into oatmeal. Serve with cream, if desired.
Serves 4

NOTE: *If using large-flake rolled oats, increase water to 4 cups (1 l) and increase rolled oats to 2 cups (500 ml). Stir oats into briskly boiling salted water. Cook 20 to 25 minutes, stirring occasionally.*

APPLE-ORANGE TOPPING FOR HOT CEREAL

Liven up your morning porridge with this apple, orange, and honey mixture.

3 apples	1 tsp (5 ml) grated orange rind
1 tbsp (15 ml) butter	2 tbsp (25 ml) honey

1. Grate or finely chop unpeeled apples.
2. Melt butter in a small saucepan. Stir in orange rind and honey. Add the grated or chopped apples and stir over medium heat until warm. Spoon over hot cereal and serve with milk or cream.
Serves 4

CAMP BREAKFAST

This is a quick muesli-type cereal to serve for breakfast at camp.

¾ cup (175 ml) uncooked rolled oats
1 can sweetened condensed milk
⅓ cup (75 ml) fresh lemon juice or undiluted frozen lemonade concentrate
3 to 4 cups (750 to 1 l) grated unpeeled apples

1. Combine oats, condensed milk, lemon juice or lemonade concentrate in a large bowl.
2. Add grated apples and stir until mixture reaches desired consistency. Serve immediately. Place any leftovers in cooler.
Serves 8

APPLE COCONUT GRANOLA

A granola baked without oil and sweetened with apple juice concentrate.

3 cups (750 ml) rolled oats
2 cups (500 ml) flaked coconut
1½ tsp (7 ml) cinnamon
⅓ cup (75 ml) undiluted apple
  juice concentrate
1 tsp (5 ml) coconut extract
1 tbsp (15 ml) vanilla
1½ cups (375 ml) dried apples
½ cup (125 ml) currants

1. Mix oats, coconut, and cinnamon in a medium bowl. Mix apple juice concentrate, coconut extract, and vanilla in a cup. Add to dry ingredients and mix until evenly moistened.
2. Spread oat mixture evenly on a cookie sheet. Bake at 350°F (180°C) for 10 minutes or until browned. Stir several times during cooking. Watch carefully because mixture can scorch quickly. Remove from oven and stir in dried apples and currants.
3. Cool completely and store in a covered container.
Yields 7 cups (1.75 l)

GRANOLA BREAKFAST APPLES

Serve these baked, cereal-stuffed apples hot or cold.

4 *large apples*
¾ cup (175 ml) *granola cereal, any flavor*
2 tbsp (25 ml) *brown sugar*

1. Core apples but do not pierce bottom. Scoop out center of apples until there is ½-inch (1-cm) thick shell. Reserve and chop ½ cup (125 ml) of the scooped out apple. Peel a strip of skin from center of apple.
2. Mix granola, reserved apple, and brown sugar in a small bowl. Stuff apples with this mixture. Place apples in a small, deep baking dish. Add water to a depth of ¼ inch (½ cm). Cover dish with foil.
3. Bake at 350°F (180°C) for 35 to 40 minutes or until apples are tender. Serve with cream if desired.
Serves 4

CREAMY RICE PUDDING CEREAL

When you have cooked more than enough rice for supper, save it to make this hot breakfast pudding. Brown rice is especially good in this cereal.

1½ cups (375 ml) *cooked rice*
2 cups (500 ml) *milk*
2 tbsp (25 ml) *white sugar*
2 tbsp (25 ml) *currants*
2 *eggs, slightly beaten*

1 cup (250 ml) *chopped peeled apples*
1 tsp (5 ml) *vanilla*
1 tbsp (15 ml) *butter*
   Freshly grated nutmeg or cinnamon

1. Combine rice, milk, sugar, and currants in top of double boiler. Cook over simmering water until hot. Stir a little of the hot rice mixture into the beaten eggs. Quickly stir eggs into hot rice mixture. Cook, stirring constantly, until mixture begins to thicken.
2. Stir in the apples, vanilla, and butter. Sprinkle each serving with nutmeg or cinnamon.
Serves 4 to 6

APPLESAUCE SCRAPPLE

Applesauce is added to a quick recipe for scrapple.

1 lb (454 g) bulk sausage meat	½ tsp (2 ml) marjoram
1 cup (250 ml) yellow cornmeal	1 cup (250 ml) applesauce
1 cup (250 ml) cold water	¼ cup (50 ml) all-purpose flour
1 cup (250 ml) boiling water	Rendered bacon fat, or salt pork fat, or butter

1. Lightly brown sausage meat, breaking it up into small pieces with a spatula while cooking. Drain off fat.
2. Mix cornmeal with cold water in a bowl and pour into a large saucepan. Add the boiling water and cook, stirring over medium heat until thickened. Fold in marjoram, applesauce, and browned sausage.
3. Spoon cornmeal mixture into a buttered 9 × 5-inch (2-l) loaf pan. Cool, cover, and chill until firm.
4. Unmold and cut in ½-inch (1-cm) slices. Dredge slices with flour. Heat enough fat or butter to generously cover bottom of large skillet. Brown slices over medium-high heat on both sides in hot fat.
Serves 6

SWEET APPLE-ALMOND COMBO

Top with yogurt and serve for breakfast, brunch, or even dessert.

2 cups (500 ml) chopped, cored, unpeeled apples	1 tbsp (15 ml) white sugar (optional)
Juice of ½ lemon	2 tbsp (25 ml) golden raisins
	¼ cup (50 ml) ground almonds

1. Toss apples with lemon juice and sugar in a small bowl.
2. Mix in raisins and ground almonds. This can be refrigerated for a short time.
Serves 3 to 4

BARLEY COOKED IN APPLE JUICE

Barley grits can be found in most health food stores. Cook the night before and reheat in the morning. Cranberry Apple Juice (see page 128) can be used instead of apple juice.

3 cups (750 ml) water	1½ cups (375 ml) apple juice
1 cup (250 ml) barley grits	½ cup (125 ml) raisins
1 strip of lemon peel	¼ cup (50 ml) white sugar

1. Bring water to a boil in a large saucepan. Stir the barley into boiling water. Add the lemon peel. Reduce heat and simmer partially covered for 30 minutes. Stir frequently.
2. Stir in the apple juice, raisins, and sugar. Cook over low heat, uncovered, for 30 minutes or until thick. Remove lemon peel. It may be necessary to add a little apple juice when reheating cereal.
3. Serve with cream.
Serves 4

SWISS APPLE OATMEAL

A tasty break from hot porridge or commercial cereal. It is easy to prepare in the morning, if you soak the grain overnight. This recipe can be doubled.

2 tbsp (25 ml) rolled wheat flakes or old fashioned rolled oats	1 tbsp (15 ml) finely chopped hazelnuts or almonds
2 medium apples	3 tbsp (45 ml) milk or light cream
Juice of ½ orange	1 tbsp (15 ml) honey
Juice of ½ lemon	Cinnamon (optional)

1. Soak the wheat flakes or rolled oats overnight in about ¼ cup (50 ml) cold water. In the morning, drain flakes if all water is not absorbed.

2. Coarsely grate or chop unpeeled apples into a medium bowl. Sprinkle with orange and lemon juice.

3. Add wheat or oats, nuts, milk or cream, and honey to apples and toss.

4. Sprinkle a little cinnamon over each serving if desired.

Serves 2

SKILLET APPLE BREAD PUDDING

Serve this main-course breakfast or brunch dish with cinnamon sugar or maple syrup.

3 to 4 slices day-old white bread	4 eggs
2 cups (500 ml) milk	2 tbsp (25 ml) white sugar
1 cup (250 ml) chopped, cored, peeled apples	1 tsp (5 ml) vanilla
	2 tbsp (25 ml) raisins
1/3 cup (75 ml) melted butter	2 tbsp (25 ml) ground almonds

1. Tear bread into small pieces. Place in a small bowl with milk to cover for 10 minutes.

2. Butter a 9- or 10-inch (22.5- or 25-cm) cast iron or ovenproof skillet. Lightly squeeze bread and place in skillet. Sprinkle with chopped apples. Discard milk.

3. Process butter, eggs, sugar, vanilla, and almonds in a blender or food processor until smooth. Pour over bread and sprinkle with raisins.

4. Place in a cold oven; turn heat to 350°F (180°C). Bake for 15 to 20 minutes or until puffy and lightly browned.

5. Remove from oven. Cut in wedges to serve.

Serves 4

Pancakes

APPLE-COTTAGE CHEESE PANCAKES

These pancakes are lightened with stiffly beaten egg whites. Serve with maple syrup and yogurt.

1 cup (250 ml) grated unpeeled apples
1 cup (250 ml) creamed cottage cheese
¾ cup (175 ml) all-purpose flour
1 tbsp (15 ml) white sugar
½ tsp (2 ml) cinnamon
⅛ tsp (½ ml) allspice
¼ tsp (1 ml) salt
4 eggs

1. Combine apples, cottage cheese, flour, sugar, spices, and salt in a large bowl.
2. Separate eggs and beat yolks into apple mixture. Beat whites until stiff and fold into batter.
3. Pour about ¼ cup (50 ml) batter for each pancake on an oiled, medium-hot griddle or frying pan. Spread batter evenly with back of spoon. Brown on both sides.
Yields 10 to 12 pancakes

OVEN-PUFFED APPLE PANCAKES

Impress your guests with these Yorkshire-pudding style pancakes.

8 apples
3 tbsp (45 ml) butter
6 eggs
1 cup (250 ml) milk

1 cup (250 ml) all-purpose flour
½ tsp (2 ml) baking powder
4 tbsp (50 ml) butter
⅓ cup (75 ml) brown sugar
½ tsp (2 ml) cinnamon

1. Preheat oven to 450°F (250°C). Peel, quarter, and core apples. Cut into thin slices. Melt butter in a large saucepan. Add apples and cook over medium heat, stirring occasionally, until partially cooked. Remove from heat.
2. Whisk eggs and milk in a large bowl. Add flour and baking powder. Blend well, but do not overbeat.
3. You will need two 9 x 13-inch (3 l) baking pans. Place 2 tbsp (25 ml) butter in each pan. Place in oven to melt butter and preheat pan (2 to 3 minutes).
4. Carefully remove pans from oven. Tip pans to distribute butter evenly.
5. Working quickly, pour half of batter into each pan. Spread half of apple slices in center of each pan to within 2 inches (5 cm) of edges.
6. Sprinkle brown sugar and cinnamon over apples. Bake for 10 to 12 minutes or until puffed and brown. Serve immediately, as pancakes deflate quickly.
Serves 4

WHOLE-WHEAT APPLE PANCAKES

Top with the traditional maple syrup or Apple Syrup (see page 226).

1   cup (250 ml) whole-wheat flour
½ cup (125 ml) all-purpose flour
2   tbsp (25 ml) white sugar
1   tbsp (15 ml) baking powder
½ tsp (2 ml) salt

1   egg
1¾ cup (425 ml) milk
2   tbsp (25 ml) vegetable oil or
    melted butter
¾ cup (175 ml) finely chopped
    peeled apples

1. Blend whole-wheat flour, all-purpose flour, sugar, baking powder, and salt in a large bowl.
2. Beat egg, milk, and vegetable oil or melted butter in a medium bowl. Add to flour mixture and beat only until combined. Fold in chopped apples. If batter thickens, add a little more milk.
3. Heat a griddle or skillet over medium heat. Lightly oil griddle or skillet. Use about ¼ cup (50 ml) batter for each pancake. Bake until edges of pancakes look dry. Turn and bake until golden brown. Serve hot, with butter and syrup.
Yields about 12 pancakes

APPLESAUCE PANCAKES

A fine-grained pancake.

1½ cups (375 ml) all-purpose flour
2   tbsp (25 ml) sugar
½ tsp (2 ml) cinnamon
¼ tsp (1 ml) nutmeg
⅛ tsp (½ ml) ground cloves
1   tsp (5 ml) baking powder

½ tsp (2 ml) baking soda
1   egg
1   cup (250 ml) milk
¾ cup (175 ml) applesauce
¼ cup (50 ml) chopped raisins
2   tbsp (25 ml) vegetable oil or
    melted butter

1. Blend flour, sugar, cinnamon, nutmeg, cloves, baking powder, and baking soda in a large bowl.

2. Beat egg, milk, applesauce, raisins, and vegetable oil or melted butter in a medium bowl. Add to flour mixture. Beat only until combined. If batter thickens, add a little more milk.

3. Heat a griddle or skillet over medium-high heat. Lightly oil griddle or skillet. Use about ¼ cup (50 ml) batter for each pancake. Bake until edges of pancakes look dry. Turn and bake until golden brown. Serve hot with butter and syrup.

Yields about 12 pancakes

MOLASSES-GINGER PANCAKES

Spicy pancakes that taste like gingerbread.

2½ cups (625 ml) all-purpose flour	*¼ cup (50 ml) molasses*
2 tbsp (25 ml) baking powder	*2 cups (500 ml) milk*
1 tsp (5 ml) salt	*2 eggs, beaten*
1 tsp (5 ml) baking soda	*½ cup (125 ml) butter, melted*
1 tsp (5 ml) cinnamon	*1 cup (250 ml) diced, cored,*
½ tsp (2 ml) ground ginger	*peeled apples*
⅛ tsp (½ ml) ground cloves	*¼ cup (50 ml) raisins*

1. Mix flour, baking powder, salt, baking soda, and spices in a large bowl.

2. Combine molasses, milk, eggs, and butter in a medium bowl. Add to flour mixture, and stir until evenly moistened.

3. Fold in apples and raisins.

4. Cook on a lightly greased hot griddle, using about ¼ cup (50 ml) batter for each pancake. Spread batter evenly with back of spoon. Cook until golden brown on both sides. Serve hot with butter and molasses.

Yields 20 pancakes

Brunch Dishes

APPLE-CHEDDAR EGG SCRAMBLE

Round out this brunch dish with buttered toast and browned sausages.

2 eggs	2 tbsp (25 ml) butter
1 tsp (5 ml) honey	¼ cup (50 ml) cubed cheddar
½ cup (125 ml) grated unpeeled apples	cheese

1. Lightly beat eggs with honey in a small bowl. Stir in the grated apples.
2. Heat butter in a skillet and when butter foams, add the egg mixture and cheese cubes.
3. Stir a few times until eggs are cooked, about 3 minutes.
Serves 1 to 2

CELERY APPLE SANDWICHES

A colorful, crunchy sandwich filling.

½ cup (125 ml) finely chopped celery	2 tbsp (25 ml) mayonnaise
½ cup (125 ml) finely chopped unpeeled apple	2 tsp (10 ml) butter
	4 slices of oatmeal bread

1. Mix celery, apple, and mayonnaise in a small bowl.
2. Butter bread. Spread filling evenly over two slices of bread. Slice diagonally and serve immediately.
Serves 1 to 2

CHEESE-APPLE RAREBIT

For a crunchy contrast to the smooth cheese sauce, stir in diced apples at the last moment.

1 tbsp (15 ml) unsalted butter	¼ tsp (1 ml) nutmeg
1 tsp (5 ml) all-purpose flour	1 cup (250 ml) diced unpeeled
3 cups (750 ml) grated medium	apples
cheddar cheese	4 thick slices lightly toasted
½ tsp (2 ml) dry mustard	bread

1. Melt butter in a medium saucepan over low heat. Stir in flour.
2. Add cheese, cream, mustard, and nutmeg to saucepan. Stir over medium-low heat until cheese has melted.
3. When mixture begins to bubble, stir in apples. Spoon over toasted bread.
Serves 4

BROILED APPLES AND CHEESE ON PUMPERNICKEL

Sliced apples on pumpernickel toast are topped with cottage cheese, sprinkled with cinnamon sugar, and broiled.

1 slice pumpernickel bread	¼ cup (50 ml) cottage cheese
1 tsp (5 ml) butter	1 tbsp (15 ml) white or brown
½ cup (125 ml) thinly sliced	sugar
apples	⅛ tsp (½ ml) cinnamon

1. Lightly toast the pumpernickel bread. Spread with butter.
2. Arrange apple slices over bread. Spread cottage cheese over apples.
3. Mix sugar with cinnamon and sprinkle over cheese. Broil until sugar begins to caramelize and cheese is softened. Serve immediately.
Serves 1

TUNA-APPLE-SPROUT SALAD IN PITA BREAD

A satisfying but light lunch dish.

1   7 oz (200 g) can of tuna
1   cup (250 ml) finely diced
    unpeeled apples
2   tsp (10 ml) fresh lemon juice

1   cup (250 ml) lightly packed
    alfalfa sprouts
½ cup (125 ml) mayonnaise
3   pita bread

1. Drain tuna. Sprinkle apples with lemon juice. Combine tuna, apples, sprouts, and mayonnaise, and toss lightly until evenly mixed.
2. Cut pita bread in half. Stuff each half with tuna mixture and serve immediately.
Serves 3

SPICED APPLE-HAM PATTIES

This is a nice brunch dish.

2   cups (500 ml) ground cooked
    ham
½ cup (125 ml) dry breadcrumbs
2   eggs
2   tsp (10 ml) prepared mustard

3   tbsp (45 ml) butter or bacon
    drippings
2   tbsp (25 ml) apple juice
4   cups (1 l) sliced, peeled, cored
    apples
¼ tsp (1 ml) cloves
¼ cup (50 ml) brown sugar

1. Combine ham, breadcrumbs, eggs, and mustard in a medium bowl. Shape into six thin patties.
2. Heat butter or bacon drippings in a large skillet over medium-high heat. Brown ham patties on both sides. Drain on paper towels. Transfer to a baking dish. Sprinkle with apple juice.
3. Cover ham patties with apple slices.
4. Mix cloves and brown sugar. Sprinkle over apples. Bake at 375°F (190°C) for 10 to 15 minutes or until apples and patties are heated through.
Serves 6

SAUSAGE AND APPLE PATTIES

Try this on an English muffin topped with an egg sunny side up.

½ lb (250 g) bulk sausage meat
1 ¼ cup (300 ml) fine breadcrumbs
1 cup (250 ml) grated unpeeled
    apples
2 tbsp (250 ml) flour

1 egg
2 tbsp (25 ml) shortening or bacon
    fat
Salt and freshly ground pepper

1. Using your hands, mix together sausage meat, ¾ cup (175 ml) bread crumbs, grated apples, flour, and egg.
2. Form into thin patties. Coat with remaining bread crumbs.
3. Melt shortening or bacon fat in a large skillet over medium heat. Fry patties about 8 minutes on each side until browned. Season with salt and pepper just before serving.
Serves 4

FRENCH TOAST SANDWICHES

Apple marmalade or preserves are sandwiched between sliced or whole-wheat bread, dipped in beaten egg, and sautéed in butter.

8 slices day-old whole-wheat bread
⅔ cup (150 ml) Apple Marmalade
    (see page 246) or
    Apple Preserves
    (see page 245)

4 eggs, well beaten
¼ cup (50 ml) milk
½ tsp (2 ml) vanilla
3 tbsp (45 ml) butter
    Icing sugar

1. Spread 4 slices of bread with apple marmalade or preserves. Top with remaining slices of bread.
2. Combine eggs, milk, and vanilla in a pie plate. Dip sandwiches in egg mixture, coating both sides.
3. Melt butter in an electric frying pan or large skillet over medium-high heat and fry sandwiches until golden brown on both sides.
4. Sprinkle with icing sugar and serve hot.
Serves 4

BACON-APPLE PIE

Thin slices of back bacon are cooked with onions and apples for a
hearty breakfast or brunch.

Crust
1 cup (250 ml) all-purpose flour
½ tsp (2 ml) salt
⅓ cup (75 ml) shortening or lard
2 to 3 tbsp (25 to 45 ml) cold
   water

Filling
1 tbsp (15 ml) butter
1 lb (454 g) sliced lean bacon
   (Canadian back or home cured)
3 medium onions, chopped
2 cups (500 ml) chopped peeled
   apples
⅓ cup (75 ml) cider
   Freshly ground pepper

1. Mix flour and salt in a medium bowl. Cut in shortening until
mixture resembles coarse meal. Sprinkle water over flour and mix
with a fork until evenly moistened. Gather into a ball. Cover with
plastic wrap and chill while preparing filling.
2. Melt butter in a large skillet. Add the bacon and onions. Sauté
until bacon is cooked and onions are tender. Drain off any excess
fat.
3. Transfer bacon and onions to a 2-quart (2-l) ovenproof casserole.
Mix in the chopped apples and add cider. Season to taste with pepper.
4. Roll dough on a lightly floured surface to fit over casserole.
Crimp edges and cut a vent in center of pastry. Bake at 375°F (190°C)
for 25 to 30 minutes or until pastry is golden brown.
Serves 4

APPLE-RAISIN QUICHE

Serve this rich, sweet quiche for brunch or dessert.

1½ cups (375 ml) all-purpose
   flour
¼ tsp (1 ml) salt
¼ cup (50 ml) cold butter
¼ cup (50 ml) cold shortening
3 tbsp (45 ml) ice water
⅓ cup (75 ml) golden raisins

3 large apples
2 eggs
1 cup (250 ml) whipping cream
⅓ cup (75 ml) white sugar
½ tsp (2 ml) vanilla
1½ tsp (7 ml) cinnamon

1. Mix flour and salt in a medium bowl. Cut in butter and shortening until mixture resembles coarse breadcrumbs. Sprinkle with water and mix with a fork until mixture is evenly moistened. Gather dough into a ball, and roll on a lightly floured surface to fit a 9-inch (22.5-cm) pie plate or flan dish. Be careful not to stretch dough. Crimp edges and prick pastry all over with fork. Bake at 400°F (200°C) oven for 15 to 20 minutes. Remove from oven. Reduce oven temperature to 375°F (190°C).
2. Sprinkle raisins over bottom of quiche shell.
3. Peel, quarter, and core apples. Slice into thin wedges and arrange over raisins.
4. Beat eggs, cream, sugar, vanilla, and cinnamon until blended. Pour over apples. Bake at 375°F (190°C) for 50 to 60 minutes or until custard is nearly set.
5. Serve lukewarm or at room temperature.
Serves 6

CRANBERRY-OATMEAL COFFEE CAKE

A wholesome addition to brunch.

Cake
½ cup (125 ml) shortening
1 cup (250 ml) white sugar
2 eggs
1 cup (250 ml) applesauce
1½ cups (375 ml) all-purpose flour
¾ tsp (4 ml) baking soda
½ tsp (2 ml) salt
1 tsp (5 ml) cinnamon

½ tsp (2 ml) ground cloves
¼ tsp (1 ml) nutmeg
1 cup (250 ml) rolled oats
¾ cup (175 ml) whole cranberry
  sauce

Glaze
1 cup (250 ml) icing sugar
1½ tbsp (22 ml) milk

1. Cream shortening, sugar, and eggs until light. Beat in applesauce. (Mixture may look curdled.)
2. Sift flour, soda, salt, and spices into a medium bowl. Add to creamed mixture and mix thoroughly. Fold in oats and cranberry sauce. Pour into a buttered 9-inch (2.5-l) square baking pan.
3. Bake at 350°F (180°C) for 40 to 45 minutes or until cake tester comes out clean.
4. Beat icing sugar and milk until smooth in a small bowl. Drizzle over cake while still warm.
Serves 9

CHAPTER FOUR

Apples at Tea

Cakes

APPLE-ALMOND CHEESECAKE

An almond shortbread crust is filled with luscious cheesecake and a whorl of apple slices.

Shortbread Crust
½ cup (125 ml) butter
½ cup (125 ml) ground almonds
¼ cup (50 ml) white sugar
⅛ tsp (½ ml) almond extract
1 cup (250 ml) all-purpose flour

Cheesecake Filling
16 oz (500 g) cream cheese, at room
    temperature
⅔ cup (150 ml) white sugar
2 eggs
1 tsp (5 ml) vanilla

Apple Topping
⅓ cup (75 ml) brown sugar
1 tbsp (15 ml) all-purpose flour
½ tsp (2 ml) cinnamon
4 cups (1 l) sliced peeled apples
⅓ cup (75 ml) sliced almonds

1. To make shortbread crust, cream butter until light and fluffy. Add ground almonds, sugar, and almond extract, and beat until combined. Add flour and knead until evenly mixed.
2. Roll dough between two sheets of waxed paper to a 10-inch (25-cm) circle. Remove paper and fit pastry into a 9-inch (22.5-cm) springform pan. Press pastry against side of pan. Cover and chill while preparing filling and topping.
3. To make cheesecake filling, beat cream cheese, sugar, eggs, and vanilla until smooth. Pour into chilled crust.
4. To prepare apple topping, combine sugar, flour, and cinnamon in a large bowl. Add apple slices and toss lightly to coat. Arrange apple slices in a circular pattern over cheesecake filling.
5. Bake at 425°F (220°C) for 10 minutes, reduce heat to 350°F (180°C) and bake for 25 to 30 minutes longer or until apples are

tender and cheesecake is set. Sprinkle with almonds 5 minutes before cheesecake is done. Cool, remove rim, and transfer to a serving plate.
Serves 8

APPLESAUCE CAKE

For the cholesterol-conscious, this cake recipe uses oil instead of shortening.

½ cup (125 ml) vegetable oil
1¼ cups (300 ml) white sugar
2 eggs
1 cup (250 ml) applesauce
½ tsp (2 ml) baking soda
1½ cups (375 ml) all-purpose flour

1 tsp (5 ml) baking powder
¼ tsp (1 ml) salt
1 tsp (5 ml) cinnamon
½ tsp (2 ml) ground cloves
¼ tsp (1 ml) nutmeg
1 cup (250 ml) raisins

1. Beat oil, sugar, and eggs in a large bowl until light.
2. Dissolve soda in applesauce.
3. Sift flour, baking soda, salt, cinnamon, cloves, and nutmeg into a large bowl. Stir into egg mixture alternately with applesauce. Fold in raisins.
4. Pour batter into a buttered 8-inch (1.2-l) square baking pan. Bake at 350°F (180°C) for 40 to 45 minutes or until a cake tester comes out clean. Cool on a wire rack. Leave in pan and ice if you wish.
Serves 9

APPLESAUCE RAISIN CAKE

Applesauce cakes are moist and spicy, and this one is no exception.

2½ cups (625 ml) all-purpose flour   ½ cup (125 ml) butter
1½ tsp (7 ml) baking soda   1 cup (250 ml) brown sugar
½ tsp (2 ml) salt   ½ cup (125 ml) white sugar
1 tsp (5 ml) cinnamon   2 large eggs
   Pinch of ground cloves   1½ cups (375 ml) applesauce
                                       ½ cup (125 ml) raisins

1. Mix flour, baking soda, salt, cinnamon, and cloves in a medium bowl.
2. Cream butter and sugars in a large bowl until light and fluffy. Add eggs and beat until well mixed.
3. Add dry ingredients to creamed mixture, alternately with applesauce. Beat well after each addition. Fold in raisins.
4. Divide batter between two greased and floured 8-inch (1.2-l) round cake pans. Bake at 350°F (180°C) for 40 minutes or until cake tester comes out clean.
5. Invert on to wire rack and cool. Ice when cool if desired.
Serves 8

APPLE-WALNUT BUNDT CAKE

A good, old-fashioned, spice-and-apple cake.

Cake
½ cup (125 ml) white sugar
1 cup (250 ml) vegetable oil
3 eggs
1 tsp (5 ml) vanilla
2 cups (500 ml) all-purpose flour
1 tsp (5 ml) baking soda
1 tsp (5 ml) nutmeg
1 tsp (5 ml) allspice
1 tsp (5 ml) cinnamon
1 cup (250 ml) cultured buttermilk

1 cup (250 ml) finely chopped
   walnuts
2 cups (500 ml) diced peeled apples

Glaze
½ cup (125 ml) white sugar
½ tsp (2 ml) vanilla
¼ cup (50 ml) buttermilk
4 tbsp (60 ml) butter
1 tbsp (15 ml) corn syrup
⅛ tsp (½ ml) baking soda

1. Beat sugar and vegetable oil in a large bowl. Beat in eggs and vanilla.

2. Sift flour, soda, and spices in a medium bowl. Add dry ingredients alternately with buttermilk to sugar mixture. Mix until evenly blended but do not beat.

3. Stir in walnuts and apples. Pour into a buttered and lightly floured bundt pan. Bake for one hour at 350°F (180°C) or until a cake tester comes out clean.

4. Fifteen minutes before the cake is done, blend together in a sauce-pan all the glaze ingredients. Stir over medium heat until sugar dissolves and the mixture is frothy. Remove from heat.

5. When cake is done, remove from oven and cool in pan for 10 minutes. Invert cake on to a cooling rack and brush the warm top-ping over the cake. When cake is cool, place on a platter to serve.
Serves 12

APPLE TORTEN

Custard apple filling is baked on a lemon-flavored cookie dough.

2 *cups (500 ml) sifted all-purpose flour*	**Filling**
½ *cup (125 ml) white sugar*	6 *apples*
Grated rind of 1 lemon	1 *cup (250 ml) white sugar*
¼ *tsp (1 ml) salt*	1 *tsp (5 ml) cinnamon*
¾ *cup (175 ml) butter*	2 *tbsp (25 ml) butter*
2 *egg yolks*	2 *egg yolks*
	6 *tbsp (90 ml) whipping cream*

1. Mix flour, sugar, lemon rind, and salt in a large bowl. Cut in butter until mixture resembles fine crumbs. Beat egg yolks and mix into flour mixture until evenly moistened.

2. Pat dough on to bottom and sides of 9 × 13-inch (3-l) baking pan.

3. Peel, quarter, and core apples. Slice into thin wedges. Arrange apples in rows on top of dough. Mix sugar and cinnamon and sprin-kle over apples. Dot with butter. Cover with foil and bake at 350°F (180°C) for 20 minutes. Mix together the egg yolks and cream until blended. Drizzle over apples. Continue baking 30 to 35 minutes uncovered until crust is golden brown and apples are tender.

4. Serve slightly warm with whipped cream or ice cream.
Serves 10

GLAZED FRESH APPLE CAKE

Hot caramel sauce is brushed over the cake as soon as it comes out
of the oven.

Cake
1½ cups (375 ml) vegetable oil
2 cups (500 ml) white sugar
3 eggs
3 cups (750 ml) all-purpose flour
1 tsp (5 ml) baking soda
2 tsp (10 ml) cinnamon
1 tsp (5 ml) nutmeg
½ tsp (2 ml) salt
3 cups (750 ml) diced, cored,
   peeled apples
1 cup (250 ml) chopped walnuts
2 tsp (10 ml) vanilla

Glaze
2 tbsp (25 ml) butter
4 tbsp (60 ml) brown sugar
2 tbsp (25 ml) whipping cream or
   cider
1 tsp (5 ml) apple brandy or
   vanilla

1. Combine oil, sugar, and eggs in a large bowl. Beat until well
blended.
2. Sift flour, baking soda, cinnamon, nutmeg, and salt into a medium
bowl. Add to sugar mixture and combine thoroughly.
3. Stir in apples, walnuts, and vanilla. Butter and flour a 10-inch
(25-cm) tube pan or bundt pan. Pour batter into pan and bake at
325°F (160°C) for 1¼ hours or until cake tester comes out clean.
4. Remove from oven and let cool in pan for 10 minutes. Meanwhile, melt the butter in a small saucepan. Add the brown sugar
and cream or cider. Stir until sugar is dissolved. Boil for 1 minute.
Remove from heat and stir in apple brandy or vanilla.
5. Invert cake on to a wire rack. Brush hot glaze over warm cake
until glaze is absorbed. Cool completely and transfer to a serving
plate.
Serves 10 to 12

CARDAMOM APPLE CAKE

This fragrant cake needs no icing, just a dusting of icing sugar. Store
for a day before slicing.

⅔ cup (150 ml) butter
1 cup (250 ml) white sugar
¾ cup (175 ml) brown sugar
2 eggs
1 tsp (5 ml) vanilla
2 cups (500 ml) sifted all-purpose
   flour
2 tsp (10 ml) baking soda

1 tsp (5 ml) ground cardamom
2 tsp (10 ml) cinnamon
1 tsp (5 ml) nutmeg
½ tsp (2 ml) salt
1 cup (250 ml) chopped pecans or
   unblanched almonds
4 cups (1 l) chopped, cored, peeled
   apples
¼ cup (50 ml) icing sugar

1. Butter a bundt pan, and dust with a little flour.
2. Cream butter, white and brown sugars, eggs, and vanilla in a
large bowl until light. Sift the flour, soda, spices, and salt into a
medium bowl. Place nuts in a small bowl and dust with ¼ cup (50
ml) flour mixture.
3. Beat dry ingredients into creamed mixture. Stir in nuts and apples.
4. Pour batter into bundt pan. Bake at 350°F (180°C) for 50 minutes or until cake tester comes out clean.
5. Cool in pan for 15 minutes, then invert and finish cooling on a
wire rack. Wrap in plastic and store for a day before serving.
6. Dust with icing sugar before serving.
Serves 10 to 12

RAISED APPLE CAKE

Poached apple wedges top this unusual cake. Serve still warm from
the oven.

4 *large apples*
1 *cup (250 ml) water*
½ *cup (125 ml) white sugar*
½ *lemon, sliced*

Topping
2 *tbsp (25 ml) brown sugar*
½ *tsp (2 ml) cinnamon*
¼ *tsp (1 ml) nutmeg*
2 *tbsp (25 ml) butter*
2 *tbsp (25 ml) icing sugar*

Cake
1¼ *to 1½ cups (300 to 375 ml)*
    all-purpose flour
¼ *cup (50 ml) white sugar*
½ *tsp (2 ml) salt*
1 *package active dry yeast*
3 *tbsp (45 ml) butter*
½ *cup (125 ml) water*
1 *large egg*

1. Peel, quarter, and core apples. Cut each apple quarter into 3 slices.
Combine water, sugar, and lemon slices in a large saucepan. Stir
over medium heat until sugar dissolves. Add apple slices and simmer until tender, but do not overcook or they will become mushy.
Remove from heat and set aside to cool.
2. Mix ½ cup (125 ml) flour, sugar, salt, and dry yeast in a large
bowl.
3. Heat butter and water in a small saucepan over medium heat
until butter has melted and water is very warm, but not boiling.
Gradually add this mixture to flour mixture and beat for 2 minutes
with an electric mixer. Add the egg, beat until mixture is smooth.
Let sit for 5 minutes to allow yeast to soften. Beat in just enough
flour to make a soft batter. Spread batter in a buttered 8-inch (2-l)
square baking pan.
4. Drain apples and pat dry with paper towel. Arrange apples over
batter.
5. Combine the brown sugar, cinnamon and nutmeg. Cut in butter
finely. Sprinkle apples evenly with brown sugar mixture. Cover and
let rise in a warm place until double in bulk (about 1 hour).
6. Bake at 400°F (200°C) for 25 to 30 minutes. Remove from oven
and cool in pan for 10 minutes. Sift icing sugar over top of cake.
Serve warm.
Serves 8

APPLE BUCKLE

Serve this cake warm with sour cream, whipped cream, or vanilla ice cream.

Cake
½ cup (125 ml) butter
½ cup (125 ml) white sugar
1 egg
1 tsp (5 ml) vanilla
2 cups (500 ml) sifted all-purpose flour
1 tbsp (15 ml) baking powder
½ tsp (2 ml) salt
¾ cup (175 ml) milk
3 cups (750 ml) chopped peeled apples

Topping
½ cup (125 ml) brown sugar
6 tbsp (90 ml) all-purpose flour
½ tsp (2 ml) cinnamon
¼ cup (50 ml) chilled butter

1. Butter a 9 × 13-inch (3.5-l) baking dish.
2. To make cake batter, cream butter and sugar in a large bowl, until light and fluffy. Beat in egg and vanilla.
3. Sift flour, baking powder, and salt into a medium bowl. Add to creamed mixture alternately with milk. Spread batter in baking dish. Sprinkle chopped apples evenly over batter.
4. To make topping, combine brown sugar, flour, and cinnamon in a small bowl. Cut in chilled butter until mixture resembles fine crumbs. Sprinkle over apples.
5. Bake at 350°F (180°C) for 45 minutes or until cake tester comes out clean. Leave cake in pan.
Serves 10 to 12

VARIATION: APPLE-CRANBERRY BUCKLE

Proceed as for Apple Buckle but substitute 1½ cups (425 ml) finely chopped apples and 1½ cups (425 ml) cranberries. Increase brown sugar in topping to ¾ cup (175 ml).

APPLE UPSIDE-DOWN CAKE

Delicious by itself or with whipped cream or ice cream.

¼ cup (50 ml) butter
¼ cup (50 ml) brown sugar
2½ cups (325 ml) sliced, cored,
    peeled apples

Cake
¼ cup (50 ml) butter
⅔ cup (150 ml) white sugar

2 eggs
1 tsp (5 ml) vanilla
1½ cups (325 ml) sifted
    all-purpose flour
½ tsp (2 ml) salt
1 tbsp (15 ml) baking powder
½ cup (125 ml) milk

1. Melt ¼ cup (50 ml) butter in 8-inch (2-l) square baking pan. Sprinkle brown sugar over butter. Arrange apple slices over brown sugar.
2. To prepare cake, cream butter and sugar in a large bowl until light and fluffy. Beat in eggs and vanilla.
3. Sift flour, salt, and baking powder into a small bowl. Add flour mixture to creamed mixture alternately with milk. Stir just until mixed. Spread batter over apples.
4. Bake at 375°F (190°C) for 35 minutes or until top is browned. Let cool for 5 minutes, then invert on to a plate.
Serves 6

WHOLE-WHEAT APPLESAUCE RAISIN CAKE

Honey and applesauce make this a moist whole-wheat cake. Frost with Applesauce Icing (see page 92) or a cream cheese icing.

1¾ cups (425 ml) whole-wheat
    flour
¼ tsp (1 ml) cream of tartar
¼ tsp (1 ml) salt
1 tsp (5 ml) baking soda
1 tsp (5 ml) cinnamon

½ tsp (2 ml) ground cloves
½ cup (125 ml) butter
½ cup (125 ml) liquid honey
1 large egg
1 cup (250 ml) applesauce
½ cup (125 ml) raisins

1. Mix flour, cream of tartar, salt, soda, cinnamon, and cloves in a medium bowl.
2. Cream butter and honey until light and fluffy. Beat in egg. Mix in applesauce. Add flour mixture and stir until evenly moistened. Fold in raisins.
3. Pour batter into an 8-inch (2-l) square baking pan. Bake at 350°F (180°C) 30 to 35 minutes or until golden brown and cake springs back when touched.
Serves 9

COCONUT APPLE CAKE

This cake doesn't need any icing.

⅓ cup (75 ml) butter
⅔ cup (150 ml) white sugar
2 eggs
1⅔ cups (400 ml) all-purpose flour
1 tbsp (15 ml) baking powder

¼ tsp (1 ml) salt
1 tsp (5 ml) cinnamon
1 tsp (5 ml) vanilla
⅔ cup (150 ml) milk
1 cup (250 ml) angel-flake coconut
2 cups (500 ml) diced unpeeled apples

1. Cream butter and white sugar until light and fluffy. Add the eggs and beat until combined.
2. Sift together the flour, baking powder, salt, and cinnamon. Add flour mixture to creamed mixture alternately with milk. Beat until smooth after each addition.
3. Fold in coconut and apples. Pour batter into a buttered 9-inch (2.5 l) square baking pan. Bake at 350°F (180°C) for 50 to 60 minutes or until a cake tester comes out clean.
Serves 9

CHOCOLATE-CHIP APPLESAUCE CAKE

Moist and chocolatey.

1 cup (250 ml) all-purpose flour
2 tbsp (25 ml) cocoa
1 tsp (5 ml) baking soda
¾ cup (175 ml) white sugar
⅓ cup (75 ml) melted butter

1 egg
1 tsp (5 ml) vanilla
1 cup (250 ml) applesauce
⅓ cup (75 ml) chocolate chips
⅓ cup (75 ml) chopped walnuts

1. Sift flour, cocoa, soda, and sugar into a large bowl.
2. Combine butter, egg, vanilla, and applesauce in a medium bowl.
Beat until blended. Add to the dry ingredients and stir until mixed.
Fold in the chocolate chips and walnuts.
3. Pour batter into a greased 8- or 9-inch (2 or 2.5 l) square baking
pan. Bake at 350°F (180°C) for 25 to 30 minutes or until cake tester
comes out clean.
4. Let cool in pan on rack.
Serves 9

MICROWAVE APPLESAUCE CAKE

A chocolate cake that bakes in 10 to 12 minutes!

1⅓ cups (325 ml) all-purpose
   flour
1 cup (250 ml) white sugar
1 tsp (5 ml) baking soda
½ tsp (2 ml) salt
½ tsp (2 ml) cinnamon
½ tsp (2 ml) nutmeg

¼ tsp (1 ml) allspice
1½ tbsp (22 ml) cocoa
⅓ cup (75 ml) vegetable oil
1 egg
1 cup (250 ml) applesauce
½ cup (125 ml) raisins
½ cup (125 ml) walnuts

1. Place all ingredients, except raisins and nuts, in a large bowl.
Using an electric mixer, beat for 2 minutes or until smooth. Scrape
bowl frequently.

2. Fold in raisins and walnuts. Pour batter into a buttered 8 × 12-inch (2.5-l) pan or a buttered microwave tube pan.

3. Bake at maximum power for 10 to 12 minutes. Rotate ½ turn after 5 minutes. Cake is done when a toothpick or cake tester stuck in several places comes out clean. Remove from oven and cool in pan.

Serves 9 to 10

YOGURT APPLE CAKE

A lightly spiced butter cake.

½ cup (125 ml) butter
¾ cup (175 ml) white sugar
2 eggs
2 cups (500 ml) all-purpose flour
1 tsp (5 ml) baking powder
1 tsp (5 ml) baking soda

¼ tsp (1 ml) salt
1 tsp (5 ml) cinnamon
1 cup (250 ml) plain yogurt
1 tsp (5 ml) vanilla
2 cups (500 ml) diced unpeeled apples
Icing sugar

1. Cream butter and sugar in a large bowl until light and fluffy. Beat in eggs until smooth.

2. Sift flour, baking powder, baking soda, salt, and cinnamon.

3. Combine yogurt and vanilla.

4. Add the flour mixture to creamed mixture alternately with yogurt. Stir until blended. Add the diced apples.

5. Pour batter into a buttered 9-inch (2.5-l) square baking pan. Bake at 350°F (180°C) for 45 minutes or until a cake tester comes out clean.

6. Cool in pan on a wire rack. Ice if desired or sprinkle with icing sugar.

Serves 9

DRIED APPLE CAKE WITH BUTTERMILK CARAMEL SAUCE

This moist spice cake is soaked with a caramel sauce after baking.

¾ cup (175 ml) lightly packed
   dried apples
¼ cup (50 ml) water
¼ cup (50 ml) white sugar
½ cup (125 ml) vegetable oil
1 egg
1 tsp (5 ml) vanilla
1 cup (250 ml) all-purpose flour
½ tsp (2 ml) baking soda
½ tsp (2 ml) cinnamon
½ tsp (2 ml) allspice
½ tsp (2 ml) nutmeg
   Dash salt
½ cup (125 ml) buttermilk
½ cup (125 ml) chopped walnuts

Buttermilk Caramel Sauce
¾ cup (175 ml) white sugar
⅓ cup (75 ml) buttermilk
3 tbsp (45 ml) butter
1 tbsp (15 ml) corn syrup or
   molasses
1 tsp (5 ml) vanilla
⅛ tsp (½ ml) baking soda

1. Pick over dried apples and discard any bits of core or peel. Place dried apples in a small saucepan with water. Cover and cook over low heat until all water is absorbed. Remove from heat and set aside.
2. Blend sugar, oil, egg, and vanilla in a large bowl until thoroughly mixed.
3. Sift flour, baking soda, cinnamon, allspice, nutmeg, and salt in a medium bowl. Add to oil mixture alternately with buttermilk.
4. Fold in walnuts and apples. Pour batter into a buttered 9-inch (2.5-l) glass pie plate. Bake at 300°F (150°C) for 25 to 30 minutes, or until cake tester comes out clean.
5. When cake is almost done, prepare Buttermilk Caramel Sauce. Blend sugar, buttermilk, butter, corn syrup or molasses, vanilla, and baking soda in a small saucepan. Stir over medium heat until sugar is dissolved. Increase heat to medium-high and cook, stirring until mixture forms a soft ball when a little is dropped into cold water.
6. When cake is removed from oven, prick top in several places with a skewer. Spoon sauce over cake. Serve warm or at room temperature.

Serves 6

STREUSEL UPSIDE-DOWN APPLE CAKE

A large, apple-topped coffee cake with streusel throughout.

Streusel

½ cup (125 ml) chopped walnuts
⅓ cup (75 ml) brown sugar
¼ cup (50 ml) all-purpose flour
½ tsp (2 ml) cinnamon
3 tbsp (45 ml) chilled butter

Topping

¼ cup (50 ml) melted butter
½ cup (125 ml) brown sugar
3 apples

Cake

2 cups (500 ml) all-purpose flour
1 cup (250 ml) white sugar
1 tbsp (15 ml) baking powder
½ tsp (2 ml) salt
⅓ cup (75 ml) melted butter
1 cup (250 ml) milk
1 beaten egg

1. Mix nuts, brown sugar, flour, and cinnamon for streusel in a medium bowl. Cut in butter until mixture is crumbly. Set aside.
2. Pour melted butter into a 9 × 13-inch (3-l) baking pan. Sprinkle brown sugar evenly over butter. Peel, quarter, and core apples. Slice into thin wedges. Arrange apple slices over brown sugar. Set aside while preparing batter.
3. To make cake, mix flour, sugar, baking powder, and salt in a large bowl. Combine butter, milk, and egg, and add to flour mixture. Beat until smooth.
4. Spread half of the batter over apple slices. Sprinkle with half of the streusel. Top with remaining batter, sprinkle with remaining streusel.
5. Bake at 350°F (180°C) for 35 minutes or until cake tester comes out clean. Immediately invert pan on heatproof serving platter. Scrape any remaining sauce over cake.
6. Serve warm or at room temperature.
Serves 9

VARIATION: WHOLE-WHEAT STREUSEL UPSIDE-DOWN APPLE CAKE
Substitute 1 cup (250 ml) whole-wheat flour for 1 cup (250 ml) all-purpose flour when making cake batter. Substitute whole-wheat flour for the all-purpose flour in streusel. Proceed as above.

CREAM FILLED SPICE ROLL

Cream cheese and applesauce fill this light, rolled sponge cake.

3 eggs
¾ cup (175 ml) white sugar
½ cup (125 ml) applesauce
1 cup (250 ml) all-purpose flour
½ tsp (2 ml) baking powder
½ tsp (2 ml) baking soda
1 tsp (5 ml) cinnamon
¼ tsp (1 ml) nutmeg
¼ tsp (1 ml) ground cloves
¼ tsp (1 ml) salt
¼ cup (50 ml) sifted icing sugar

Filling
8 oz (225 g) cream cheese, at room
    temperature
¼ cup (50 ml) applesauce
3 tbsp (45 ml) brown sugar
½ tsp (2 ml) vanilla
½ cup (125 ml) raisins

1. Grease a jelly roll pan or rimmed cookie sheet. Line pan with waxed paper.
2. Beat eggs and white sugar until light and fluffy. Fold in applesauce.
3. Sift flour, baking powder, baking soda, cinnamon, nutmeg, cloves, and salt into a small bowl. Fold flour mixture into creamed mixture. Pour batter onto the waxed paper and spread evenly. Bake at 375°F (190°C) for 8 to 10 minutes or until lightly browned.
4. Spread a clean tea towel on a flat surface and dust with icing sugar. When cake is done, remove from oven and immediately invert onto the towel. Remove the waxed paper and roll up cake in towel from the short end.
5. Meanwhile to make filling, beat cream cheese, applesauce, brown sugar, and vanilla in a medium bowl until light and fluffy. Fold in raisins.
6. Unroll cake and spread with cream cheese filling. Reroll the cake. Wrap and chill before slicing.
Serves 8

APPLE BUNDT COFFEE CAKE

A coffee cake to be served at room temperature.

⅓ cup (75 ml) white sugar
2 tsp (10 ml) cinnamon

Cake
1 cup (250 ml) white sugar
1 cup (250 ml) vegetable oil
4 eggs

¼ cup (50 ml) fresh orange juice
2 tsp (10 ml) vanilla
3 cups (750 ml) all-purpose flour
1 tbsp (15 ml) baking powder
½ tsp (2 ml) salt
5 medium apples, peeled, quartered
  and cored

1. Combine sugar and cinnamon in a small bowl and set aside.
2. To make cake, beat sugar, oil, eggs, orange juice, and vanilla in a large bowl. Sift flour, baking powder, and salt into a medium bowl. Add to oil mixture and beat until smooth.
3. Peel, quarter, and core apples. Cut quarters into thin wedges.
4. Butter a bundt or 10-inch (25-cm) tube pan. Pour in ⅓ of cake batter. Spread ½ of the apples over batter and sprinkle with ⅓ of the cinnamon sugar. Repeat until all ingredients are used.
5. Bake at 350°F (180°C) for 70 minutes or until cake tester comes out clean. Cool in pan, on a wire rack, then invert onto a serving platter.
Serves 10 to 12

CHOCOLATE-APPLE JUICE ICING

2 tbsp (25 ml) apple juice
1 tbsp (15 ml) butter

2 tbsp (25 ml) cocoa
1 cup (250 ml) unsifted icing sugar

1. Heat butter and apple juice in a small saucepan over low heat until butter melts.
2. Place cocoa and icing sugar in a small bowl. Beat in the butter and apple juice mixture with an electric beater. It may be necessary to add a little more liquid.
Yields enough for a one-layer 8-inch (2-l) square cake

APPLESAUCE ICING

The beauty of this icing is that it does not dry out quickly.

2 tbsp (25 ml) butter
¼ cup (50 ml) thick unsweetened
    applesauce

1 tsp (5 ml) undiluted apple juice
   concentrate, or vanilla, or apple
   brandy
2 cups (500 ml) icing sugar

1. Beat butter, applesauce, and apple juice concentrate (or vanilla or apple brandy) in a medium bowl until blended.
2. Beat in icing sugar until smooth. Add more icing sugar if a stiffer icing is preferred.
Yields 1 cup (250 ml)

Pies

CLASSIC APPLE PIE

Top this traditional dessert with vanilla ice cream or a slice of cheddar cheese.

Pastry for a 9-inch (22.5-cm)
double-crust pie (see page 94)
½ to ⅔ cup (125 to 150 ml)
white sugar (depending on
sweetness of apples)
Pinch of salt
1 tbsp (15 ml) cornstarch (if
apples are juicy)

½ tsp (2 ml) cinnamon
⅛ tsp (½ ml) nutmeg
7 cups (1.75 ml) thinly sliced,
cored, peeled apples
1½ tbsp (22 ml) butter
1 tbsp (15 ml) lemon juice (if
apples are bland)
1 tbsp (15 ml) water or cream (if
apples are very dry)

1. Roll out half of dough on a lightly floured surface to fit a 9-inch (22.5-cm) pie plate with about a ½-inch (1-cm) overhang.
2. Blend sugar, salt, cornstarch, and spices in a large bowl. Add apple slices and toss lightly until coated. Mound apple slices in pie shell. Dot with butter and sprinkle with lemon juice and water or cream if necessary.
3. Roll out remaining dough to fit top of pie. Moisten rim of bottom crust with water. Cover pie with upper crust. Crimp edges and cut several vents in top crust.
4. Bake in preheated 425°F (220°C) oven for 10 minutes; reduce heat to 350°F (180°C) and bake 30 to 40 minutes more or until the apples are tender when pierced with a skewer and the crust is golden brown.
Serves 6

BASIC PASTRY

Single-Crust Pie
1½ cups (375 ml) all-purpose
    flour
¼ tsp (1 ml) salt
½ cup (125 ml) shortening (mix-
    ture of lard, butter, or vegetable
    shortening)
3 to 4 tbsp (45 to 60 ml) ice water

Double-Crust Pie
2½ cups (625 ml) all-purpose
    flour
½ tsp (2 ml) salt
¾ cup (175 ml) shortening (mixture
    of lard, butter, or vegetable
    shortening)
6 to 7 tbsp (90 to 105 ml) ice water

1. Mix flour and salt in a medium bowl. Cut in shortening with a
pastry blender or two knives until mixture resembles coarse meal.
2. Sprinkle water over the flour mixture 1 tbsp (15 ml) at a time,
and mix lightly with a fork. Use only enough water so that the pastry
will hold together when pressed gently into a ball.
3. Don't handle pastry dough any more than necessary or it will be
tough.

CINNAMON PASTRY

A brown flaky pastry for pies and dumplings.

1¾ cups (425 ml) all-purpose
    flour
1 tsp (5 ml) cinnamon

½ cup (125 ml) lard
¼ cup (50 ml) butter
⅓ cup (75 ml) ice water

1. Mix flour and cinnamon in a large bowl until thoroughly blended.
2. Cut in lard and butter until mixture resembles coarse meal.
3. Sprinkle water over dough and mix with a fork until evenly moistened. Gather into a ball, then flatten into a disk. Wrap in plastic and
chill for 30 minutes.
*Yields enough pastry for double-crust 9-inch (22.5-cm) pie or four large
dumplings.*

NEVER-FAIL PASTRY

A tender, flaky, foolproof pastry.

5 cups (1.25 l) all-purpose flour	1 tbsp (15 ml) vinegar
1 tbsp (15 ml) salt	1 egg
1 lb (454 g) lard	Ice water

1. Mix flour and salt in a large bowl. Cut in half the lard with a pastry blender or two knives until mixture resembles fine meal. Cut in remaining lard until mixture resembles coarse crumbs.
2. Lightly beat egg and vinegar in a measuring cup. Add enough ice water to make 1 cup (250 ml). Gradually stir liquid into flour mixture. Knead lightly and gather into a ball. Divide into 6 portions.
Yields 3 double-crust pies or 6 pie shells

SOUTHERN APPLE PIE

This diced apple pie is flavored with fresh orange juice, butter, and lots of nutmeg.

Pastry for a 9-inch (22.5-cm) single-crust pie (see page 94)	½ tsp (2 ml) nutmeg (freshly grated is best)
1 cup (250 ml) white sugar	½ cup (125 ml) fresh orange juice
2 tbsp (25 ml) cornstarch	6 large apples
	3 tbsp (45 ml) butter

1. Mix sugar, cornstarch, nutmeg, and orange juice in a 2-quart (2-l) baking dish.
2. Peel, quarter, core, and dice apples. Add the diced apples and mix until coated. Dot with butter.
3. Roll out pastry on a lightly floured surface and drape over top of apples. Trim and crimp edges.
4. Bake at 375°F (190°C) for 40 to 50 minutes or until pastry is golden and apples are tender when pierced with a skewer.
Serves 6 to 8

CREAM CHEESE APPLE PIE

This scrumptious pie has a cookie crust, cream cheese filling, and an apple and almond topping.

Crust
½ cup (125 ml) butter
⅓ cup (75 ml) white sugar
1 tsp (5 ml) vanilla
1 cup (250 ml) all-purpose
   flour

Topping
¼ cup (50 ml) white sugar
½ tsp (2 ml) cinnamon
4 cups (1 l) sliced peeled apples
¼ cup (50 ml) sliced blanched
   almonds

Filling
8 oz (225 g) cream cheese, at
   room temperature
¼ cup (50 ml) white sugar
¼ tsp (1 ml) grated lemon rind
1 egg

1. To make crust, cream butter, sugar, and vanilla in a medium bowl. Blend in flour. Pat dough on bottom and sides of a 9-inch (22.5-cm) pie plate.
2. For filling, beat cream cheese, sugar, lemon rind, and egg in a medium bowl until smooth. Spread evenly on crust in pie plate.
3. Combine sugar, cinnamon, and apple slices in a large bowl. Toss to coat with sugar. Spread over cream cheese mixture and sprinkle with almonds.
4. Bake at 400°F (200°C) for 10 minutes; reduce heat to 375°F (190°C) for 20 to 25 minutes or until crust is golden and apples are tender.
5. Cool on a wire rack, then chill for 3 to 4 hours before serving.
Serves 6 to 8

UPSIDE-DOWN APPLE PIE

In this delectable pie, apple wedges are simmered in a sugar syrup until slightly caramelized, then topped with a buttery crust. A cast iron or ovenproof skillet is essential to prepare this dessert.

Pastry
1 cup (250 ml) all-purpose flour
1 tbsp (15 ml) white sugar
½ cup (125 ml) chilled butter
1 egg yolk
2 tbsp (25 ml) ice water

Filling
8 to 10 apples
⅓ cup (75 ml) butter
1 cup (250 ml) white sugar
¼ tsp (1 ml) grated lemon rind

1. Blend flour and sugar in a large bowl. Cut in butter until mixture resembles coarse meal.
2. Mix egg yolk and water in a cup and drizzle over flour mixture. Using a fork, mix until pastry is evenly moistened. Gather into a ball, wrap in plastic, and chill while preparing filling.
3. Melt butter in the bottom of a 9-inch (22.5-cm) skillet over low heat. Sprinkle evenly with sugar.
4. Peel, quarter, and core apples. Arrange apple wedges upright in sugar, in a circular pattern. Slice some of the apple quarters in half and use to fill any gaps. (The apples shrink as they cook.)
5. Cook, uncovered, over medium-low heat for about 30 minutes or until syrup is golden and thick. As apples cook, baste with syrup. Reduce heat if necessary to prevent scorching. Remove from heat and let cool for 30 minutes or until no longer steaming. Sprinkle with lemon rind.
6. Roll out pastry on a floured surface into a circle slightly larger than skillet. Place pastry over apples. Fold pastry to inside to smooth the edges.
7. Bake at 425°F (220°C) for 10 minutes, reduce heat to 375°F (190°C) and bake for 20 minutes or until crust is golden. Remove from oven and let cool for 5 minutes.
8. Invert a large plate over skillet. Using oven mitts, carefully invert skillet on to plate. Sometimes apple wedges stick to skillet; remove and place on pie. Cool for 5 minutes before serving. Serve warm with cheese or unsweetened whipped cream.

Serves 6

CRANBERRY-APPLE-RAISIN PIE

Red cranberries, plump raisins, and crisp apples combine to make one of the tastiest of fruit pies.

Pastry
1 cup (250 ml) all-purpose flour
½ tsp (2 ml) salt
⅓ cup (75 ml) shortening
1 tbsp (15 ml) butter
2 to 3 tbsp (25 to 45 ml) ice water

Filling
1 cup (250 ml) fresh or frozen
   cranberries
¾ cup (175 ml) white sugar
2 tbsp (25 ml) water
2 large apples
½ cup (125 ml) raisins
4 tsp (20 ml) cornstarch
½ tsp (2 ml) cinnamon

1. Combine flour and salt in a bowl. Cut in shortening and butter until mixture resembles coarse crumbs. Sprinkle with ice water and mix lightly with a fork until evenly moistened. Gather into a ball, wrap, and chill while preparing filling.
2. Combine cranberries, sugar, and 1 tbsp (15 ml) water in a medium saucepan. Cook over medium heat for about 10 minutes or until cranberries pop.
3. Peel, quarter, and core apples. Dice or slice apples. Add apples and raisins to cranberries. Combine cornstarch and remaining water and blend into apple-cranberry mixture. Cook, stirring for about 5 minutes or until mixture thickens slightly. Stir in cinnamon.
4. Roll out ⅔ of pastry on a lightly floured surface to fit an 8-inch (20-cm) pie plate. Spoon filling into pie plate. Roll out remaining pastry to fit top and crimp edges to seal. Cut vents in top of pie.
5. Bake at 400°F (200°C) for 35 minutes or until crust is golden.
Serves 4 to 6

ALMOND-APPLE MERINGUE PIE

This buttery almond pastry is filled with jam and apples and crowned with meringue.

Crust
⅓ cup (75 ml) butter
2 tbsp (25 ml) white sugar
2 egg yolks
¾ cup (175 ml) all-purpose flour
⅓ cup (75 ml) finely chopped
   almonds
2 tsp (10 ml) grated lemon rind

Filling
5 cups (1.25 l) sliced, cored, peeled
   apples
¼ cup (50 ml) white sugar
1 tbsp (15 ml) fresh lemon juice
½ cup (125 ml) sieved raspberry or
   apricot jam

Meringue
2 egg whites
4 tbsp (60 ml) white sugar
   Dash of salt

1. Cream butter and 2 tbsp (25 ml) sugar in a medium bowl. Add the egg yolks and beat until combined. Blend in flour, almonds, and lemon rind. Pat dough over bottom and sides of a 9-inch (22.5-cm) pie plate.
2. Bake at 350°F (180°C) for 15 minutes or until golden brown.
3. For the filling, mix apples, sugar, and lemon juice in a medium saucepan. Cover and cook over medium heat until tender. Stir occasionally.
4. Spread jam over crust. Arrange apples over jam.
5. Beat egg whites until foamy. Gradually add sugar and salt. Continue beating until stiff but not dry. Spread over apples. Return to oven and bake until meringue is lightly browned, about 15 minutes.
Serves 6 to 8

SOUR CREAM CRUMBLE PIE

A rich, creamy pie with a buttery crumb topping.

Pastry for a 9-inch (22.5-cm) single-crust pie (see page 94)

Filling
¾ cup (175 ml) white sugar
1 tbsp (15 ml) all-purpose flour
½ tsp (2 ml) cinnamon
½ cup (125 ml) sour cream
1 tsp (5 ml) vanilla
5 cups (1.25 l) sliced peeled apples

Crumb Topping
½ cup (125 ml) all-purpose flour
½ tsp (2 ml) cinnamon
6 tbsp (90 ml) brown sugar
¼ cup (50 ml) cold butter

1. Roll out pastry on a lightly floured surface to fit a 9-inch (22.5-cm) pie plate. Crimp edges and set aside.
2. To make filling, combine sugar, flour, and cinnamon in a large bowl. Blend in sour cream and vanilla. Add apple slices and toss lightly to coat. Spread evenly in pie shell.
3. For crumb topping, mix flour, cinnamon, and brown sugar in a medium bowl. Cut in the butter until mixture resembles fine crumbs. Sprinkle over apples.
4. Bake at 400°F (200°C) for 10 minutes. Reduce heat to 350°F (180°C) and bake for 25 to 30 minutes longer, or until apples are tender and crust is browned. If crust browns too quickly, cover lightly with strips of foil.
Serves 6

BLUEBERRY-APPLE MERINGUE TART

Apples and blueberries are a delicious combination. Use a juicy apple when you make this tart. Serve warm or at room temperature.

Shortbread Crust
2 cups (500 ml) all-purpose flour
½ cup (125 ml) white sugar
   Pinch salt
¾ cup (175 ml) butter
3 egg yolks
1 tbsp (15 ml) water

Blueberry-Apple Filling
6 cups (1.5 l) sliced peeled apples
2 cups (500 ml) fresh or frozen
   blueberries
⅔ cup (150 ml) white sugar
2 tbsp (25 ml) cornstarch
¼ tsp (1 ml) nutmeg
¼ tsp (1 ml) cinnamon

Meringue
3 egg whites
⅛ tsp (½ ml) cream of tartar
⅔ cup (150 ml) white sugar

1. To make crust, combine flour, sugar and salt in a medium bowl. Cut in butter until mixture resembles fine bread crumbs. Mix egg yolks and water and stir into flour mixture. Stir until evenly moistened. Gather into a ball and roll between two long pieces of waxed paper to fit bottom and sides of a buttered 9 × 13-inch (3-l) baking dish.
2. Combine apples and blueberries in a bowl. Combine sugar, cornstarch, and spices and sprinkle evenly over fruit. Toss to coat. Spread fruit mixture into baking dish.
3. Bake at 350°F (180°C) for 35 minutes or until apples are tender.
4. Meanwhile, prepare the meringue by beating egg whites and cream of tartar until soft peaks form. Gradually add the sugar and beat until stiff peaks form and sugar is dissolved.
5. Spoon meringue over fruit, leaving a space between each spoonful. Increase heat to 400°F (200°C). Bake for 8 minutes or until meringue is golden.
Serves 8 to 10.

CROW'S NEST (DEEP DISH) APPLE PIE

An old favorite for people who like a lot of filling in their pies.

Pastry for a 9-inch (22.5-cm)   ½ tsp (2 ml) cinnamon
single-crust pie (see page 94)   ½ tsp (2 ml) nutmeg
10 cups (2.5 l) sliced peeled apples   Dash of salt
1 cup (250 ml) white sugar   2 tbsp (25 ml) fresh lemon juice
1 tbsp (15 ml) cornstarch (if apples   3 tbsp (45 ml) butter
   are very juicy)

1. Place apple slices in a deep buttered baking dish at least 3-inches (7.5 cm) deep. Mix sugar, cornstarch, cinnamon, nutmeg, and salt in a dish and sprinkle over apples. Sprinkle with lemon juice and dot with butter.
2. Roll out dough on a lightly floured surface to fit top of deep baking dish with a 1-inch (2.5-cm) overhang. Drape pastry over top of baking dish and fold overhang under to make rim. Crimp edges. Cut a vent in center of pastry.
3. Bake at 400°F (200°C) for 45 to 60 minutes or until apples are tender and juices are bubbling. The crust should be golden brown.
4. Remove from oven and cool on a wire rack. Serve warm or at room temperature.
Serves 8 to 10

TROPICAL APPLE PIE

Toasted coconut, pineapple juice, and sweet apple slices make a delightfully different apple pie.

1 9-inch (22.5-cm) baked pie shell   ⅔ cup (150 ml) white sugar
½ cup (125 ml) toasted coconut   8 cups (2 l) cored, peeled apples in
1 cup (250 ml) unsweetened pine-   ¼-inch (½-cm) slices
   apple juice   3 tbsp (45 ml) cornstarch
½ cup (125 ml) cream of coconut   1 tbsp (15 ml) butter
   (Look in mixed drink section of   ¾ cup (175 ml) whipping cream
   supermarket.)

1. Sprinkle ¼ cup (50 ml) coconut over bottom of pie shell. Set aside.

2. Mix pineapple juice and cream of coconut in a large saucepan. Remove ¼ cup (50 ml) and reserve. Add sugar to mixture in saucepan. Bring to a boil and add apple slices. Simmer uncovered for 8 to 10 minutes or until barely tender. Do not overcook. Pour apples into a large sieve or colander over a bowl. Drain for 10 minutes. Return juices to saucepan.

3. Mix cornstarch and reserved juice mixture. Add to juices in saucepan. Cook over high heat, stirring until thickened and clear. Add butter and cool. Add apples and toss to coat. Spoon apples into pie shell. Chill.

3. Just before serving, whip cream and spoon over top of pie. Sprinkle with remaining coconut.

Serves 6 to 8

RAISIN CIDER PIE

The raisins for this pie are plumped in hot cider.

Pastry for double-crust 8- or 9-inch (20- or 22.5-cm) pie (see page 94)	⅓ *cup (75 ml) white sugar*
	3 *tbsp (45 ml) all-purpose flour*
	3 *tbsp (45 ml) fresh lemon juice*
2 *cups (500 ml) raisins*	1 *tbsp (15 ml) butter*
2 *cups (500 ml) sweet cider*	¼ *tsp (1 ml) cinnamon*
1 *tbsp (15 ml) grated lemon rind*	¼ *tsp (1 ml) nutmeg*

1. Place raisins in a large saucepan. Add cider and lemon rind. Bring to a boil, then reduce heat and simmer for 5 minutes.

2. Blend together the sugar and flour in a cup. Stir briskly into raisin mixture and cook until thickened. Remove from heat and stir in lemon juice, butter, cinnamon, and nutmeg. Cool.

3. Meanwhile, roll out pastry on a lightly floured surface to fit an 8- or 9-inch (20- or 22.5-cm) pie plate. Pour cooled filling into pie plate. Cover with top crust. Crimp edges.

4. Bake at 400°F (200°C) for 25 to 30 minutes or until crust is golden brown.

Serves 6

APPLE PIZZA

Not *really* a pizza, more like an open-faced pie.

Pastry for a 9-inch (22.5-cm)
double-crust pie (see page 94)
6 medium apples, peeled, quartered
and cored
½ cup (125 ml) white sugar
1 tsp (5 ml) cinnamon

Crumb Topping
¾ cup (175 ml) all-purpose flour
½ cup (125 ml) white or brown
sugar
⅓ cup (75 ml) chilled butter

1. Roll out pastry on a lightly floured surface to fit a 15-inch (37.5-cm) pizza pan. Turn edge of dough under and crimp.
2. Peel, quarter, and core apples. Slice apple quarters into thin wedges. Arrange wedges in a circular pattern over dough. Combine sugar and cinnamon in a cup and sprinkle evenly over apples.
3. To make the crumb topping, mix flour and sugar in a medium bowl. Cut butter into small pieces then, using a pastry blender, cut in butter until mixture resembles bread crumbs. Sprinkle crumbs evenly over the apples.
4. Bake at 425°F (220°C) for 10 minutes, then reduce heat to 350°F (180°C) and continue cooking for 25 minutes until pastry is golden brown and apples are tender. Serve warm or at room temperature, with cheese or ice cream.
Serves 8

GLAZED APPLE PIZZA

Apple slices are arranged over jam on a flaky crust and served pizza-style in large wedges.

Pastry
1½ cups (375 ml) all-purpose
flour
½ tsp (2 ml) salt
⅓ cup (75 ml) cold lard
¼ cup (50 ml) cold butter
3 to 4 tbsp (45 to 60 ml) ice water

Topping
4 large apples
2 tbsp (25 ml) fresh lemon juice
½ cup (125 ml) apricot or peach
    jam, or orange marmalade
2 tbsp (25 ml) white sugar
1 tbsp (15 ml) butter

Glaze
2 tbsp (25 ml) apricot or peach jam,
    or orange marmalade
1 tbsp (15 ml) apple brandy or
    Apple Cordial (see page 131)

1. Combine flour and salt in a medium bowl. Cut in lard and butter until mixture resembles coarse meal. Add ice water 1 tbsp (15 ml) at a time, and mix with a fork until mixture is evenly moistened. Gather into a ball, wrap, and chill while preparing apples.
2. Peel, quarter, and core apples. Slice into thin wedges. Place in a large bowl and sprinkle with lemon juice. Toss lightly to coat.
3. Roll out dough on a lightly floured surface to fit a 12-inch (30-cm) pizza pan. Crimp edges. Spread ½ cup (125 ml) jam or marmalade over dough. Arrange apple slices in a circular pattern over jam. Sprinkle with sugar and dot with butter.
4. Bake at 400°F (200°C) for 40 to 50 minutes or until crust is golden. If apples are browning too quickly, lay a sheet of foil over top.
5. Heat remaining jam or marmalade and apple brandy or cordial in a small saucepan. Brush top of apples with warm jam. Cut into wedges and serve warm or at room temperature.
Serves 6

GRATED APPLE TART

This shortbread tart with spiced grated apples is very rich. Serve with Crème Fraîche (see page 231) or sharp cheese.

1 cup (250 ml) sifted all-purpose
  flour
½ tsp (2 ml) salt
½ cup (125 ml) butter
1 tbsp (15 ml) cider vinegar
1 cup (250 ml) white sugar

2 tbsp (25 ml) all-purpose flour
½ tsp (2 ml) cinnamon
½ tsp (2 ml) grated orange or
  lemon rind
¼ tsp (1 ml) nutmeg
3 cups (750 ml) coarsely grated
  unpeeled apples
1 tbsp (15 ml) icing sugar

1. Combine 1 cup (250 ml) flour and salt in a small bowl. Mix lightly with a fork. Cut in butter until mixture resembles coarse meal. Blend in vinegar.

2. Spread dough with a spatula on the bottom and ½ inch (1 cm) up the side of a 9-inch (22.5-cm) springform pan. Pat smooth with your hand.

3. Combine 1 cup (250 ml) sugar, 2 tbsp (25 ml) flour, cinnamon, grated rind, nutmeg, and apples in a medium bowl. Spread mixture evenly over the dough.

4. Bake at 400°F (200°C) for 1 hour. Cool on a wire rack for 30 minutes then remove side of pan. Sift icing sugar over top of tart. When completely cool, slide tart on to a serving platter.

Serves 6 to 8

DRIED APPLE PIE

A pie with a dark spicy filling.

Pastry for a double-crust 9-inch   4 cups (1 l) cold water
(22.5-cm) pie (see page 94)   White sugar to taste
4 cups (1 l) lightly packed, dried   1 tsp (5 ml) cinnamon
   apples   ¼ tsp (1 ml) allspice

1. Pick over apples and remove any bits of core or peel. Place apples
and water in a large saucepan. Bring to a boil, reduce heat and simmer for about 20 minutes or until apples are tender. Lightly mash
apples, then sweeten to taste and stir in spices. Place in a bowl,
cover, and chill.
2. Roll out pastry on a lightly floured surface to fit pie plate. Spread
cold filling over pastry. Roll out top crust and place on top of filling.
Crimp edges and cut vents in top crust.
3. Bake at 425°F (220°C) for 10 minutes. Reduce heat to 350°F
(180°C) and bake for about 25 minutes longer, or until crust is golden.
Serves 6 to 8

Muffins and Quick Breads

SPICY APPLE MUFFINS

These moist muffins are topped with apples and cinnamon sugar.

2 cups (500 ml) all-purpose flour   ¾ cup (175 ml) white sugar
1 tbsp (15 ml) baking powder   1 egg
½ tsp (2 ml) salt   1 cup (250 ml) milk
½ tsp (2 ml) nutmeg   ¼ cup (50 ml) melted butter
2 tsp (10 ml) cinnamon   1½ cups (375 ml) finely chopped
⅛ tsp (½ ml) ground cloves   unpeeled apples

1. Sift flour, baking powder, salt, nutmeg, 1 tsp (5 ml) cinnamon, cloves, and ½ cup (125 ml) sugar into a large bowl.
2. Beat egg, milk, and melted butter in a medium bowl. Blend into flour mixture and stir just until combined.
3. Fold in 1 cup (250 ml) chopped apple. Fill buttered muffin cups ⅔ full.
4. Combine remaining ¼ cup (50 ml) sugar and 1 tsp (5 ml) cinnamon in a cup. Top muffins with remaining chopped apple, then sprinkle with cinnamon sugar.
5. Bake at 400°F (200°C) for 15 to 20 minutes.
Yields 12 large muffins

HEARTY GRATED APPLE MUFFINS

Enjoy these moist muffins with butter, cheese, and a cup of tea.

1 cup (250 ml) sifted all-purpose   ½ tsp (2 ml) nutmeg
    flour   1 egg
1 cup (250 ml) whole-wheat flour   ¾ cup (175 ml) apple juice or milk
½ cup (125 ml) brown sugar   1 cup (250 ml) grated unpeeled
1 tbsp (15 ml) baking powder   apples
½ tsp (2 ml) salt   ¼ cup (50 ml) vegetable oil
1 tsp (5 ml) cinnamon   1 tbsp (15 ml) white sugar
                                       ½ tsp (2 ml) cinnamon

1. Place both kinds of flour, brown sugar, baking powder, salt, cinnamon, and nutmeg in a large bowl. Stir to combine thoroughly.
2. Beat egg lightly in a medium bowl and stir in apple juice or milk, apples, and oil. Add to flour mixture and stir just enough to moisten.
3. Fill buttered muffin cups ⅔ full.
4. Mix white sugar and cinnamon. Sprinkle over top of muffins. Bake at 375°F (190°C) for 25 minutes or until golden brown.
Yields 12 muffins

CHEDDAR OAT MUFFINS

These spicy applesauce muffins have the tang of aged cheddar cheese.

½ cup (125 ml) butter
½ cup (125 ml) white sugar
2 eggs
1½ cups (375 ml) all-purpose
   flour
½ tsp (2 ml) salt
1 tsp (5 ml) baking soda

½ tsp (2 ml) allspice
¾ cup (175 ml) rolled oats
1 cup (250 ml) grated aged cheddar
   cheese
½ cup (125 ml) chopped walnuts
1 cup (250 ml) applesauce
¼ cup (50 ml) milk

1. Cream butter and sugar in a medium bowl until light. Beat in eggs.
2. Mix flour, salt, baking soda, and allspice in a small bowl. Add to creamed mixture and mix thoroughly. Mix in rolled oats, ¾ cup (175 ml) cheese, applesauce, and walnuts. Add milk and stir to blend.
3. Spoon batter into buttered muffin cups, filling ¾ full. Top each with a little grated cheese. Bake at 400°F (200°C) for 20 minutes or until cake tester comes out clean.
4. Invert on a wire rack and cool slightly. Serve warm.
Yields 12 muffins

APPLESAUCE MUFFINS

Spicy and very moist, these muffins are particularly good with roast pork.

¼ cup (50 ml) butter
½ cup (125 ml) brown sugar
1 egg
1 cup (250 ml) applesauce
½ cup (125 ml) milk
1½ cups (375 ml) all-purpose
    flour

½ tsp (2 ml) salt
2 tsp (10 ml) baking powder
½ tsp (2 ml) baking soda
1 tsp (5 ml) cinnamon
½ tsp (2 ml) nutmeg
½ tsp (2 ml) ground cloves
½ cup (125 ml) raisins or chopped
    pitted dates

1. Beat butter, brown sugar, and egg in a large mixing bowl until creamy. Stir in applesauce and milk.
2. Sift flour, salt, baking powder, baking soda, and spices into a medium bowl. Add flour mixture to applesauce mixture and stir just until batter is barely smooth. Fold in raisins or dates.
3. Fill buttered muffin cups ¾ full. Bake at 400°F (200°C) for 15 minutes or until a cake tester comes out clean.
Yields 12 muffins

APPLESAUCE SCONES

A cake-like scone. Serve hot with butter and cheese.

1 cup (250 ml) all-purpose flour
4 tsp (20 ml) baking powder
½ tsp (2 ml) salt
2 tbsp (25 ml) white sugar
¼ tsp (1 ml) cinnamon

⅛ tsp (½ ml) nutmeg
2 tbsp (25 ml) butter
1 tbsp (15 ml) currants (optional)
½ cup (125 ml) cold, thick apple-
    sauce

1. Sift flour, baking powder, salt, 1 tbsp (15 ml) sugar, and spices into a medium bowl. Cut in butter until mixture resembles fine crumbs.

2. Add the currants. Stir in applesauce. Turn dough onto a lightly floured surface and knead lightly. Pat dough into a buttered glass 9-inch (22.5-cm) pie plate. Score lightly with a knife into 6 wedges. Sprinkle with remaining sugar.

3. Bake at 375°F (190°C) for 15 to 18 minutes.
Serves 6

APPLE-BIT BANANA BREAD

An interesting variation on basic banana bread.

½ cup (125 ml) shortening
1½ cups (375 ml) white sugar
2 large eggs
2 cups (500 ml) all-purpose flour
1 tsp (5 ml) baking soda
1 tsp (5 ml) baking powder
1 tsp (5 ml) cinnamon
½ tsp (2 ml) salt
2 finely mashed ripe bananas
2 cups (500 ml) finely chopped peeled apples
1 tsp (5 ml) vanilla

1. Cream shortening and sugar in a large bowl. Beat in eggs until light and fluffy.

2. Sift flour, soda, baking powder, cinnamon, and salt into a medium bowl. Beat flour mixture into shortening mixture.

3. Stir in bananas, apples, and vanilla. Pour batter into a greased 9 × 5-inch (2-l) loaf pan. Let sit while oven heats.

4. Bake at 350°F (180°C) for 50 to 60 minutes or until a cake tester comes out clean.
Yields 1 loaf

LIGHT APPLE-OAT LOAF

Moist with grated apple, this bread is delicious served with sharp cheese.

2 cups (500 ml) sifted all-purpose flour	⅓ cup (75 ml) rolled oats
1 tsp (5 ml) baking powder	¾ cup (175 ml) buttermilk or sour milk
1 tsp (5 ml) baking soda	1 lightly beaten egg
½ tsp (2 ml) salt	1 cup (250 ml) grated, cored, un-peeled apples
½ cup (125 ml) white sugar	¼ cup (50 ml) melted butter

1. Blend flour, baking powder, baking soda, salt, sugar, and oats in a large bowl.
2. Combine buttermilk, beaten egg, grated apples, and melted butter in a medium bowl. Add to dry ingredients, stirring only enough to blend.
3. Spoon into buttered 9 × 5-inch (2-l) loaf pan. Bake at 350°F (180°C) for 50 to 60 minutes or until a cake tester comes out clean.
4. Remove from oven and cool in pan for 10 minutes, then invert on wire rack. When completely cooled, wrap in plastic for several hours before slicing.
Yields 1 loaf

ANGOSTURA APPLESAUCE BREAD

Aromatic bitters were first made in Angostura, Venezuela, about 1824. They add a special aroma and flavor to this bread.

½ cup (125 ml) shortening	1¾ cups (425 ml) sifted all-purpose flour
1 cup (250 ml) brown sugar	
1 cup (250 ml) warm applesauce	1 tsp (5 ml) cinnamon
1 tsp (5 ml) baking soda	½ tsp (2 ml) ground cloves
½ tsp (2 ml) orange extract	½ tsp (2 ml) salt
1 tsp (5 ml) Angostura bitters	1 cup (250 ml) raisins

1. Cream shortening and brown sugar in a large bowl. Beat in applesauce, baking soda, orange extract, and bitters.
2. Sift flour, cinnamon, cloves, and salt into a small bowl. Add to creamed mixture and beat until combined. Fold in raisins.
3. Spread batter in a greased 8 × 4-inch (1.5-l) loaf pan. Bake at 350°F (180°C) for 35 minutes or until a cake tester comes out clean. Cool for 5 minutes in pan then invert on to a wire rack and finish cooling.
Yields 1 loaf

APPLE CORNBREAD

This cornbread has a sweet apple topping.

1 cup less 2 tbsp (225 ml) all-purpose flour	**Topping**
¼ cup (50 ml) white sugar	2 cups (500 ml) sliced, peeled, cored apples
4 tsp (20 ml) baking powder	2 tbsp (25 ml) white sugar
¼ tsp (1 ml) salt	1 tsp (5 ml) cinnamon
1 cup (250 ml) cornmeal	
1 beaten egg	
1 cup (250 ml) milk	
¼ cup (50 ml) melted butter	

1. Blend flour, sugar, baking powder, salt, and cornmeal in a large bowl.
2. Combine beaten egg, milk, and melted butter in a small bowl. Make a well in center of flour mixture and pour in liquid mixture. Stir until mixture is evenly moistened.
3. Pour into a buttered 8- or 9-inch (2- or 2.5 l) square baking pan. Cover batter with apple slices. Mix sugar and cinnamon in a cup and sprinkle over apples.
4. Bake at 375°F (190°C) for 25 to 30 minutes or until cake tester comes out clean. Serve warm.
Serves 9

APPLE CHEDDAR LOAF

Old cheddar cheese adds tang to this moist bread. It freezes well.

½ cup (125 ml) butter
⅔ cup (150 ml) brown sugar
2 eggs
1½ cups (375 ml) grated
   unpeeled apples
½ cup (125 ml) grated aged
   cheddar cheese

½ cup (125 ml) chopped walnuts
2 cups (500 ml) all-purpose flour
1½ tsp (7 ml) baking powder
½ tsp (2 ml) baking soda
½ tsp (2 ml) salt

1. Cream butter and sugar in a large bowl. Add eggs and beat until fluffy.
2. Stir in apples, cheese, and walnuts.
3. Sift flour, baking powder, soda, and salt into a medium bowl. Stir into apple mixture just until mixed.
4. Spoon into a buttered 9 × 5-inch (2-l) loaf pan. Bake at 350°F (180°C) for 50 to 60 minutes or until a cake tester comes out clean.
Yields 1 loaf

GLAZED APPLESAUCE LOAF

A delicious fine textured quick bread.

½ cup (125 ml) butter
1 cup (250 ml) white sugar
2 eggs
1¾ cups (425 ml) sifted
   all-purpose flour
½ tsp (2 ml) salt
1 tsp (5 ml) baking powder

½ tsp (2 ml) baking soda
½ tsp (2 ml) cinnamon
½ tsp (2 ml) nutmeg
¼ tsp (1 ml) ground cloves
1 cup (250 ml) applesauce
½ cup (125 ml) chopped walnuts
½ cup (125 ml) raisins

Glaze
½ cup (125 ml) icing sugar
1 tbsp (15 ml) milk or apple juice

1. Cream butter and sugar in a large bowl. Beat in eggs. Sift flour, salt, baking powder, baking soda, and spices into a medium bowl.
2. Add flour mixture to creamed mixture alternately with applesauce. Beat after each addition.
3. Fold in nuts and raisins. Pour into a buttered 9 × 5-inch (2-l) loaf pan. Bake at 350°F (180°C) for 50 to 60 minutes or until cake tester comes out clean.
4. Cool in pan for 10 minutes. Invert onto a wire rack.
5. Mix icing sugar and milk or apple juice in a cup. While loaf is still warm, spoon glaze over top.
Yields 1 loaf

LEMON APPLE-WALNUT BREAD

A glazed quick loaf.

¼ cup (50 ml) butter or shortening
⅔ cup (150 ml) white sugar
2 beaten eggs
2 cups (500 ml) sifted all-purpose flour
1 tsp (5 ml) baking powder
1 tsp (5 ml) baking soda
½ tsp (2 ml) salt

2 cups (500 ml) grated peeled apples
2 tsp (10 ml) grated lemon rind
⅔ cup (150 ml) chopped walnuts

Glaze

¼ cup (50 ml) white sugar
2 tbsp (25 ml) fresh lemon juice

1. Cream butter or shortening and sugar in a large bowl until light and fluffy. Beat in eggs.
2. Sift flour, baking powder, baking soda, and salt into a medium bowl. Add to creamed mixture alternately with grated apple. Stir in lemon rind and nuts.
3. Bake at 350°F (180°C) for 50 to 60 minutes or until cake tester comes out clean. Remove loaf from pan. Mix sugar and lemon juice in a cup. Slowly pour over the top of loaf. Cool on a wire rack and let stand for 24 hours before slicing.
Yields 1 loaf

Cookies and Squares

BUTTERSCOTCH CHIP DROP COOKIES

Applesauce spice cookies with a butterscotch surprise.

2 cups (500 ml) all-purpose flour	½ cup (125 ml) shortening or
½ tsp (2 ml) salt	butter
½ tsp (2 ml) cinnamon	1 cup (250 ml) brown sugar
½ tsp (2 ml) nutmeg	1 egg
½ tsp (2 ml) allspice	1 cup (250 ml) applesauce
1 tsp (5 ml) baking soda	1 6 oz (170 g) package butter-
	scotch chips

1. Sift flour, salt, cinnamon, nutmeg, allspice, and baking soda into a medium bowl.
2. Cream shortening or butter and brown sugar in a large bowl. Add egg and beat.
3. Add flour mixture to creamed mixture alternately with applesauce. Fold in butterscotch chips.
4. Drop by spoonfuls about 2 inches (5 cm) apart on a buttered cookie sheet.
5. Bake at 375°F (190°C) for 12 to 15 minutes or until lightly browned and puffed.
Yields 4 dozen cookies

APPLESAUCE OATMEAL COOKIES

A good lunchbox treat.

2 cups (500 ml) all-purpose flour	1 cup (250 ml) brown sugar
½ tsp (2 ml) soda	½ cup (125 ml) shortening
½ tsp (2 ml) salt	¼ cup (50 ml) butter
¾ tsp (4 ml) cinnamon	1 egg
½ tsp (2 ml) nutmeg	1 cup (250 ml) applesauce
1½ cups (375 ml) rolled oats	½ cup (125 ml) raisins
	½ cup (125 ml) chopped walnuts

1. Sift flour, soda, salt, cinnamon, and nutmeg into a medium bowl. Mix in rolled oats.
2. Cream sugar, shortening, butter, and egg in a large bowl until light and fluffy. Add flour mixture to creamed mixture alternately with applesauce.
3. Fold in raisins and walnuts.
4. Drop by spoonfuls 2 inches (5 cm) apart on to buttered cookie sheets. Bake at 350°F (180°C) for 12 to 15 minutes.
Yields 3 dozen cookies

FROSTED APPLE-CRANBERRY COOKIES

Try these tart red-flecked cookies at Christmas.

½ cup (125 ml) butter
¾ cup (175 ml) brown or white sugar
1 egg
¼ cup (50 ml) milk
2 cups (500 ml) all-purpose flour
1 tsp (5 ml) baking powder
¼ tsp (1 ml) baking soda
1 tsp (5 ml) cinnamon
¼ tsp (1 ml) nutmeg

1 tsp (5 ml) grated orange rind
1½ cups (375 ml) grated, cored, peeled apples
1 cup (250 ml) chopped fresh or frozen cranberries

Icing

1 cup (250 ml) icing sugar
1 tbsp (15 ml) orange juice
2 tsp (10 ml) grated orange rind

1. Cream butter and sugar in a large bowl. Beat in egg and milk until fluffy.
2. Sift flour, baking powder, baking soda, cinnamon, and nutmeg into a medium bowl. Blend into creamed mixture. Stir in orange rind, apples, and cranberries.
3. Drop by spoonfuls 2 inches (5 cm) apart on to buttered cookie sheets. Bake at 375°F (190°C) for 12 to 15 minutes.
4. Beat icing sugar, orange juice, and rind in a small bowl until smooth. Add more orange juice if necessary. Ice cookies while still warm.
Yields 3½ dozen cookies

WHOLE-WHEAT APPLESAUCE COOKIES

A moist, wholesome cookie with nuts and raisins.

1 cup (250 ml) all-purpose flour	½ cup (125 ml) butter
¾ cup (175 ml) whole-wheat flour	¾ cup (175 ml) brown sugar
1 tsp (5 ml) baking soda	1 egg
½ tsp (2 ml) salt	1 cup (250 ml) applesauce
½ tsp (2 ml) cinnamon	1 tsp (5 ml) vanilla
½ tsp (2 ml) allspice	¾ cup (175 ml) chopped walnuts
½ tsp (2 ml) nutmeg	¾ cup (175 ml) raisins

1. In a medium bowl, mix the flours, baking soda, salt, and spices until blended.
2. Cream the butter and brown sugar until light and fluffy. Beat in the egg, applesauce, and vanilla. Stir in the flour mixture until evenly mixed. Fold in the walnuts and raisins.
3. Drop by spoonfuls (tsp or 5-ml size) on to a lightly buttered cookie sheet.
4. Bake at 350°F (180°C) for 12 to 15 minutes or until browned. Cool on a wire rack.
Yields 4 dozen

APPLE BEIGNETS

To make the vanilla sugar called for in this recipe, slit a vanilla bean and bury in a jar of white sugar for several days.

1 cup (250 ml) beer	3 to 4 firm apples
1 cup (250 ml) all-purpose flour	White sugar or vanilla sugar
Dash of salt	Oil or vegetable shortening for
1 tsp (5 ml) vanilla	deep frying

1. Process beer, flour, salt, and vanilla in a blender until smooth.
2. Peel and core apples. Cut apples into rings or wedges ½-inch (1 cm) thick. Pat dry with paper towels.
3. Pour 2 inches (5 cm) oil into a deep fryer. Heat oil or shortening to 370°F (185°C). Dip apple into batter and let excess drip off. Fry a

few slices at a time. Turn once during frying. Drain on paper towels.
Keep in a warm oven until all the apples are cooked.

4. Pile on to a serving platter and sprinkle thickly with ½ cup plain
or vanilla sugar. Serve warm.

Serves 4

APPLESAUCE DROP DOUGHNUTS

Spicy nuggets coated with cinnamon sugar.

2¼ cups (550 ml) sifted
   all-purpose flour
1½ tsp (7 ml) baking powder
½ tsp (2 ml) baking soda
½ tsp (2 ml) cinnamon
½ tsp (2 ml) nutmeg
¼ tsp (1 ml) ground cloves
¼ tsp (1 ml) salt
½ cup (125 ml) white sugar
¼ cup (50 ml) brown sugar

2 eggs
2 tbsp (25 ml) vegetable oil
¼ cup (50 ml) milk
1 cup (250 ml) unsweetened
   applesauce
½ tsp (2 ml) vanilla
   Peanut oil

Cinnamon Sugar
½ cup (125 ml) white sugar
½ tsp (2 ml) cinnamon

1. Sift flour, baking powder, baking soda, spices, and salt into a
medium bowl.

2. Beat white and brown sugars, eggs, and vegetable oil in a medium
bowl until light and fluffy. Beat in milk, applesauce, and vanilla.
Add to flour mixture and stir until evenly moistened.

3. Heat 3 inches (7.5 cm) peanut oil in a large deep saucepan or
electric deep fryer to 360°F (185°C). Carefully drop heaping spoonfuls (tsp or 5-ml size) of batter into hot oil. Cook 3 to 4 doughnuts at
a time. Fry for about 2 minutes or until golden brown, turning once.
Drain on paper toweling. Be careful to maintain frying temperature; if oil is too hot, doughnuts will be browned but uncooked in
middle.

4. Place white sugar and cinnamon in a paper bag and shake a few
doughnuts at a time until coated. Serve warm.

Yields approximately 4 dozen

APPLE SHORTBREAD WEDGES

Imagine these buttery shortbread triangles topped with spicy cooked apples and whipped cream.

Shortbread Base
1 cup (250 ml) butter, at room
  temperature
½ cup (125 ml) brown sugar
2 cups (500 ml) all-purpose
  flour
1 tsp (5 ml) vanilla

Topping
3 cups (750 ml) diced, peeled apples
½ cup (125 ml) brown sugar
¼ tsp (1 ml) cinnamon
1 tbsp (15 ml) all-purpose flour

1. Mix ingredients for shortbread base in a bowl. Knead until smooth and form into a ball. Roll dough on a cookie sheet into 10-inch (25-cm) circle. Dough should be ¼-inch (6-mm) thick. Pinch edges to form a rim.
2. Mix apples, brown sugar, cinnamon, and flour in a bowl. Spread on top of uncooked shortbread, leaving a 1-inch (2.5-cm) border. Bake at 375°F (190°C) for 25 minutes or until golden brown.
3. Cut carefully while still hot from the oven, into wedges. Serve hot or cold with whipped cream or ice cream, dusted with cinnamon. *Serves 8*

PEANUT-APPLE BARS

Kids like these moist peanut squares.

¾ cup (175 ml) all-purpose flour
1 tsp (5 ml) baking powder
½ tsp (2 ml) cinnamon
1 egg
¾ cup (175 ml) brown sugar
¼ cup (50 ml) milk

1 tsp (5 ml) vanilla
½ cup (125 ml) smooth or crunchy
  peanut butter
1 cup (250 ml) grated, cored, unpeeled apples
  Icing sugar

1. Sift flour, baking powder, and cinnamon into a small bowl.
2. Beat egg until light. Beat in sugar, milk, vanilla, and peanut butter. Blend in the flour and stir in the grated apple.
3. Spread batter in buttered 8- or 9-inch (2- or 2.5-l) square baking pan.
4. Bake at 350°F (180°C) for 20 to 25 minutes or until a cake tester comes out clean. Do not overbake.
5. Cool until lukewarm, cut into bars, and roll in icing sugar. Place on wire rack to finish cooling.
Yields 24 bars

CRUNCHY COCONUT APPLE SQUARES

Apples are sandwiched between a rich shortbread base and a golden coconut topping.

Pastry
⅓ cup (75 ml) butter
2 tbsp (25 ml) brown sugar
1 cup (250 ml) all-purpose flour

Topping
¾ cup (175 ml) white sugar
1 egg
3 tbsp (45 ml) melted butter
1¼ cups (300 ml) flaked coconut

Filling
⅓ cup (75 ml) white sugar
2½ cups (625 ml) sliced peeled apples
¼ cup (50 ml) fresh lemon or orange juice
½ tsp (2 ml) grated lemon rind
1 tsp (5 ml) butter

1. Cream butter and brown sugar in a medium bowl. Blend in flour. Mix until smooth. Pat into an 8-inch (2-l) square baking pan.
2. Combine ingredients for filling in a medium saucepan. Cook over medium-high heat until thick, stirring frequently. Cool slightly.
3. To make topping, beat sugar and egg in a medium bowl until light and fluffy. Beat in melted butter. Fold in coconut.
4. Spread cooled filling over dough. Spread topping over filling. Bake at 350°F (180°C) for 20 to 25 minutes or until topping is golden.
Serves 8

APPLE-WALNUT SQUARES

A light sponge cake studded with apples and walnuts on a short-bread base.

1½ cups (325 ml) all-purpose
    flour
¼ cup (50 ml) icing sugar
½ cup (125 ml) butter
2 eggs

¾ cup (175 ml) brown sugar
1 tsp (5 ml) vanilla
2 cups (500 ml) diced peeled
    apples
¼ cup (50 ml) chopped walnuts
1 tsp (5 ml) baking powder

1. Sift 1 cup (250 ml) flour and icing sugar into a small bowl. Melt butter and blend into flour mixture. Press mixture into an 8-inch (2-l) square baking pan. Bake at 350°F (180°C) for 20 minutes.
2. Meanwhile, beat eggs and brown sugar together in a medium bowl until thick. Stir in vanilla, apples, and walnuts.
3. Sift remaining flour and baking powder into a small bowl. Stir into egg mixture. Spread over baked pastry. Bake at 350°F (180°C) for 35 minutes or until browned. Cut into squares when cool. Serve at room temperature.
Serves 8

MICROWAVE APPLE-FUDGE BROWNIES

A rich moist brownie.

½ cup (125 ml) butter
⅓ cup (75 ml) cocoa powder
1 cup (250 ml) brown sugar
½ cup (125 ml) applesauce
1 tsp (5 ml) vanilla

2 eggs
1 cup (250 ml) all-purpose flour
1 tsp (5 ml) baking powder
1 cup (250 ml) finely chopped,
    peeled apples

1. Melt butter in a medium microproof bowl, on maximum power for 1½ minutes. Blend in cocoa, sugar, applesauce, eggs, and vanilla.
2. Mix flour and baking powder in a small bowl and add to applesauce mixture. Add a little milk if batter seems too thick.
3. Fold in chopped apples and spread batter evenly in a buttered 8-inch (2-l) square microproof baking dish. Bake on maximum power for 10 minutes. Turn once after 5 minutes.
4. Remove from oven and let stand for 5 minutes. Ice with Chocolate Apple Juice Icing (see page 91).
Serves 6 to 8

BEST-EVER APPLESAUCE BARS

A moist, spicy bar with creamy icing.

½ cup (125 ml) butter	½ tsp (5 ml) ground cloves
1 cup (250 ml) white sugar	¾ cup (175 ml) raisins
1 cup (250 ml) applesauce	½ cup (125 ml) chopped walnuts
1 tsp (5 ml) vanilla	
2 cups (500 ml) all-purpose flour	Butter-Cream Icing
¼ tsp (1 ml) salt	¼ cup (50 ml) melted butter
1 tsp (5 ml) cinnamon	¼ cup (50 ml) whipping cream
1 tsp (5 ml) nutmeg (freshly grated is best)	1¾ cups (425 ml) icing sugar
	½ tsp (2 ml) vanilla

1. Cream butter and sugar until light and fluffy. Add applesauce and vanilla; stir until combined.
2. Sift flour, salt, cinnamon, nutmeg, and cloves into a medium bowl. Add to creamed mixture and stir until combined. Batter will be thick.
3. Fold in the raisins and walnuts. Spread batter in a 9 × 13-inch (3-l) baking pan. Bake at 350°F (180°C) for 35 to 40 minutes or until cake tester comes out clean.
4. To make Butter-Cream Icing, beat butter, whipping cream, icing sugar, and vanilla in a medium bowl until smooth. Ice bars while still warm. Leave in pan and cut when cool.
Yields 24 bars

CHEESE DREAM SQUARES

Delicious when spread with apple jelly or marmalade.

1¾ cups (425 ml) sifted
  all-purpose flour
1 tbsp (15 ml) brown sugar
¼ tsp (1 ml) baking powder
1 cup (250 ml) grated cheddar
  cheese

½ cup (125 ml) chilled butter
1 cup (250 ml) Apple Jelly (see
  page 236) or Apple Marmalade
  (see page 246) or Crabapple
  Jelly (see page 237)

1. Sift flour, brown sugar, and baking powder into a large bowl.
Add cheese and stir to combine.
2. Cut in butter until mixture resembles fine crumbs. Spread half
of the mixture in a lightly buttered 8-inch (2-l) baking pan. Spread
generously with apple jelly, marmalade, or crabapple jelly. Cover
with remaining cheese mixture.
3. Bake at 350°F (180°C) for 25 to 30 minutes or until golden brown.
Cool on wire rack. Cut into fingers or squares when cool.
Serves 9 or more

YOGURT APPLE SQUARES

These are thin, tart, and very tasty squares. Best served the same
day you make them.

¼ cup (50 ml) melted butter
1½ cups (375 ml) graham
  cracker crumbs
1 can (397 g) sweetened condensed
  milk

1 cup (250 ml) plain yogurt
¼ cup (50 ml) fresh lemon juice
¼ tsp (1 ml) grated lemon rind
3 medium apples
  Cinnamon

1. Mix butter with graham cracker crumbs in a small bowl. Pat into a 9 × 13-inch (3-l) baking pan.

2. Combine condensed milk, yogurt, lemon juice, and rind in a medium bowl. Set aside (the mixture will thicken).

3. Peel, quarter, and core apples. Cut in ¼-inch (½-cm) wedges. Arrange apple slices over crust. Pour yogurt mixture evenly over apples. Bake at 350°F (180°C) for 25 minutes.

4. Remove from oven and dust with cinnamon. Cool to room temperature, then chill.

Serves 8 to 10

ROLLED-OAT APPLE SQUARES

Spiced apples are layered between sweet buttered oats. Serve as a dessert with whipped cream.

1¾ cups (425 ml) rolled oats	¾ cup + 2 tbsp (200 ml) butter
1½ cups (375 ml) all-purpose flour	2½ cups (625 ml) sliced, cored, peeled apples
¼ tsp (1 ml) baking soda	2 tbsp (25 ml) white sugar
1 cup (250 ml) brown sugar	1 tsp (5 ml) cinnamon

1. Mix oats, flour, baking soda, and brown sugar in a large bowl. Rub in ¾ cup (175 ml) butter. Pat half of oat mixture in a buttered 9-inch (2.5-l) square pan.

2. Arrange apples over top of oat mixture and dot with 2 tbsp (25 ml) butter.

3. Mix together sugar and cinnamon. Sprinkle sugar over apples and top with remaining oat mixture.

4. Bake at 350°F (180°C) for 45 minutes or until golden brown. Cut into squares.

Serves 9

GLAZED APPLE TRIANGLES

One of our favorite recipes. It can be used to make individual turnovers.

Pastry
2½ cups (625 ml)
    all-purpose flour
½ tsp (2 ml) salt
1 cup (250 ml) butter
1 egg, separated
¾ cup (175 ml) milk

Filling
5 cups (1.25 l) sliced, cored, peeled
    apples
½ cup (125 ml) white sugar
1 tbsp (15 ml) cornstarch
1 tsp (5 ml) cinnamon
¼ tsp (1 ml) nutmeg

Glaze
1 cup (250 ml) icing sugar
1 tbsp (15 ml) apple juice or milk
½ tsp (2 ml) vanilla

1. Blend flour and salt together in a medium bowl. Cut in butter until mixture resembles coarse meal.

2. Beat egg yolk with milk in a cup, and stir into flour mixture. Gather into a ball. Divide dough in half, and roll one half on a lightly floured surface to fit a rimmed 10½-inch by 15½-inch (26 cm by 39 cm) cookie sheet or jelly roll pan.

3. Arrange apple slices evenly over pastry to within 1 inch (2.5 cm) from edge. Mix sugar, spices, and cornstarch. Sprinkle sugar mixture over apples.

4. Roll out remaining pastry and cover apples. Moisten edges of dough and press together. Beat egg white in a small bowl until soft peaks form. Brush beaten egg white over top. Bake at 350°F (180°C) for 30 to 35 minutes until golden brown. Remove from oven.

5. Mix icing sugar, apple juice or milk, and vanilla in a small bowl. Add a little more liquid if necessary. Drizzle pastry with glaze. Cool. Cut into 6 squares, then cut each square diagonally.

Yields 12 pastries

CHAPTER FIVE

Apples for Dinner

Beverages

CRANBERRY APPLE JUICE

Make your own fruit juice combinations. This juice can be made in quantity and frozen into cubes for drinks or for kids' popsicles.

2 cups (500 ml) fresh or frozen cranberries
1 cup (250 ml) water

¼ cup (50 ml) white sugar (optional)
4 cups (1 l) apple juice

1. Place cranberries and water in a large saucepan. Bring to a boil; cover and reduce heat. Cook for 5 minutes or until cranberries pop.
2. Strain juice through a fine sieve. Add sugar if you wish, and stir to dissolve. Pour into saucepan and boil for 3 minutes. Cool.
3. Stir apple juice into cranberry juice. Chill before serving.
Yields 5 cups (1.25 l)

BLUEBERRY APPLE JUICE

Children love drinking blue juice. Use it to make ice cream floats.

1 cup (250 ml) fresh or frozen blueberries
½ cup (125 ml) water

2 tbsp (25 ml) white sugar (optional)
3 cups (750 ml) apple juice

1. Place blueberries and water in a saucepan. Bring to a boil; cover and reduce heat. Cook for 5 minutes.
2. Strain juice through a fine sieve. Add sugar if you wish, and stir to dissolve. Pour juice into a saucepan and boil 3 minutes. Cool.
3. Stir the blueberry juice into apple juice. Chill before serving.
Yields 3¾ cups (925 ml)

RED RASPBERRY SHRUB

This is a real thirst quencher, not too sweet.

3   tbsp (45 ml) Red Raspberry Vinegar (see page 253)
    Crushed ice
    Ice water, cider, club soda, orange juice or ginger ale

1. Pour vinegar over ice in a glass. Dilute to taste with water, cider, club soda, orange juice, or ginger ale.
Serves 1

WITCHES' SPECIAL BREW

Make a punch-bowlful to serve trick-or-treaters or serve at a harvest party.

8   cups (2 l) sweet cider or apple   1½ cups (375 ml) undiluted
    juice   frozen orange juice
1   3-inch (7.5-cm) cinnamon stick   concentrate
2   tsp (10 ml) whole allspice   ½ cup (125 ml) white sugar
1   whole nutmeg   4   cups (1 l) gingerale
                                         1   large orange
                                             Whole cloves

1. Simmer 1 cup (250 ml) cider in a small saucepan with cinnamon stick, allspice, and nutmeg for 10 minutes. Discard spices.
2. Combine remaining cider with orange juice concentrate, spiced cider, and sugar in a large container. Stir until sugar has dissolved. Chill.
3. Just before serving, stir in ginger ale.
4. Cut orange into ½-inch (1-cm) slices. Stud with whole cloves to resemble a smiling jack-o'-lantern.
Serves 10 to 12

CIDER FLIP

Refreshing on a hot day.

2 egg yolks
2 tsp (10 ml) white sugar
¼ tsp (1 ml) freshly grated nutmeg

1½ cups (375 ml) light cream
½ cup (125 ml) sweet cider
2 jiggers whiskey
½ cup (125 ml) crushed ice

1. Beat egg yolks, sugar, and nutmeg in a small bowl until thick and light. Beat in milk, cider, whiskey.
2. Add crushed ice and stir until mixture is cold. Strain into glasses and serve immediately.
Serves 2 to 3

MULLED CIDER

For an extra touch, float clove-studded red crabapples or small apples in the punch bowl.

8 cups (2 l) sweet apple cider
5 3-inch (7.5-cm) cinnamon sticks

8 cloves
2 tbsp (25 ml) white sugar

1. Place ingredients in a large saucepan and stir over low heat until sugar dissolves. Simmer uncovered for 30 minutes.
2. Remove cinnamon sticks and cloves. Pour into a heatproof punch bowl and garnish with crabapples.
Serves 8

MICROWAVE MULLED CIDER

This recipe is designed for one serving; if doubling or tripling amount, add 2 minutes for each additional serving.

1 cup (250 ml) apple cider
2 tsp (10 ml) brown sugar
   (optional)
¼ tsp (1 ml) butter

1 2-inch (5-cm) cinnamon stick
1 clove
1 tbsp (15 ml) rum or brandy

1. Place cider, sugar if desired, butter, and spices in a large microproof mug. Heat on maximum power for 2 minutes or until simmering.
2. Add rum or brandy and stir. Serve hot.
Serves 1

NON-ALCOHOLIC CRAN-APPLE PUNCH

Freeze 3 to 4 cups (75 to 100 ml) apple juice in a ring mold and float it in this punch to keep it chilled. This recipe can easily be halved.

6   cups (1.5 l) water
1   cup (250 ml) white sugar
1   cup (250 ml) strong tea
4   cups (1 l) cranberry cocktail

1   6-ounce (160 ml) frozen
    lemonade concentrate, thawed
2   cups (500 ml) apple juice
1   cup (250 ml) fresh orange juice

1. Chill all ingredients. Mix all ingredients in a large punch bowl just before serving.
Serves 25

APPLE CORDIAL

Once this cordial has been infused with apple flavor, store in the freezer. You can make it without the spices if you wish.

4   cups (1 l) finely chopped unpeeled
    apples
1   cup (250 ml) white sugar

1   3-inch (7.5-cm) cinnamon stick
4   allspice berries
2   cups (500 ml) vodka or brandy

1. Combine all ingredients in a screw-top jar.
2. Secure lid and shake until sugar is distributed evenly. Store in refrigerator for a month.
3. Strain through several thicknesses of cheesecloth or a paper coffee filter. Return to a smaller screw-top jar.
Yields 2½ cups (625 ml)

SPICED APPLE-APRICOT MIXER

Just the thing to mix with a little vodka, rum, brandy, or ginger ale.

½ cup (125 ml) water
¼ cup (50 ml) white sugar
3 3-inch (7.5-cm) cinnamon sticks

6 whole cloves
3 cups (750 ml) apple juice
1½ cups (375 ml) apricot nectar
¼ cup (50 ml) fresh orange juice

1. Place water, sugar, and spices in a small saucepan. Simmer covered for 10 minutes. Cool and strain.
2. Combine spiced syrup, apple juice, apricot nectar, and orange juice in a pitcher. Cover and chill.
Yields about 4 cups (1 l)

APPLE EGGNOG

Rich custard forms the base for this holiday drink.

3 beaten eggs
3 cups (750 ml) whole milk
2 cups (500 ml) light cream

½ cup (125 ml) white sugar
½ to ¾ cup (125 ml to 175 ml)
    apple brandy
    Grated nutmeg or cinnamon

1. Combine eggs, milk, cream, and sugar in top of double boiler. Stir until sugar dissolves.
2. Place over simmering water and cook, stirring constantly, until slightly thickened. Remove from heat and cool. Chill.
3. Just before serving, stir in desired amount of apple brandy. Add brandy gradually or mixture may curdle. Sprinkle each serving with a little nutmeg or cinnamon.
Serves 6

MAPLE-APPLE LIQUEUR

Mixed in a minute. Make this special liqueur to serve after dinner.

1 tbsp (15 ml) apple juice concentrate
2 tbsp (25 ml) maple syrup
3 tbsp (45 ml) whiskey

1. Combine ingredients in a small jar and shake for 30 seconds.
2. Refrigerate for an hour. Serve in chilled liqueur glasses.
Serves 2

DRIED APPLE LIQUEUR

The soft apple slices are a bonus; add to fruit salads or use as a topping for cake or ice cream.

2 cups (500 ml) lightly packed   ½ cup (125 ml) brandy
   dried apples   1 cup (250 ml) white sugar
2 cups (500 ml) dry white wine

1. Place all ingredients in a 1 quart (1 l) jar. Seal and let stand for 4 to 6 weeks in a cool dark place. Shake once a day to dissolve sugar.
2. Strain liqueur into a clean jar. Pack apple slices into another jar. Store apple slices in the refrigerator and use within a week.
Yields 2 cups (500 ml) liqueur and 3 cups (750 ml) apple slices

Appetizers

APPLE ANTIPASTO PLATTER

Arrange this platter according to what you have on hand. Here is a list of suggested foods that complement apples.

Red, green, and yellow skinned
   apples, with fruit knives
Smoked turkey slices
Pickled herring
Hard-boiled eggs
Thinly sliced ham
Sardines

Liverwurst sausage
Pâté
Blue cheese spread
Stilton cheese spread
Tomato wedges or cherry
   tomatoes
Celery sticks
Black and stuffed olives

1. Dip apple slices in lemon juice.
2. Wrap apple wedges in slices of smoked turkey or ham. Spread some of the apple wedges with liverwurst, pâté, or blue cheese or Stilton cheese spread.
3. Arrange ingredients on a platter with some or all of the other foods listed. Accompany with thin slices of rye bread, Melba toast, or assorted crackers.

CARAWAY-CHEESE SPREAD

Spread on crackers or Melba toast as an appetizer.

½ cup (125 ml) cream cheese, at
   room temperature
1 tsp (5 ml) caraway seed

1 tsp (5 ml) prepared mustard
½ cup (125 ml) finely chopped
   unpeeled apples

1. Beat cream cheese until smooth in a small bowl. Blend in the caraway seed and mustard.
2. Fold in apple. Serve immediately.
Serves 4

CHICKEN LIVER APPLE PÂTÉ

Spoon this mellow pâté into a crock and swirl a design with a fork over top.

1 cup (250 ml) butter
½ cup (125 ml) finely minced onion
1 large apple
1 lb (454 g) chicken livers

¼ cup (50 ml) apple brandy or
   apple juice
2 tbsp (25 ml) whipping cream
2 tsp (10 ml) fresh lemon juice
½ tsp (2 ml) salt
¼ tsp (1 ml) freshly ground pepper

1. Melt ¼ cup (50 ml) butter in a skillet over medium heat. Sauté onions until translucent. Peel, core, and chop apples. Add chopped apple to onions and sauté until soft. Place onions and apple into blender or food processor container. Do not process yet.
2. Remove fat and any gristle from chicken livers. Cut in half. Melt ¼ cup (50 ml) butter in the same skillet. Increase heat to high and cook livers until browned but still slightly pink inside. Add apple brandy or apple juice and cook for 1 minute.
3. Add chicken livers to onions and apples and process until smooth adding cream to thick mixture. Add lemon juice, salt, and pepper. Process again until blended. Cool to room temperature.
4. Cream remaining butter and beat in cooled liver mixture. Taste and adjust seasoning if necessary.
Yields 2¼ cups (300 ml)

GLAZED MINI-MEATBALLS

Grated apple keeps these appetizers moist; cider vinegar contributes
to the sweet-sour glaze.

1 lb (454 g) finely ground pork or beef	**Glaze**
¾ cup (175 ml) grated peeled apples	⅓ cup (75 ml) white sugar
1 tbsp (15 ml) finely minced peeled fresh ginger	⅓ cup (75 ml) cider vinegar
	1 tbsp (15 ml) soy sauce
1 tbsp (15 ml) soy sauce	
1 egg	
Peanut oil	

1. Combine pork or beef, apples, ginger, soy sauce, and egg in a
medium bowl. Shape mixture with wet hands into 1-inch (2.5-cm)
balls.
2. Cover bottom of a large skillet with oil. Heat over medium heat.
3. Place as many meatballs in skillet as will fit without crowding.
Cook 5 to 8 minutes, turning often, until browned and there is no
trace of pink. Drain meatballs on paper toweling. Keep in a warm
oven until all the meatballs are cooked.
4. Meanwhile, place sugar, vinegar, and soy sauce in a small saucepan. Bring to a boil and cook until sauce is a thick syrup.
5. Place meatballs in a serving dish. Pour glaze over and turn meatballs to coat. Serve immediately.
Serves 8

MINI BACON-APPLE APPETIZERS

These are irresistible one-bite sandwiches. Watercress adds a pep-
pery flavor.

8 slices firm white bread	¼ cup (50 ml) finely chopped
⅔ cup (150 ml) mayonnaise	watercress leaves
	11 slices bacon
	2 to 3 apples

1. Remove crusts from each slice of bread. Cut each slice into quarters, either in squares or triangles. Place on a baking sheet and toast in a 325°F (160°C) oven for 10 minutes, or until lightly browned and very crisp. Cool.

2. Blend mayonnaise with chopped watercress and spread on cooled toast.

3. Cut each slice of bacon into thirds. Fry bacon until crisp. Drain on paper towels.

4. Quarter and core apples. Slice apples into thin wedges. Arrange 2 or more apple wedges on each square of bread. Top with a piece of bacon.

5. Serve immediately.

Makes 32 appetizers

APPLES WITH CHEDDAR MAYONNAISE

These little packets are made by dabbing apple wedges with a special mayonnaise and wrapping them in lettuce leaves.

1 *large egg*	1 *cup (250 ml) vegetable oil*
3 *tbsp (45 ml) lemon juice*	¾ *cup (175 ml) grated cheddar*
1 *tsp (5 ml) salt*	*cheese*
1 *tsp (5 ml) white sugar*	6 *apples*
	Leaf lettuce

1. Process egg, 2 tbsp (25 ml) lemon juice, salt, and sugar in a blender or food processor until thoroughly mixed.

2. With blender or food processor running, add the vegetable oil very gradually. Process just until the mixture has thickened. Add the cheese and process briefly, just enough to combine. Chill if not serving immediately.

3. Quarter and core apples. Slice each quarter into three wedges and brush with 1 tbsp (15 ml) lemon juice. Place an apple wedge on a lettuce leaf. Top with a spoonful of mayonnaise. Wrap lettuce leaf around apple wedge and secure with a toothpick if necessary. Serve immediately.

Serves 6

Soups

CUCUMBER APPLE YOGURT SOUP

Perfect supper on a hot summer's night. Chill cucumber and apple before preparing this soup.

½ English cucumber
1 large red apple
2 cups (500 ml) plain yogurt
¾ cup (175 ml) whipping cream or whole milk

1 tbsp (15 ml) snipped fresh chives
2 tbsp (25 ml) finely chopped fresh mint
Salt and freshly ground pepper

1. Cut unpeeled cucumber into matchstick pieces. Quarter, core, and dice apple.
2. Combine cucumber, apple, yogurt, whipping cream or milk, chives, and 1 tbsp (15 ml) mint in a large bowl. Stir until thoroughly mixed. Season with salt and pepper to taste.
3. To serve, ladle soup into chilled serving dishes. Garnish with remaining mint.
Serves 6

DRIED FRUIT SOUP

A sweet, amber-colored fruit soup you serve hot. Any leftovers can be served over ice cream.

¾ cup (175 ml) chopped dried apples
½ cup (125 ml) chopped dried pears
½ cup (125 ml) golden raisins
2 cups (500 ml) apple juice or water, or a combination of the two

¼ cup (50 ml) chopped dried peaches or apricots
3 whole cloves
1 2-inch (5-cm) cinnamon stick
½ cup (125 ml) white sugar
¾ cup (175 ml) fresh orange juice
2 tbsp (25 ml) cornstarch

1. Place fruit and apple juice and/or water in a medium non-metallic bowl for 2 hours or overnight. Pour into a large saucepan. Add cloves, cinnamon, and sugar. Cook covered on medium-low heat until fruit is tender, about 30 minutes.

2. Blend cornstarch and orange juice in a cup. Stir into soup and continue cooking, stirring until thickened. Serve hot with a dollop of sour cream or Crème Fraîche (see page 231).

Serves 6

MULLIGATAWNY SOUP

A curried chicken soup to serve with hot cooked rice and chopped unpeeled apples.

3 tbsp (45 ml) butter	5 cups (1.25 l) chicken broth
1 thinly sliced Spanish onion	2 whole cloves
¼ cup (50 ml) diced carrot	1 cup (250 ml) diced raw chicken
¼ cup (50 ml) diced celery	Salt and freshly ground pepper
2 apples, peeled and diced	1 cup (250 ml) hot cooked rice
2 tbsp (25 ml) all-purpose flour	(optional)
1 tbsp (15 ml) curry powder	1 cup (250 ml) diced unpeeled
1 cup (250 ml) chopped canned or	apples (optional)
fresh tomatoes	

1. Peel, core, and dice apples. Melt 2 tbsp (25 ml) butter in a Dutch oven or large saucepan. Sauté the onion, carrot, celery, and apples for about 10 minutes or until almost tender. Stir in the flour and curry powder and cook for 5 minutes.

2. Add the tomatoes, chicken broth, and whole cloves. Partially cover and simmer for 1 hour.

3. Meanwhile, in a small skillet melt remaining butter over medium-high heat and sauté the chicken for 4 to 5 minutes until cooked. Add to soup and simmer for 10 minutes.

4. Season to taste with salt and pepper and serve with rice and diced unpeeled apples if desired.

Serves 4 to 6

APPLE-CRANBERRY SOUP

Serve this dessert soup warm or cold with whipped cream.

3 cups (750 ml) apple juice
2 cups (500 ml) smooth cranberry
   sauce
⅓ cup (75 ml) brown sugar
2 apples

1 3-inch (7.5-cm) cinnamon stick
4 tsp (20 ml) cornstarch
¼ cup (50 ml) water
1 tsp (5 ml) vanilla

1. Combine apple juice, cranberry sauce, and sugar in a medium saucepan. Stir until sugar is dissolved.
2. Peel, quarter, and core apples. Slice into thin wedges. Add apples and cinnamon stick to saucepan. Bring to a boil; reduce heat and simmer covered for 10 minutes. Remove cinnamon stick.
3. Mix cornstarch with water until smooth. Stir into apple mixture. Bring to a boil, stirring constantly. Boil 1 minute until clear and slightly thickened. Stir in vanilla. Serve warm or chilled. It may be necessary to thin chilled soup with more apple juice.
Serves 6

GARDEN APPLE SOUP

A simple mellow soup with a tart apple surprise.

1 cup (250 ml) diced peeled potatoes
1 cup (250 ml) diced peeled winter
   squash
1 cup (250 ml) water

2 cups (500 ml) diced peeled apples
1 cup (250 ml) light cream
¼ tsp (1 ml) cinnamon or nutmeg
   Salt and freshly ground pepper

1. Place potatoes, squash, and water in a large saucepan. Bring to a boil. Cover, reduce heat, and simmer for 10 to 15 minutes or until vegetables are soft. Remove from heat and mash the vegetables in saucepan.
2. Return saucepan to heat and add remaining ingredients. Heat thoroughly but do not boil. Apples should be slightly crisp. Season to taste with salt and pepper.
Serves 4

CREAMY CIDER SOUP

Use cider that has just begun to ferment to make this lightly sweetened creamy soup.

1 quart (1 l) partially fermented cider	1 tbsp (15 ml) all-purpose flour
3 slices bread	2 tbsp (25 ml) maple syrup or brown sugar
2 tbsp (25 ml) butter	1 cup (250 ml) whipping cream
2 eggs	1 tbsp (15 ml) dark rum
	Freshly grated nutmeg

1. Dice bread. Heat butter in a skillet and when foaming add the
bread cubes and sauté until browned and crisp. Remove from heat
and set aside.
2. Beat eggs with maple syrup or brown sugar and flour until light.
Continue beating while adding cream and rum.
3. Heat cider in a large saucepan over medium heat until boiling.
Skim foam from cider. Reduce heat and simmer. Whisk in the egg
mixture and stir continuously until soup is creamy and very hot.
Remove from heat. Serve with a grating of nutmeg and croutons.
Serves 4 to 6

CREAMY RUTABAGA SOUP

A rich, smooth vegetable soup.

2   tbsp (25 ml) butter
1   cup (250 ml) chopped onions
½ cup (125 ml) chopped celery with
    leaves
2   cups (500 ml) diced rutabaga
1   cup (250 ml) sliced carrots

2   apples
2   cups (500 ml) chicken broth
1   cup (250 ml) light cream
1   cup (250 ml) milk
    Salt and freshly ground pepper
    Freshly grated nutmeg

1. Melt butter over medium heat in a large saucepan and stir in onions and celery. Cover and steam for 10 minutes.

2. Add rutabaga, carrots, apples, and broth. Bring to a boil; reduce heat and simmer, covered, for 30 minutes or until vegetables are tender.

3. Cool slightly and process in a blender or food processor until smooth. Return to saucepan and stir in cream and milk. Season to taste with salt and freshly ground pepper. Heat thoroughly but do not boil. Sprinkle a little nutmeg over each serving.

Serves 6 to 8

Salads and Side Dishes

FRUITY COLESLAW

Red apples, grapes, and white wine make this cabbage salad special.

2   cups (500 ml) shredded cabbage
1½ cups (325 ml) diced red
      apples
½ cup (125 ml) halved seedless
      green grapes
¼ cup (50 ml) mayonnaise

3   tbsp (45 ml) white wine
1   tbsp (15 ml) cider vinegar
1   tsp (5 ml) white sugar
½ tsp (2 ml) salt
½ tsp (2 ml) grated onion

1. Mix cabbage, apples, and grapes in a large bowl.
2. Blend together the mayonnaise, wine, vinegar, sugar, salt, and onion in a small bowl. Pour over the salad and toss lightly. Chill before serving.
Serves 6

RED POTATO-APPLE SALAD

Red-jacketed new potatoes are combined with apples, mayonnaise, sour cream, and chives.

4   medium red-skinned potatoes
2   apples
1   tbsp (15 ml) fresh lemon juice

⅓ cup (75 ml) mayonnaise
⅓ cup (75 ml) sour cream
¼ cup (50 ml) finely chopped chives
      Salt and freshly ground pepper

1. Boil or steam potatoes in their skins until tender. Drain and cool until lukewarm. Cut into cubes (do not peel).
2. Quarter, core, and dice apples. Sprinkle with lemon juice and toss to coat.
3. Combine mayonnaise, sour cream, and chives in a small bowl. Place potatoes and apples in a large bowl. Pour dressing over salad and toss lightly. Season with salt and freshly ground pepper to taste.
4. Serve at room temperature or chilled.
Serves 4

CRAB AND APPLE SALAD WITH BUTTERMILK DRESSING

A delightful combination of seafood and fruit. Serve with crusty rolls and white wine.

1 cup (250 ml) frozen (thawed and drained) or canned (drained) crabmeat	¼ cup (50 ml) diced celery
	¼ cup (50 ml) buttermilk
	¼ cup (50 ml) mayonnaise
1 cup (250 ml) diced unpeeled apples	1 tbsp (15 ml) whipping cream
	Salt to taste
2 tsp (10 ml) lemon juice	

1. Separate crabmeat with a fork. Remove any bits of cartilage. Mix crabmeat in a bowl with apples, lemon juice, and celery.
2. Mix buttermilk, mayonnaise, and whipping cream, and pour over crab mixture. Toss to combine. Taste and add salt if needed. Toss lightly and serve on a bed of salad greens.
Serves 4

HERRING POTATO SALAD

Serve with sliced hard-boiled eggs and apple wedges, and garnish with parsley.

6 scrubbed medium potatoes	1 jar (200 ml) marinated herring tidbits
2 apples	
4 hard-boiled eggs	½ cup (125 ml) mayonnaise
1 small onion	Salt and freshly ground pepper
	Fresh parsley

1. Place unpeeled potatoes in a large saucepan. Barely cover with water and bring to a boil. Cover and simmer until fork tender (approximately 20 minutes). Drain, cool, and peel. Dice and set aside.

2. Grate one unpeeled apple and onion into a large bowl. Mash 2 eggs with a fork or ricer. Add to apple mixture.

3. Drain the herring. Grind or mince herring with a knife, hand grinder, or food processor. Blend herring and mayonnaise into apple mixture. Stir potatoes into apple mixture. Add salt and pepper to taste.

4. Slice remaining 2 eggs; slice and core remaining apple. Arrange slices around salad and garnish with parsley.

Serves 6

SPINACH APPLE SALAD WITH HOT CIDER VINEGAR DRESSING

Smoky bacon and tart cider vinegar combine in a hot dressing which is poured over the greens just before serving.

8 cups (2 l) fresh spinach or leaf lettuce	2 tsp (10 ml) fresh lemon juice
	2 tsp (10 ml) white sugar
¼ cup (50 ml) sliced green onions	¼ tsp (1 ml) salt
3 slices bacon	1 large apple
2 tbsp (25 ml) cider vinegar	

1. Wash spinach or lettuce and drain in a colander. Tear greens and place in a large bowl. Add green onions.

2. Cut bacon into small pieces. Cook bacon in a skillet over medium heat until crisp. Do not drain off drippings. Stir in vinegar, lemon juice, sugar and salt. Remove skillet from heat.

3. Quarter and core apple. Slice into thin wedges and add to spinach. Stir dressing in skillet reheating if necessary, and pour over salad. Toss until salad is coated. Serve immediately.

Serves 6

APPLE VEGETABLE JELLIED SALAD

Red, green, and orange vegetables and diced apples are suspended in yellow apple juice.

1   envelope unflavored gelatin
2   cups (500 ml) apple juice
¼ tsp (1 ml) salt
¼ cup (50 ml) white sugar
2   tbsp (25 ml) cider vinegar
1 ½ cups (375 ml) diced, cored, unpeeled red apples

¼ cup (50 ml) finely diced celery
½ cup (125 ml) grated carrots
½ cup (125 ml) grated green cabbage
½ cup (125 ml) grated red cabbage

1. Soak gelatin in ½ cup (125 ml) apple juice for 5 minutes in a small saucepan. Place over low heat and stir until gelatin dissolves.
2. Stir in remaining apple juice, salt, sugar, and cider vinegar.
3. Chill until mixture begins to jell. Fold in apples, celery, carrots, and green and red cabbages. Pour into a 4-cup (1-l) mold or individual molds. Chill until firm.
4. Unmold and serve with salad dressing if desired.
Serves 6 to 8

WHIPPED POTATO AND APPLE SALAD

Smooth whipped potatoes are combined with crunchy apples and celery. Wrap a spoonful of salad in a thin slice of ham or smoked turkey for an easy appetizer.

2   cups (500 ml) freshly cooked mashed potatoes (no milk or butter added)
½ cup (125 ml) mayonnaise
2   tsp (10 ml) prepared mustard

1   cup (250 ml) diced unpeeled apples
½ cup (125 ml) diced celery
1   tbsp (15 ml) chopped green onions
    Salt and freshly ground pepper

1. Whip mashed potatoes with an electric beater briefly until fluffy. Let potatoes cool to room temperature.
2. Add mayonnaise and mustard. Whip briefly until combined.
3. Fold in apples, celery, and onions. Taste for seasoning and add salt and pepper if needed. Best if served immediately but can be chilled.
Serves 2 to 4

CURRIED CHICKEN AND APPLE SALAD

Mix the dressing a few hours ahead of time to allow flavors to blend.

Dressing	Salad
⅔ cup (150 ml) sour cream	1½ cups (375 ml) diced
⅔ cup (150 ml) mayonnaise	unpeeled apples
1 tbsp (15 ml) fresh lemon juice	2 diced celery stalks
2 chopped green onions	4 cups (1 l) cubed cooked chicken
1½ tsp (7 ml) curry powder	½ cup (125 ml) Thompson or
	golden raisins
	Salt and freshly ground pepper
	Lettuce and apple wedges for
	garnish

1. Whisk together sour cream, mayonnaise, lemon juice, green onions, and curry powder in a small bowl. Cover and chill.
2. Just before serving, combine apples, celery, chicken, and raisins in a large bowl. Add sour cream mixture to chicken and stir until thoroughly combined. Season to taste with salt and freshly ground pepper.
3. Serve in lettuce cups surrounded by apple wedges.
Serves 4 to 6

COOL APPLE-CUCUMBER SALAD

Thinly sliced apples are added to traditional cucumber and sour cream salad. Colorful and delicious!

1 cup (250 ml) thinly sliced, cored,   1 cup (250 ml) sour cream
   unpeeled apples   1 tbsp (15 ml) vinegar
1 thinly sliced medium English   1 tbsp (15 ml) white sugar
   cucumber   ½ tsp (2 ml) salt
2 tbsp (25 ml) chopped green
   onions

1. Combine apples, cucumber, and green onions in a bowl.
2. Whisk together sour cream, vinegar, sugar, and salt in a small bowl and pour over apple mixture. Chill briefly or serve immediately.
Serves 4

COTTAGE CHEESE APPLE-ALMOND SALAD

This refreshing salad also makes a wonderful filling for crepes.

¼ cup (50 ml) raisins   3 cups (750 ml) creamed cottage
¼ cup (50 ml) apple juice   cheese
2 cups (500 ml) chopped, cored,   ¾ cup (175 ml) chopped almonds
   unpeeled apples   2 tsp (10 ml) poppyseeds
2 tbsp (25 ml) fresh lemon juice   1 to 2 tbsp (15 to 25 ml) liquid
                                             honey

1. Heat raisins in apple juice in a small saucepan for 3 minutes. Cover and let sit for an hour or until raisins are plump. Drain.
2. Sprinkle lemon juice over apples in a large bowl. Mix in cottage cheese and raisins.
3. Meanwhile, toast nuts in a small skillet over low heat, stirring constantly, until golden. Remove from heat. Add to cheese mixture.
4. Sprinkle poppyseeds and drizzle honey over salad. Toss to combine and chill for half an hour or serve immediately.
Serves 6 to 8

CELERY APPLE RICE SALAD

Serve this salad at room temperature.

1 cup (250 ml) diced celery
¾ cup (175 ml) diced unpeeled
   apples
4 cups (1 l) freshly cooked long-
   grain rice
3 tbsp (45 ml) fresh lemon juice

4 tbsp (60 ml) vegetable oil
½ tsp (2 ml) salt
¼ tsp (1 ml) dry mustard
½ cup (125 ml) chopped green
   onions
¼ cup (50 ml) chopped parsley

1. Combine celery, apples and rice in a large bowl.
2. Combine lemon juice, vegetable oil, salt, and mustard in a measuring cup. Mix until blended and pour over rice mixture.
3. Fold in green onions and parsley. Taste and add additional lemon juice or salt if necessary.
Serves 4 to 6

APPLE-KRAUT SALAD

This sweet-sour salad completes a meal of baked beans and brown bread.

1 quart (1 l) rinsed and drained
   sauerkraut
½ cup (125 ml) chopped celery
1 cup (250 ml) grated carrots

3 large red apples
¾ cup (175 ml) white sugar
½ cup (125 ml) vegetable oil
½ cup (125 ml) vinegar

1. Combine sauerkraut, celery, and carrots in a large bowl.
2. Quarter, core, and dice apples. Mix apples with sauerkraut.
3. Stir sugar, oil, and vinegar until sugar has dissolved. Pour over salad and mix thoroughly. Chill for an hour.
4. Before serving, drain off excess dressing.
Serves 8

APPLE-DATE-CHEDDAR SALAD

Tart apples, sweet dates, cheddar cheese, and walnuts fill this salad
with delicious contrasts.

3   cups (750 ml) diced unpeeled   ½ cup (125 ml) chopped celery
    apples   ¼ cup (50 ml) chopped walnuts
2   tbsp (25 ml) fresh lemon juice   ½ cup (125 ml) mayonnaise
¾ cup (175 ml) cubed cheddar   ½ cup (125 ml) fresh orange juice
    cheese   1   tbsp (15 ml) white sugar
½ cup (125 ml) finely chopped pit-   (optional)
    ted dates   ½ tsp (2 ml) grated orange rind

1. Place apples in a large bowl and sprinkle with lemon juice. Add
the cheese, dates, walnuts, and celery.
2. Mix mayonnaise, orange juice, sugar (if desired), and orange rind in
a small bowl. Pour over apple mixture and toss lightly.
Serves 4 to 6

APPLE-CELERY SALAD WITH
BLUE CHEESE DRESSING

Mound spoonfuls of this salad on crisp crackers and serve as an
appetizer.

3½ cups (875 ml) finely diced   ¼ cup (50 ml) chopped walnuts
    unpeeled apples   1   cup (250 ml) mayonnaise
2   tbsp (25 ml) fresh lemon juice   ⅓ cup (75 ml) crumbled blue
¾ cup (175 ml) chopped celery   cheese
                                          Freshly ground pepper

1. Place apples in a large bowl and sprinkle with lemon juice. Add
celery and walnuts.
2. Combine mayonnaise and blue cheese; spoon over apple mixture. Season with pepper. Toss lightly and serve.
Serves 6 to 8 as a salad; up to 12 as an appetizer

CARROT-APPLE SALAD WITH YOGURT DRESSING

Serve this salad as soon as it is made, otherwise the carrots will soften (even if it is kept for an hour).

4 medium carrots
1½ cups (325 ml) grated unpeeled apples
2 tbsp (25 ml) fresh lemon juice

½ cup (125 ml) finely minced celery
1 cup (250 ml) plain yogurt
1 tbsp (15 ml) liquid honey
Salt and freshly ground pepper

1. Peel and coarsely grate the carrots. Combine with apples in a medium bowl and sprinkle with lemon juice.
2. Add the celery, yogurt, and honey. Stir to combine thoroughly. Season to taste with salt and pepper.
Serves 6

APPLE SALAD WITH ORANGE POPPYSEED DRESSING

The dressing for this salad is under the fruit instead of on top. Use red- and green-skinned apples for the most colorful salad.

⅓ cup (75 ml) white sugar
2 tsp (10 ml) grated orange rind
¾ cup (175 ml) plain yogurt
1 tbsp (15 ml) vegetable oil

1 tbsp (15 ml) frozen orange juice concentrate
1 tbsp (15 ml) orange liqueur
1 tbsp (15 ml) poppyseeds
4 apples
4 oranges

1. Process sugar, orange rind, yogurt, vegetable oil, orange juice concentrate, and liqueur in a blender or food processor until combined. Stir in poppyseeds.
2. Quarter, core, and slice apples into 12 wedges. Peel and section oranges.
3. Spoon about ⅓ cup (75 ml) dressing onto individual salad plates and arrange fruit artistically over dressing.
Serves 4

RASPBERRY VINAIGRETTE

Dress up a fruit salad with this luscious pink vinaigrette.

¼ cup (50 ml) Red Raspberry Vinegar (see page 253)
½ cup (125 ml) Crème Fraîche (see page 231) or sour cream
   Pinch freshly grated nutmeg

1. Blend vinegar and Crème Fraîche or sour cream in a small bowl.
Add nutmeg and stir to blend. Serve immediately.
Yields ¾ cup (175 ml)

CARROT CHEESE DRESSING

A naturally sweetened orange dressing for fruit salads.

1 medium carrot
1 large apple
1 cup (250 ml) creamed cottage
   cheese
¼ cup (50 ml) undiluted apple juice
   concentrate
1 tsp (5 ml) grated orange rind
¼ tsp (1 ml) cinnamon (optional)

1. Peel and slice carrot. Peel, core, and dice apple.
2. Process all ingredients in a blender or food processor until smooth,
about 3 minutes. Pour over fruit salad.
Yields 1½ cups (375 ml)

BAKED BEANS WITH MAPLE SYRUP

These "sugarbush" beans have a crisp topping of brown sugar and sliced apples.

1 lb (454 g) dried yellow-eye or navy beans	¼ cup (50 ml) molasses
8 cups (2 l) water	4 apples
¼ lb (125 g) salt pork	½ cup (125 ml) brown sugar
1 chopped onion	½ cup (125 ml) butter
½ tsp (2 ml) dry mustard	1 tbsp (15 ml) all-purpose flour
½ cup (125 ml) maple syrup	¼ cup (50 ml) sweet cider (optional)

1. Pick over beans and wash in cold water. Place in a large saucepan and add water. Bring to a boil and cook for 1 minute. Remove from heat and cover. Let stand for 1 hour.

2. Uncover, then bring to a boil in the same water. Partially cover, then reduce heat and simmer for about 1½ hours, until the beans are tender but not mushy. (Time will vary according to the dryness of the beans.) Do not salt cooking water or the beans will harden. If beans need water during cooking, add boiling not cold water.

3. Slice salt pork and place in bottom of pot. Pour in undrained beans and add onion, mustard, maple syrup, and molasses. Cover and bake at 325°F (160°C) for 3 hours.

4. Peel, quarter, and core apples. Slice into thick wedges. Arrange on top of beans.

5. Cream brown sugar, butter, and flour. Spread on top of apples. Return to oven and bake uncovered for about an hour or until apples are tender and topping is browned. Pour cider over apples just before serving.

Serves 10 to 12

TURNIP-APPLE SCALLOP

Layers of turnips, apples, and onions are baked in cream.

¼ cup (50 ml) butter
½ cup (125 ml) thinly sliced onions
3 cups (750 ml) thinly sliced
   turnips
1½ cups (325 ml) sliced peeled
   apples

2 tbsp (25 ml) all-purpose flour
1 tsp (5 ml) sugar
1 cup (250 ml) milk
½ cup (125 ml) cream

1. Butter a 1½-quart (1.5-l) casserole.
2. Sauté onions in 1 tbsp (15 ml) butter until translucent. Layer turnips, onions and apples, sprinkling each layer with a bit of flour and dot with remaining butter.
3. Mix sugar with milk and cream. Pour over apples. Cover and bake at 350°F (180°C) for 30 minutes, then uncover and bake for 25 minutes or until tender and browned.
Serves 4

MAPLE-STUFFED BAKED APPLES

These apples are served as a side dish rather than a dessert. You can make them well in advance and serve them at room temperature.

12 small perfect apples
¾ cup (175 ml) fine dry breadcrumbs

6 tsp (30 ml) butter
12 tsp (60 ml) maple syrup

1. With a melon ball scoop or knife, scoop out a ball of apple at the stem end. Reserve for topping the apple after filling. Remove the core.
2. Fill each apple with approximately 1 tbsp (15 ml) of breadcrumbs until ¾ full. Spoon on 1 tsp (5 ml) maple syrup and ½ tsp (2 ml) butter. Plug the hole with the small apple ball, reversed skin side down.
3. Place apples in a 9 × 13-inch (3-l) dish. Bake at 350°F (180°C) for 40 minutes or until tender.
Serves 12

CIDER-BRAISED TURNIPS

Sliced carrots can be substituted for turnip.

1 ½ lbs (750 g) turnips
¼ cup (50 ml) butter
½ cup (125 ml) sweet cider or apple
   juice

1 apple
¼ tsp (1 ml) freshly grated nutmeg
   Salt and freshly ground pepper

1. Peel turnips and slice into ½-inch (1-cm) slices.
2. Melt butter in a medium saucepan. Add turnip slices and toss to coat lightly with butter. Add cider; cover pan tightly and cook over low heat for 15 minutes or until turnips are tender but not mushy.
3. Meanwhile, peel, quarter, and core apple. Cut into thick wedges. Remove turnip slices to a casserole and keep warm. Add apple slices and nutmeg to saucepan. Boil vigorously to reduce liquid and pour over turnips.
4. Season lightly with salt and pepper.
Serves 4 to 6

CIDER-BRAISED CARROTS AND APPLES

Serve with roast chicken or pork.

1 ½ cups (325 ml) grated
   unpeeled apples
4 cups grated carrots
¼ cup (50 ml) light brown sugar

½ tsp (2 ml) salt
½ cup (125 ml) apple cider
2 tbsp (25 ml) butter

1. Combine the apples, carrots, brown sugar, salt, and cider in a small buttered casserole. Dot with the butter.
2. Cover and bake at 350°F (180°C) for 35 to 40 minutes. Stir once during cooking time.
Serves 4

APPLE KUGEL (NOODLE PUDDING)

Apples, plump raisins, and noodles are bound together with eggs
and baked until golden and crisp.

¼ cup (50 ml) raisins
   Boiling water
4 cups (1 l) cooked wide egg
   noodles
¼ cup (50 ml) butter or rendered
   chicken fat, melted

2 apples
1 to 3 tbsp (15 to 45 ml)
   brown sugar
¼ tsp (1 ml) cinnamon
4 to 5 beaten eggs
   Salt and pepper

1. Place raisins in a small bowl. Cover with boiling water and set
aside. Peel and coarsely chop apples.
2. Rinse cooked noodles and mix in a buttered 9-inch (2.5-l) square
baking dish with melted butter, apples, brown sugar, cinnamon, eggs,
salt, pepper, and drained raisins.
3. Place baking dish on top rack of 350°F (180°C) oven.
4. Pour boiling water into a small cake pan and place on lower rack
in oven. Bake for 30 to 45 minutes until top is slightly brown. Cut in
squares and serve.
Serves 9

WILD RICE PILAF

Dried apples, golden raisins, and toasted almonds complement the
nutty flavor of wild rice.

½ cup (125 ml) chopped dried
   apples
¼ cup (50 ml) golden raisins
⅓ cup (75 ml) dry sherry or cider
½ cup (125 ml) wild rice
2⅓ cups (575 ml) hot chicken
   broth

3 tbsp (45 ml) butter
1 cup (250 ml) brown rice
½ cup (125 ml) slivered blanched
   almonds
¼ cup (50 ml) chopped fresh parsley
   Salt and freshly ground black
   pepper

1. Heat apples and raisins in sherry or cider in a small saucepan to boiling. Reduce heat; cover and simmer 5 minutes. Set aside.
2. Place wild rice, 1 cup (250 ml) of hot chicken broth, and 1 tbsp (15 ml) butter in top of double boiler. Cook covered over boiling water for 1 hour.
3. Meanwhile, place brown rice, remaining chicken broth, and 1 tbsp (15 ml) butter in a medium saucepan. Bring to a boil; reduce heat and cook until all the water is absorbed, about 40 minutes.
4. Sauté almonds in a small skillet in remaining 1 tbsp (15 ml) butter until lightly browned.
5. When wild rice is cooked, combine with cooked brown rice, fruit, almonds, and parsley in a casserole.
6. Season to taste with salt and pepper. Serve immediately.
Serves 4 to 6

HEAVEN AND EARTH

Potatoes and apples seem to have a natural affinity for one another. Serve with sausages or pork roast.

6 *medium potatoes*	2 *tbsp (25 ml) butter*
1 *cup (250 ml) milk*	1 *tsp (5 ml) sugar*
2 *cups (500 ml) diced peeled apples*	*Ginger or nutmeg*

1. Peel potatoes and slice into ¼-inch (½-cm) thick slices. Place in a heavy skillet and add milk. Slowly bring to a boil; reduce heat, cover, and simmer for 15 minutes or until potatoes are almost tender.
2. Add apples and stir to combine. If necessary, add a little more milk or water. Cover and cook for 10 minutes until apples and potatoes are tender. Milk should be mostly absorbed.
3. Stir potatoes and apples to combine and turn into a serving dish. Drizzle with melted butter and sprinkle with sugar and a dusting of ginger or nutmeg.
Serves 4

BEETS AND APPLESAUCE

Serve with chicken or steak and kidney pie.

6 *medium beets*   1 *tbsp (15 ml) butter*
1 *cup (250 ml) thick applesauce*   *Salt and freshly ground pepper*

1. Scrub beets and place in a large saucepan. Cover with boiling water and cook over medium-low heat for 30 to 40 minutes or until tender. Drain and place under cold running water until cool enough to handle. Peel beets.
2. Mash beets or put through a ricer and place in a medium saucepan. Add butter and applesauce. Heat until steamy and butter melts. Season with salt and pepper. Serve immediately.
Serves 4

APPLE JUICE BEETS

An interesting variation on Harvard beets.

2 *tbsp (25 ml) cornstarch*   ⅔ *cup (150 ml) apple juice*
1 *tbsp (15 ml) white sugar*   ½ *cup (125 ml) cider vinegar*
½ *tsp (2 ml) salt*   2 *to 3 cups (500 to 750 ml)*
                                        freshly cooked diced beets

1. Mix cornstarch, sugar, salt, apple juice, and vinegar in a medium saucepan. Cook, stirring constantly, over medium-high heat, until mixture thickens and is clear. Continue to cook, still stirring for 1 minute more. Fold in the beets and heat thoroughly. Serve hot.

MICROWAVE METHOD

1. Combine cornstarch, sugar, salt, apple juice, and vinegar in a 4-cup (1-l) microproof dish. Stir until smooth.
2. Cook for 2 to 3 minutes on maximum power until thick and clear. Fold in the beets and heat covered for 3 to 4 minutes on maximum power until hot.
Serves 6

Main Dishes

COUNTRY CHICKEN

A tasty combination of apples, vegetables, and curry sauce.

2½ to 3 lb (1 to 1.5 kg)
   chicken pieces
¼ cup (50 ml) all-purpose flour
1 tsp (5 ml) salt
½ tsp (2 ml) freshly ground pepper
3 tbsp (45 ml) butter
1 diced onion
1 sweet red pepper, diced
2 crushed cloves garlic

2 cups (500 ml) diced, cored, peeled
   apples
2 tsp (10 ml) curry powder
½ tsp (2 ml) thyme
2 cups (500 ml) drained canned
   tomatoes
2 tbsp (25 ml) currants
½ cup (125 ml) apple juice

1. Dredge chicken pieces with flour, salt, and pepper. Heat butter in a large skillet over medium-high heat and brown chicken. Transfer chicken to a 9 × 13-inch (3-l) casserole.
2. Drain all fat except for 1 tbsp (15 ml). Sauté onion, green pepper, garlic, apples, and curry powder until vegetables begin to soften.
3. Add thyme, tomatoes, currants, and apple juice. Cook for 2 minutes. Pour sauce over chicken in casserole. Bake uncovered at 350°F (180°C) for 40 minutes or until chicken is tender. Baste during cooking with pan juices.
Serves 4 to 6

DRIED APPLE CHICKEN

Marmalade and ginger form an amber glaze while the dried fruit absorbs pan juices. Perfect for a buffet dinner with a mound of fluffy white or wild rice.

5 to 6 lb (2 to 2.5 kg)
  chicken breast halves
    Salt and freshly ground pepper
1 tsp (5 ml) ginger

1½ cups (375 ml) orange
  marmalade
⅔ cup (150 ml) apple juice or cider
2 cups (500 ml) dried apples
1 cup (250 ml) currants

1. Place chicken halves skin side up in a shallow roasting pan and sprinkle with salt and pepper.
2. Mix ginger and marmalade in a small bowl and spread over the chicken. Pour apple juice into pan. Bake at 325°F (160°C) for 15 minutes.
3. Add dried apples and currants to the pan. Bake for 30 minutes or until chicken is tender and glazed. Baste chicken frequently.
4. Remove chicken and fruit to a serving platter. Skim fat from pan juices. Pour some juices over the chicken and serve remainder in a sauceboat.
Serves 6 to 8

CIDER SAUCED CHICKEN

Cider marinade is combined with brown sugar, applejack, and apple slices to make a rich sauce to serve with the chicken.

2 quartered fryer chickens
2 cups (500 ml) sweet cider
¾ cup (175 ml) all-purpose flour
2 tsp (10 ml) ginger
1 tsp (5 ml) cinnamon

½ tsp (2 ml) allspice
1 tsp (5 ml) salt
½ tsp (2 ml) freshly ground pepper
3 tbsp (45 ml) brown sugar
⅓ cup (75 ml) applejack
2 cups (500 ml) sliced peeled apples

1. The day before serving, place chicken quarters in large glass baking dish. Pour cider over the chicken. Cover and marinate overnight in the refrigerator. Turn pieces several times during marinating.
2. Next day, remove chicken from cider. Reserve cider marinade. Mix flour, ginger, cinnamon, allspice, salt, and pepper in a small bowl. Dredge the chicken pieces with the flour mixture. Place chicken skin side up in a single layer in a large baking dish.
3. Bake at 350°F (180°C) for 40 minutes. Skim off excess fat.
4. Combine cider marinade, brown sugar, applejack and apple slices in a medium bowl. Pour over the chicken and bake for 20 minutes more. Baste chicken several times with pan juices.
Serves 6 to 8

ROAST CHICKEN WITH APPLE-RYE STUFFING

Rye bread and apples have an affinity for each other.

4 tbsp (60 ml) butter	½ tsp (2 ml) marjoram
1 cup (250 ml) diced onions	1 lightly beaten egg
¾ cup (175 ml) sliced celery	½ tsp (2 ml) salt
4 cups (1 l) cubed day-old rye bread	¼ tsp (1 ml) freshly ground pepper
2 cups (500 ml) diced, cored, peeled apples	1 5 to 6-lb (2 to 2.5-kg) roasting chicken

1. To prepare stuffing, melt butter in a Dutch oven over medium heat. Sauté onion and celery until tender, stirring occasionally. Remove from heat.
2. Add bread, apple, marjoram, egg, salt, and pepper. Mix until evenly moistened. If dressing is too dry, add a tbsp (15 ml) of water or chicken broth.
3. Stuff chicken and place on a rack in a roasting pan. Bake at 325°F (160°C) for 2½ to 3 hours or until chicken is golden and juices are clear when thigh is pierced with a fork. Baste chicken often with pan drippings during last hour.
Serves 6

CORNISH HENS WITH CURRIED RICE STUFFING

This hot and spicy stuffing will delight lovers of piquant food.

2   tbsp (25 ml) butter
¼ cup (50 ml) chopped onions
1   small green chili pepper, minced
½ cup (125 ml) slivered almonds
1   tsp (5 ml) minced peeled ginger
    root
1   tsp (5 ml) curry powder
1   cup (250 ml) chopped apples

½ cup (250 ml) raisins
1½ cups (375 ml) cooked white
    or brown rice
    Salt and freshly ground pepper
4   1 to 1½ lb (454 to 750 g)
    Cornish game hens
2   tbsp (25 ml) vegetable oil or
    melted butter

1. Melt butter in a large saucepan over medium heat. Sauté onions, chili pepper, almonds, ginger, and curry powder until onions are tender.

2. Remove from heat and add apple, raisins, and rice. Season to taste with salt or pepper. Toss to mix thoroughly.

3. Sprinkle cavities of hens with salt. Lightly stuff with rice mixture. Pull neck skin, if present, to back of each hen. Twist wing tips under back to hold skin in place. Tie legs to tail with a piece of cotton twine. Place hens on a rack in a roasting pan. Brush with cooking oil or melted butter.

4. Cover loosely with foil and roast at 375°F (190°C) for 30 minutes. Uncover and roast for 40 to 50 minutes longer or until drumsticks can be twisted easily in sockets.

5. Transfer hens to a platter and serve.

Serves 4

CURRIED STUFFED CHICKEN BREASTS

In the center of each chicken breast is a spicy apple filling. Serve with steamed rice, green salad, and a bowl of yogurt.

4 chicken breast halves, skinned and boned
½ cup (125 ml) grated peeled apples
½ tsp (2 ml) curry powder
1 small clove garlic, crushed
½ tsp (2 ml) coconut milk or vegetable oil

¼ tsp (1 ml) salt
¼ cup (50 ml) all-purpose flour
1 beaten egg
1 cup (250 ml) desiccated unsweetened coconut
½ cup (125 ml) unsalted butter

1. Place each chicken breast between waxed paper and flatten with a mallet to a thickness of ¼ inch (6 mm). Set aside.
2. Mix grated apples, curry powder, garlic, coconut milk or vegetable oil, and salt in a small bowl.
3. Place ¼ apple mixture in center of each breast. Fold over edges and roll into a cylinder. Dust rolled breasts with flour, dip in beaten egg, and roll in coconut. Set aside for 10 minutes to allow coating to set.
4. Heat butter in a skillet over medium heat until it foams. Fry the chicken rolls until golden on all sides. Turn carefully. Transfer to a casserole and bake at 300°F (150°C) for 10 to 15 minutes.
Serves 4

ALLSPICE BRANDY CHICKEN

Apples, onions, Calvados, and allspice combine in this fragrant sauce.

6 tbsp (90 ml) butter	½ tsp (2 ml) allspice
2 diced onions	2 cups (500 ml) apple juice
4 chicken breast halves	½ tsp (2 ml) salt
2 apples	¼ tsp (1 ml) freshly ground pepper
½ cup (125 ml) Calvados	2 tbsp (25 ml) all-purpose flour

1. Melt 3 tbsp (45 ml) butter over medium heat in a large skillet. Add the onions and sauté until tender. Remove from pan and reserve.
2. Peel, quarter, and core apples.
3. Melt 1 tbsp (15 ml) butter in skillet and brown chicken breasts on both sides.
4. Add apples, Calvados, allspice, apple juice, salt, and pepper to skillet. Cover and cook chicken over low heat for 20 minutes. Remove chicken to a platter and keep warm.
5. Blend together remaining butter and flour. Stir into sauce and cook for 5 minutes or until thickened. Pour over chicken and serve immediately.
Serves 4

APPLE-PORT GLAZED CHICKEN LIVERS

Serve these sweet-sour tidbits on a mound of fluffy white rice.

½ cup (125 ml) undiluted apple juice concentrate	1 lb (500 g) chicken livers
½ cup (125 ml) port	½ cup (125 ml) all-purpose flour
3 tbsp (45 ml) butter	½ tsp (2 ml) salt
	¼ tsp (1 ml) freshly ground pepper

1. Prepare sauce by combining apple juice concentrate, port, and 1 tbsp (15 ml) butter in a small saucepan. Boil until sauce is reduced to ½ cup (125 ml). Set aside.
2. Remove any bits of fat or gristle from liver and cut each in half. Combine flour, salt, and pepper in a plastic bag. Drop in liver pieces a few at a time, and toss to coat.
3. Melt 2 tbsp (25 ml) butter over medium-high heat, and brown liver pieces, turning once. Cook until no pink shows when liver is cut, but do not overcook.
4. Place livers in a serving dish and top with warmed sauce.
Serves 4

CHICKEN LIVERS AND APPLE SLICES

The apples complement the natural sweetness of the liver and onions.

1 lb (500 g) chicken livers	2 tbsp (25 ml) apple brandy or cider
3 tbsp (45 ml) all-purpose flour	½ cup (125 ml) finely chopped onions
1 tsp (5 ml) paprika	
½ tsp (2 ml) salt	
½ tsp (2 ml) freshly ground pepper	3 cups (750 ml) sliced unpeeled apples
6 tbsp (90 ml) butter	2 tbsp (25 ml) brown sugar

1. Cut chicken livers in half and remove any fat and gristle. Blend flour, paprika, salt, and pepper in a paper or plastic bag. Add chicken livers and shake to coat.
2. Heat butter over medium-high heat until it foams. Add chicken livers and sauté until browned on all sides. Pour apple brandy or cider over livers. Stir and scoop livers into a warm serving dish.
3. Add onions to same skillet and stir over medium heat until onions are tender. Transfer to same dish as livers.
4. Heat remaining butter in same skillet and add apples and sugar. Stir over medium heat until apples are barely tender, 3 to 5 minutes. Return livers and onions to apples and toss together to reheat livers. Season to taste with more salt and pepper.
Serves 4

DRIED FRUIT AND APPLE STUFFING

Dried fruit, candied ginger, apples, and nuts are combined in this moist and distinctive stuffing—perfect for a duck or a small turkey.

1 ½ cups (375 ml) dried apricots	⅓ cup (75 ml) apple brandy or
¾ cup (175 ml) pitted dates	orange liqueur
1 ¼ cups (300 ml) pitted prunes	2 cups (500 ml) chopped peeled
½ cup (125 ml) candied ginger	apples
⅓ cup (75 ml) apple juice or cider	½ cup (125 ml) chopped blanched
	almonds

1. Coarsely chop dried fruit and ginger. Combine dried fruit with apple juice, cider, and apple brandy or orange liqueur in a large bowl. Cover with plastic wrap and marinate overnight.
2. Next day, toast chopped almonds in a small skillet over low heat or bake at 350°F (180°C) for 10 minutes or until golden.
3. Add apples and almonds to marinated fruit. Mix thoroughly and use to stuff bird. If serving as a side dish, add a cup (250 ml) hot chicken broth and bake in a covered casserole at 350°F (180°C) for 30 minutes.
Yields about 5 cups (1.25 l)

CAPE ISLAND DUCK

This dressing and rather long roasting method is used traditionally with wild sea duck. It is delicious with domestic duck or turkey, too.

4 large apples	2 heaping tbsp (35 ml) white sugar
16 carrots	½ tsp (2 ml) salt
1 ½ slices turnip ½-inch	¼ tsp (1 ml) freshly ground pepper
(1-cm) thick	1 ½ to 2 cups (375 to 500 ml)
1 parsnip	water
1 onion	1 5-lb (2-kg) duck
1 slice day-old bread	

1. Peel, quarter, and core apples. Peel carrots, turnip slices, parsnip and onion.

2. Grind apples and vegetables separately in a meat grinder or process in a food processor to a finely ground consistency. Grind or process bread separately and last.

3. Mix apples, vegetables, bread, sugar, salt, pepper, and enough water so the mixture will stick together.

4. Stuff duck cavity loosely. Line a rack in a roasting pan with tin foil overlapping the sides. Pierce foil in several places to allow fat to drain. Place duck on lined rack and mound remaining dressing around bird.

5. Bake at 350°F (180°C) for 3 hours. Cover for the first 1½ hours; bake uncovered for remaining time. Water may be added as necessary.

Serves 4 to 6

ROAST GOOSE WITH APPLE PRUNE STUFFING

Sweet stuffing is delicious with goose. Save the rendered goose fat for frying golden brown potatoes.

24 *large pitted prunes*	1 *8 to 10-lb (3 to 4-kg) goose*
1½ *cups (375 ml) cider*	2 *tbsp (25 ml) all-purpose flour*
6 *apples*	1½ *cups (375 ml) chicken*
2 *inches (5 cm) fresh peeled ginger root*	*Salt and freshly ground pepper*

1. Combine prunes and cider in a bowl. Let soak for 1 hour. Peel, quarter, and core apples. Add apples to prunes and toss to combine.

2. Pull out all the fat inside the body cavity. Rub goose inside and out with slices of ginger. Sprinkle inside and out with salt. Stuff goose with prunes and apples. Skewer cavities closed.

3. Place goose on a rack in a roasting pan. Prick the skin all over. Bake at 325°F (160°C) for 3 to 3½ hours or until internal temperature reaches 185°F (85°C). During roasting, remove fat from pan every 20 minutes using a spoon or bulb baster. Remove goose from oven and transfer to a serving platter. Cover with foil and let stand for 10 to 15 minutes while preparing gravy.

4. Remove all but 1 tbsp (15 ml) fat from the roasting pan. Place over medium heat and stir in the flour. Add the chicken broth and stir until thickened. Season to taste with salt and pepper.
5. Transfer dressing into a serving dish. Carve the goose and serve with gravy and dressing.
Serves 8

HOLIDAY TURKEY

A fruit-stuffed turkey basted with red wine and orange juice.

1 *8 to 9-lb (*3.75 *to* 4-kg*) turkey*
   Salt
   Freshly ground pepper
½ *tsp (*2 *ml) marjoram*

Basting Sauce
½ *cup (*125 *ml) red wine*
½ *cup (*125 *ml) orange juice*
   Juice of 1 *lemon*
⅛ *tsp (*½ *ml) Tabasco sauce*
½ *cup (*125 *ml) sour cream*

Stuffing
1 *cup (*250 *ml) finely chopped*
   mixed dried fruit (apricots,
   pears, peaches)
2 *tbsp (*25 *ml) raisins*
2½ *cups (*625 *ml) diced peeled*
   apples
1 *cup (*250 *ml) day-old bread-*
   crumbs

1. Rinse turkey under cold running water and dry with paper towels. Sprinkle cavity with salt, pepper, and marjoram.
2. Mix dried fruit, raisins, apples, and breadcrumbs in a large bowl. Stuff turkey and skewer openings closed. Rub skin with salt.
3. Place turkey in a roasting pan. Cover with aluminum foil and bake on lowest rack in a 350°F (180°C) oven for about 2¾ to 3 hours or until internal temperature registers 190°F (88°C) when inserted in turkey thigh.
4. Mix red wine, orange juice, lemon juice, and Tabasco sauce in a small bowl. After one hour cooking time, baste turkey with sauce. Cover again with foil. Continue baking, basting turkey every 30 minutes.

5. When turkey is cooked, transfer to a platter and keep in a warm place for 20 minutes before carving. Skim excess fat from pan. Stir in sour cream and add a little water if necessary to make a thin sauce. Heat over low heat; season with salt and pepper. Serve with turkey and stuffing.
Serves 12

BAKED FISH WITH APPLE DILL SAUCE

A tart dill sauce, with crunchy bits of diced apple.

2 lb (1 kg) whole haddock or salmon, head and tail removed
   Salt
2 tbsp (25 ml) butter
1 tsp (5 ml) cornstarch

1 tsp (5 ml) prepared mustard
2 tbsp (25 ml) chopped fresh dill
½ cup (125 ml) apple juice
½ cup (125 ml) finely diced un-peeled apples
1 tbsp (15 ml) fresh lemon juice

1. Wash fish and pat dry. Sprinkle all over with salt. Wrap fish in 2 layers of aluminum foil. Fold over and seal seam and ends. Place on a cookie sheet. Bake at 375°F (190°C) for 40 to 45 minutes, or until fish flakes easily.
2. Meanwhile, melt butter in a small saucepan. Stir in cornstarch, mustard, and dill. Gradually add apple juice. Stir until smooth and thickened. Add the diced apples and lemon juice.
3. Open foil packet, remove skin from fish, and transfer to a platter. Serve sauce over fish or in a sauceboat.
Serves 4

CIDER CREAM HALIBUT

Salmon steaks can be used in this recipe too.

¼ cup (50 ml) butter
3 finely minced green onions
6 halibut steaks, about 3 lb
   (1.5 kg)
½ tsp (2 ml) salt
½ tsp (2 ml) freshly ground pepper

1¾ cups (425 ml) sweet or hard
   cider or apple juice
3 egg yolks
¾ cup (175 ml) whipping cream
1½ tbsp (22 ml) fresh lemon
   juice
1 tbsp (15 ml) minced fresh
   parsley

1. Preheat oven to 375°F (190°C). Melt 3 tbsp (45 ml) butter in a small skillet. Sauté the onions in the butter for 1 minute. Pour butter and onions into a 9 × 13-inch (3-l) ovenproof casserole.
2. Add the halibut steaks. Sprinkle with salt and pepper. Pour the cider or apple juice over the steaks. Dot with remaining butter. Cover with a sheet of waxed paper. Bake for 15 to 20 minutes until the fish is opaque and flakes easily.
3. Remove the steaks to a warm serving platter. Pour the cooking liquids into a stainless steel or enamel saucepan. Bring to a boil and reduce liquid by half.
4. Whisk the egg yolks and cream in another small saucepan. Stir in the reduced liquid and cook over low heat, stirring constantly, until slightly thickened. Stir in the lemon juice and parsley.
5. Taste for seasoning and pour over the halibut steaks. Serve immediately.
Serves 6

SOUSED MACKEREL

Fresh mackerel are cooked in cider vinegar and pickling spice. This is a general recipe you can follow to make one serving or ten.

Fresh cleaned mackerel   Mixed pickling spice
Cider vinegar   Salt and freshly ground pepper
                                Butter

1. Cut mackerel in half lengthwise then cut in serving-size pieces. Place in a buttered baking dish.
2. Pour in enough vinegar to cover fish. Sprinkle with ½ tsp (2 ml) pickling spice for each mackerel. Season with a little salt and pepper. Dot with butter.
3. Bake at 350°F (180°C) for 30 minutes or until fish flakes easily. Serve hot or cold.

PICADILLO

This is one version of a favorite South American ground beef dish. The jalapeño chilies make it hot!

2 tbsp (25 ml) olive oil   2 canned jalapeño chilies, chopped
2 lb (1 kg) lean ground beef   (optional)
2 chopped onions   ½ cup (125 ml) sliced pimento-
2 crushed garlic cloves   stuffed olives
2 cups (500 ml) chopped peeled   ⅛ tsp (½ ml) thyme
   apples   ⅛ tsp (½ ml) oregano
2 large tomatoes, peeled and   Pinch ground cloves
   chopped   Salt and freshly ground pepper
½ cup (125 ml) raisins

1. Heat oil in a large skillet over medium-high heat. Brown the meat then add the onions and garlic, and sauté until onions are soft.
2. Add remaining ingredients and simmer uncovered for 20 minutes. Serve with rice and a salad.
Serves 6

BEEF CIDER STEW

Adding cider to a stew enhances the natural sweetness of the vegetables.

2 lb (1 kg) stewing beef
3 tbsp (45 ml) all-purpose flour
1 tsp (5 ml) salt
1 tsp (5 ml) pepper
¼ cup (50 ml) vegetable oil
2 sliced onions

2 cups (500 ml) sweet cider or apple juice
½ cup (125 ml) beef broth or water
2 tbsp (25 ml) cider vinegar
½ tsp (2 ml) thyme
4 small potatoes
4 medium carrots
½ cup (125 ml) sliced celery

1. Cut stewing meat into 1-inch (2.5-cm) cubes. Combine flour, salt, and pepper in a plastic bag. Add meat and shake to coat. Heat oil in a Dutch oven over medium-high heat and brown meat on all sides, in two batches. Add sliced onions and sauté for 3 minutes or until soft. Drain off excess fat.
2. Return meat to Dutch oven and add cider or apple juice, beef broth or water, vinegar, and thyme. Bring to a boil; reduce heat and simmer covered for 1 hour or until meat is nearly tender.
3. Peel potatoes and carrots. Quarter potatoes and carrots. Add vegetables to stew and simmer covered for 30 minutes or until vegetables and meat are tender.
Serves 6

PERSIAN LAMB STEW

A sweet-sour stew.

2½ lb (1 kg) lean lamb
3 tbsp (45 ml) butter
1 large onion, finely chopped
1 tsp (5 ml) saffron
1¼ cups (300 ml) beef broth
1 tsp (5 ml) salt

¼ tsp (1 ml) freshly ground pepper
¼ cup (50 ml) fresh lemon juice
¼ cup (50 ml) yellow split peas
6 large cooking apples
   ¼ cup (50 ml) white sugar

1. Trim any excess fat from lamb. Cut into ½-inch (1-cm) pieces. Heat butter in a Dutch oven and when foaming, brown the lamb. Add the onion and sauté until tender.
2. Stir in saffron. Add beef broth, salt, pepper, and lemon juice. Cover and simmer over low heat for 30 minutes. Add yellow peas; cover and simmer for another hour or until peas are tender.
3. Peel, quarter, and core apples. Cut each quarter in half lengthwise. Add the apple wedges and sugar to stew. Cover and simmer for 15 minutes. Do not overcook or apples will be mushy. Serve with rice.
Serves 6

CURRIED LAMB CHOPS

Make this curry sauce as spicy as you like. Serve on a bed of rice with Cool Apple-Cucumber Salad (see page 148).

3 tbsp (45 ml) butter	1 ½ cups (325 ml) chopped
8 lamb shoulder chops	peeled apples
1 finely chopped onion	1 cup (250 ml) chicken broth
⅓ cup (75 ml) chopped celery	½ cup (125 ml) drained canned
2 large cloves garlic, crushed	tomatoes, chopped
2 tbsp (25 ml) curry powder or to taste	½ cup (125 ml) raisins

1. Melt 2 tbsp (25 ml) butter in a large skillet and brown chops on both sides. Transfer to a Dutch oven.
2. Melt remaining butter in skillet and sauté onion, celery, and garlic for 2 minutes. Stir in curry powder and cook, stirring, for 1 minute.
3. Add apples, chicken broth, tomatoes, and raisins. Simmer for 2 minutes, then pour curry sauce into Dutch oven. Cover and simmer until chops are tender, about 30 minutes.
Serves 4 to 6

LAMB AND APPLE CURRY

For a milder flavor, substitute sweet green peppers for the chili peppers.

2 lb (1 kg) stewing lamb
1 tbsp (15 ml) vegetable oil
2 chopped onions
2 crushed cloves garlic
2 hot chili peppers
1 tbsp (15 ml) curry powder
½ tsp (2 ml) salt

1 tbsp (15 ml) diced peeled ginger root
4 whole cloves
3 cups (750 ml) chopped peeled fresh tomatoes or chopped, drained canned tomatoes
3 cups (750 ml) chopped peeled apples

1. Trim excess fat from meat and cut into 1-inch (2.5-cm) cubes. Heat oil in a Dutch oven over medium-high heat. Brown meat, then push it to one side and sauté the onions, garlic, chili peppers, curry powder, salt, ginger, and whole cloves. Cook for 3 minutes.
2. Add the tomatoes and apples. Reduce heat and simmer, covered, for 1 hour or until meat is tender. If sauce is not thick enough, remove meat and cook sauce over medium-high heat until it reaches the desired consistency.
3. Taste and add a little more salt if desired. Serve with rice.
Serves 6

APPLESAUCE-GLAZED PORK CHOPS

Spiced applesauce forms a golden brown glaze over the chops. This recipe is great company fare!

2 tbsp (25 ml) all-purpose flour	3 tbsp (45 ml) vegetable oil
½ tsp (2 ml) dry mustard	1 cup (250 ml) unsweetened
¼ tsp (1 ml) freshly ground pepper	applesauce
6 loin pork chops, about 2 lb	⅓ cup (75 ml) brown sugar
(1 kg)	¼ tsp (1 ml) ground cloves
	2 tsp (10 ml) cider vinegar

1. Mix flour, mustard, and pepper in a paper or plastic bag. Add one pork chop at a time and shake to coat.
2. Heat oil in a large skillet and brown chops on both sides. Transfer chops to an ovenproof casserole and arrange in a single layer.
3. Combine applesauce, sugar, cloves, and vinegar in a small bowl. Spread applesauce mixture over chops and bake uncovered at 350°F (180°C) for 35 to 40 minutes or until meat is tender and glaze is golden brown.
Serves 4 to 6

APPLE PEANUT BARBECUED PORK

These pork steaks can be broiled or barbecued. The sauce makes a succulent glaze for a pork roast as well.

4 pork steaks	¼ cup (50 ml) smooth peanut
½ cup (125 ml) Apple Butter (see	butter
page 242)	2 tbsp (25 ml) fresh orange juice

1. Beat apple butter, peanut butter, and orange juice in a small bowl until smooth.
2. Trim fat from pork steaks. Broil or grill steaks over medium-hot coals for 15 minutes. Turn and brush steaks with sauce. Cook for 15 minutes more. Brush other side with remaining sauce. Grill for a few minutes longer, then serve.
Serves 4

APPLE BAKED HAM

A simple dish you can serve to guests.

1½ lb (750 g) ham steak
8 whole cloves
¼ cup (50 ml) brown sugar

¾ cup (175 ml) sweet cider or apple
    juice
4 apples

1. Slash fat diagonally on ham steak. Stick cloves in fat. Place ham in a shallow baking dish. Bake at 350°F (180°C) for 30 minutes.
2. Remove from oven and cover with brown sugar. Add cider or juice to pan. (Be careful; it may splatter.) Return to oven and continue baking for 30 minutes.
3. Peel, quarter, and core apples. Slice into thick wedges. Remove ham to a platter and keep warm. Place apple slices in syrup in baking dish and bake for 10 minutes. Baste often with syrup.
4. Serve apple slices on each portion of ham.
Serves 4 to 6

GLAZED PORK ROAST

Spiced applesauce forms a golden brown glaze.

4-lb (2.2-kg) pork loin roast
2 tbsp (25 ml) all-purpose flour
1 tsp (5 ml) salt
1 tsp (5 ml) white sugar
¼ tsp (1 ml) freshly ground pepper

1 tsp (5 ml) dry mustard
1 cup (250 ml) thick applesauce
¼ cup (50 ml) brown sugar
2 tsp (10 ml) cider vinegar
¼ tsp (1 ml) allspice

1. Trim fat on roast so there is a thin even layer.
2. Mix flour, salt, sugar, pepper, and mustard in a small dish. Rub mixture over meat. Place roast on a rack in a roasting pan. Bake at 325°F (160°C) for 2 hours or until juices run clear and a meat thermometer registers 170°F (77°C).
3. During last thirty minutes of roasting time, mix applesauce, brown sugar, vinegar, and allspice. Brush applesauce mixture on roast several times until nicely glazed.
Serves 6 to 8

CORIANDER ROAST PORK WITH APPLES AND ONIONS

This herb-flavored pork is delicious hot or cold the next day. Raisin-and-walnut–stuffed apples are baked in the oven at the same time as the roast.

4 lb (2.2-kg) boned pork shoulder roast	¼ cup (50 ml) chopped walnuts
1 ½ tsp (7 ml) ground coriander	½ cup (125 ml) white sugar
½ tsp (2 ml) dried thyme	⅓ cup (75 ml) melted butter
6 medium onions	½ cup (125 ml) water
6 apples	¾ cup (175 ml) chicken broth
½ cup (125 ml) raisins	Salt and freshly ground pepper

1. Rub meat with coriander and thyme. Place on a rack in a roasting pan and roast in a 325°F (160°C) oven for 1¼ hours.
2. Parboil onions in boiling water for 10 minutes. Drain and arrange around roast. Baste with pan juices.
3. Meanwhile core apples and cut a center band of skin from each. Mix the raisins, walnuts, ⅓ cup (75 ml) sugar, and half the melted butter in a small bowl. Stuff apples with raisin mixture. Bake in a separate baking dish. Baste with melted butter and sprinkle with remaining sugar. Bake for 30 to 40 minutes or until tender.
4. When roast has reached an internal temperature of 170°F (77°C), remove from oven, place on a platter, and arrange onions around roast. Skim fat from the juices in roasting pan. Combine pan juices with chicken broth and bring to a boil. Season with salt and pepper and serve with pork.
5. Serve an apple and onion with each portion of meat.
Serves 6

CREAMED PORK CHOPS WITH GLAZED APPLES

Sautéed apple slices and white wine cream sauce make this a special dish.

3 tbsp (45 ml) butter
4 pork chops
½ cup (125 ml) chopped onion
¼ cup (50 ml) white wine
½ cup (125 ml) chicken broth

½ cup (125 ml) whipping cream
2 tbsp (25 ml) brown sugar
3 cups (750 ml) sliced unpeeled
   apples
   Salt and freshly ground pepper

1. Melt butter in a large skillet and brown pork chops on both sides. Reduce heat; cover and cook for 15 minutes or until tender and no longer pink inside. Remove pork chops and set aside.
2. Add onion to skillet and cook until tender. Stir in wine and chicken broth. Simmer for 2 minutes. Add the cream and simmer until mixture is thickened.
3. Meanwhile in another skillet, melt 1 tbsp (15 ml) butter over medium heat. Add brown sugar and stir until sugar begins to melt. Add apple slices and cook, stirring often, until apples are glazed and tender. Do not overcook.
4. Return chops to sauce and reheat. Top each pork chop with a portion of apples.
Serves 4

APPLE AND KIELBASA SAUSAGE BAKE

Assembled ahead of time, this dish makes an easy hearty family supper.

4 tbsp (50 ml) butter
4 cups (1 l) sliced peeled apples
1 sliced onion
1 cup (250 ml) sliced celery

1 lb (454 g) Kielbasa sausage
2 cups (500 ml) grated Cheddar
   cheese
⅓ cup (75 ml) fine soft breadcrumbs

1. Melt 2 tbsp (25 ml) butter in a large skillet and sauté apple slices just until tender. Arrange in a 9 × 13-inch (3-l) baking dish.
2. Melt 1 tbsp (15 ml) butter in skillet and sauté onion and celery until onion is tender. Spread over apple slices.
3. Slice sausage diagonally and arrange over onion layer. Sprinkle cheese over the sausage.
4. Melt 1 tbsp (15 ml) butter in skillet and sauté breadcrumbs for 1 minute. Sprinkle over top of cheese. Bake at 350°F (180°C) for 25 minutes or until crumbs are browned and cheese is melted.
Serves 4 to 6

SAUSAGE-APPLE CASSEROLE

The apples, tomatoes, onions, and brown sugar blend into a tangy sweet-sour sauce. Serve with fluffy mashed potatoes.

1 lb (500 g) hot and spicy Italian sausages	1 onion, thinly sliced in rings
3 apples	2½ cups (625 ml) peeled, seeded fresh tomatoes or drained
½ cup (125 ml) brown sugar	canned tomatoes
	Salt and freshly ground pepper

1. Prick sausages in several places. Broil for 5 minutes or until lightly browned.
2. Arrange sausages in 2-quart (2-l) casserole. Peel, quarter, and core apples. Place apple quarters over sausage. Sprinkle with brown sugar. Add onion rings and top with tomatoes.
3. Bake at 325°F (160°C) for 25 to 30 minutes until bubbly.
Serves 4

GLAZED APPLE PORK CHOPS

Serve these sweet and sour chops with fluffy mashed potatoes.

6 loin pork chops
1 tbsp (15 ml) vegetable oil
½ cup (125 ml) apple or crabapple
   jelly
¼ cup (50 ml) ketchup
1½ tbsp (22 ml) cider vinegar
2 large apples

1. Trim excess fat from pork chops. Heat oil in a large skillet over medium-high heat. Brown pork chops lightly on both sides.
2. Mix apple or crabapple jelly, ketchup, and vinegar in a small bowl. Add to skillet. Cover and reduce heat; simmer for 45 minutes or until pork chops are tender. Transfer pork chops to a warm platter. Cover and keep warm.
3. Peel, quarter, and core apples. Slice into thin wedges and add to sauce in skillet. Cook uncovered over medium heat for 5 to 8 minutes or until apples are tender and sauce has thickened. Spoon apples and sauce over pork chops. Serve with fluffy mashed potatoes.
Serves 3 to 6

APPLE-MOLASSES PORK CHOP BRAISE

Good company food you can prepare well in advance.

6 thick center-cut loin pork chops
½ tsp (2 ml) summer savory
2 tbsp (25 ml) butter
½ tsp (2 ml) salt
3 apples
3 tbsp (45 ml) molasses
3 tbsp (45 ml) all-purpose flour
1 cup (250 ml) hot water
1 cup (250 ml) apple juice
2 tbsp (25 ml) cider vinegar
⅓ cup (75 ml) golden raisins

1. Sprinkle chops with sage. Heat butter in a skillet over medium-high heat. Brown chops on both sides. Transfer chops to a large shallow baking dish. Reserve pan drippings. Season with salt.
2. Peel, quarter, and core apples. Cut apple wedges lengthwise into ¼-inch (6-mm) slices. Arrange slices over chops. Drizzle molasses over apples.
3. Stir flour into fat in skillet. Cook over medium heat until browned. Gradually stir in water and apple juice. Bring to a boil, stirring until smooth. Add vinegar and raisins. Pour sauce over chops and apples. Cover and bake at 350°F (180°C) for about 1 hour or until tender.
Serves 6

MARINATED LEG OF PORK

Boned leg of pork is marinated in cider with summer savory and garlic. Pork chops can be substituted, but reduce baking time accordingly.

4 lb (2.2 kg) boned rolled leg of   1 tsp (5 ml) summer savory
pork   2 crushed cloves garlic
1 cup (250 ml) cider   ¼ tsp (1 ml) freshly ground pepper
½ cup (125 ml) cider vinegar

1. Mix cider, vinegar, summer savory, garlic, and pepper in a large glass or enamel bowl. Place meat in marinade and turn to coat. Cover with plastic wrap and marinate overnight.
2. Next day, remove meat from marinade and place on a rack in a roasting pan. Pour marinade into roasting pan. Bake at 325°F (160°C) for 1½ to 2 hours or until internal temperature is 160°F (71°C) and juices run clear when roast is pierced. Baste roast frequently with marinade.
3. Remove from oven and let stand for 15 minutes before slicing.
Serves 6 to 8

APPLE-STUFFED PORK LOIN ROAST

This roast tastes just as good served cold as hot.

4 lb (2.2-kg) boneless pork loin
   roast, not tied
2 slivered garlic cloves
   Freshly ground pepper
1 tsp (5 ml) summer savory
1⅓ cups (325 ml) dried apple
   slices

3 tbsp (45 ml) dry breadcrumbs
1 tbsp (15 ml) chopped fresh
   parsley
2 cups (500 ml) sweet or hard cider
2 tbsp (25 ml) butter
2 tbsp (25 ml) molasses or honey

1. Cut roast lengthwise from the side to the center, so it will open like a book. Make tiny incisions in the meat and insert slivers of garlic. Season inside of roast with pepper and sprinkle with summer savory.
2. Lay apple slices lengthwise down the center of roast. Sprinkle with breadcrumbs, parsley, and ¼ cup (50 ml) of cider. Close roast and tie with cotton twine. Tuck in the ends of roast so fruit will not scorch.
3. Season top of roast with pepper. Rub with butter. Bake in a pan just slightly larger than roast.
4. Combine molasses and honey with remaining cider and pour over roast. Bake at 350°F (180°C), basting frequently. Allow 35 minutes per pound until juices run clear or meat thermometer inserted in thickest part registers 170°F (85°C). It may be necessary to add small amounts of cider to pan. When meat is cooked, transfer to platter and let stand in a warm place 15 minutes before slicing. Remove twine before slicing.

Serves 6 to 8

Savory Sauces

CIDER COURT BOUILLON '

Poach a ham slice, chicken, or fish in this bouillon of herb-and-vegetable–flavored cider.

½ cup (125 ml) butter
1 cup (250 ml) chopped carrot
1 cup (250 ml) chopped celery
1 chopped onion
4 cups (1 l) water
4 cups (1 l) cider

1 bay leaf
½ tsp (2 ml) thyme
4 sprigs parsley
2 tsp (10 ml) salt (omit when poaching ham)
½ tsp (2 ml) whole peppercorns

1. Melt butter in a Dutch oven over medium heat. Sauté the vegetables for 15 minutes or until tender. Do not brown.
2. Add the water, cider, and seasoning. Bring mixture to a boil; reduce heat, and simmer for 30 minutes. Strain, cool, and chill until ready to use.
Yields 7 cups (1.75 l)

CIDER TARRAGON MARINADE

Use as a marinade or basting sauce for meat or fish.

½ cup (125 ml) apple cider
¼ cup (50 ml) cider vinegar
3 sliced green onions

2 tbsp (25 ml) vegetable oil
2 tbsp (25 ml) honey
1 tsp (5 ml) crushed dried tarragon

1. Combine all ingredients in a small saucepan and bring to a boil. Remove from heat and cool before using.
Yields a scant cup (220 ml)

APPLE-MINT YOGURT SAUCE

Try this cool refreshing sauce the next time you serve lamb or a spicy curry.

⅓ cup (75 ml) apple juice
1 tbsp (15 ml) honey or to taste

2 tbsp (25 ml) minced fresh mint leaves
1 cup (250 ml) plain yogurt

1. Place apple juice, honey, and mint leaves in a small saucepan. Stir over low heat, bruising leaves with back of spoon, for 3 to 5 minutes. Remove from heat, cover, and cool to room temperature.
2. Strain juice and stir into yogurt.
Yield 1¼ cups (300 ml)

VARIATION: APPLE-GINGER YOGURT SAUCE
Instead of mint, use 1 tbsp (15 ml) finely minced fresh ginger root. Proceed as above.

RED WINE–APPLE JUICE JELLY

Serve this deep red jelly with cold roast meat.

1 envelope unflavored gelatin
¾ cup (175 ml) apple juice
⅓ cup (75 ml) white sugar

Dash of salt
1 cup (250 ml) dry red wine
1 tbsp (15 ml) fresh lemon juice

1. Sprinkle gelatin over ¼ cup (50 ml) of apple juice and let stand 5 minutes.
2. Heat remaining apple juice to boiling and stir in softened gelatin. Remove from heat and stir until gelatin is melted.
3. Add the sugar, salt, red wine and lemon juice. Stir until sugar dissolves.
4. Pour into a lightly oiled 2 cup (500 ml) mold or six small molds. Cover and chill.
Serves 6

APPLE JELLY DIPPING SAUCE

This tangy sauce goes perfectly with chicken or pork nuggets.

½ cup (125 ml) apple or crabapple jelly
½ cup (125 ml) sherry
½ cup (125 ml) ketchup

1. Process all ingredients in a blender or food processor until smooth. Pour into a small saucepan and simmer 10 minutes.
Yields 1¼ cups (300 ml) sauce

APPLE-DILL SAUCE

This tart sauce goes very well with all kinds of fish.

2 tbsp (25 ml) butter
2 tsp (10 ml) cornstarch
½ cup (125 ml) apple juice

2 tbsp (25 ml) minced fresh dill-
weed
1 tbsp (15 ml) fresh lemon juice
½ cup (125 ml) diced unpeeled
apples

1. Melt butter in a small saucepan. Stir in cornstarch and apple juice. Cook over medium heat, stirring until thickened.
2. Stir in dill, diced apples, and lemon juice. Heat until hot. Serve immediately.
Yields 1 cup (250 ml)

HORSERADISH APPLESAUCE

A tangy accompaniment for roast pork, sausages, or cold roast beef.

1 cup (250 ml) unsweetened
applesauce
¼ cup (50 ml) prepared horseradish
2 tbsp (25 ml) sour cream

1 tsp (5 ml) prepared mustard
1 tbsp (15 ml) brown sugar
Salt and freshly ground pepper
⅛ tsp (½ ml) freshly grated
nutmeg

1. Combine all ingredients in a small bowl. Cover and chill for an hour before serving.
Yields about 1⅓ cups (325 ml)

APPLE-MINT SAUCE

Serve with broiled lamb chops.

1½ cups (375 ml) applesauce   2 tsp (10 ml) fresh lemon juice
½ cup (125 ml) mint jelly   ¼ tsp (1 ml) salt

1. Place all ingredients in a medium saucepan. Bring to a simmer over medium heat, stirring until jelly has melted. Cook for 8 to 10 minutes. Serve warm or cold.
Yields 2 cups (500 ml)

ONION CONFIT

Serve this sweet-sour condiment with roast beef or pâté. It is for onion lovers only!

½ cup (125 ml) unsalted butter   ¼ cup (50 ml) dry red wine
5 cups (1.25 l) sliced onions   ¼ cup (50 ml) white sugar
½ cup (125 ml) cider vinegar   ¼ tsp (1 ml) salt
¼ cup (50 ml) apple juice   ¾ tsp (3 ml) freshly ground pepper

1. Melt butter in a large heavy saucepan over low heat. Add all ingredients and stir until sugar is dissolved.
2. Cover and cook slowly over low heat, stirring frequently, for 1 hour. Remove cover and cook uncovered for 1 hour or until mixture is brown and thick. Stir frequently especially as mixture thickens to prevent scorching.
3. Serve warm or at room temperature. Keeps well for a week in the refrigerator. Warm before serving.
Yields 2 cups (500 ml)

CHAPTER SIX

Apples for Dessert

Desserts

APPLES WITH CREAMY ORANGE DIP

A fun snack for the kids or a refreshing informal dessert for company.

4 large apples
2 tbsp (25 ml) fresh lemon juice

Orange Dip

4 eggs
⅓ cup (75 ml) butter
⅓ cup (75 ml) white sugar
4 tsp (20 ml) grated orange rind
½ cup (125 ml) fresh orange juice
1 tbsp (15 ml) fresh lemon juice

1. Process eggs, butter, sugar, and orange rind in a blender or food processor until smooth. Add orange and lemon juice and process for 20 seconds.
2. Pour mixture into top of double boiler. Place over simmering, not boiling water, and stir constantly until mixture thickens (about 10 minutes). Remove from heat. Chill dip if desired.
3. Quarter and core apples. Slice each quarter into three wedges and brush wedges with lemon juice. Arrange apple wedges on a dessert plate in a fan design with a custard cup or small dish in center. Fill cup with warm or chilled dip.
Serves 4

MIXED FRUIT SALAD

Red, green, and orange—a refreshing end to a meal.

2 tbsp (25 ml) white sugar
¼ cup (50 ml) fresh lemon juice
¼ cup (50 ml) fresh orange juice
2 tsp (10 ml) grated orange rind
2 tbsp (25 ml) almond liqueur or
   rum

3 green-skinned apples
2 cups (500 ml) fresh strawberries
2 oranges
1 grapefruit
2 cups (500 ml) green seedless
   grapes

1. Combine sugar, lemon and orange juices, orange rind, and liqueur or rum in a large bowl.

2. Quarter, core, and dice apples. Hull and cut strawberries in half. Peel and section oranges and grapefruit. Add fruit to large bowl and stir gently to coat with dressing.

3. Serve immediately at room temperature.

Serves 4 to 6

NUTTY BAKED APPLES

Tender apple wedges are topped with rich crunchy nuts and brown sugar.

6 *apples*	*½ cup (125 ml) unsalted butter*
2 *tbsp (25 ml) white sugar*	1 *cup (250 ml) finely chopped nuts*
½ tsp (2 ml) cinnamon or cardamom	*(blanched almonds, hazelnuts,*
½ cup (125 ml) brown sugar	*or walnuts)*

1. Peel, quarter, and core apples. Slice each quarter in half. Arrange apple wedges in parallel rows in a single layer in a buttered 9 × 13-inch (3-l) baking dish or individual baking dishes.

2. Combine white sugar, cinnamon, or cardamom in a cup and sprinkle over apples.

3. Cream butter and brown sugar until light and fluffy. Add nuts and blend thoroughly. Spread mixture over apples as evenly as possible.

4. Bake at 400°F (200°C) for 25 to 30 minutes or until apples are tender and topping is golden. Serve with vanilla ice cream.

Serves 4

MICROWAVE MAPLE SYRUP APPLES

Apples stuffed with raisins, nuts, and maple syrup are ready in 5 to 7 minutes.

4 large apples   2 tbsp (25 ml) finely chopped
⅓ cup (75 ml) maple syrup   walnuts
¼ cup (50 ml) raisins   4 tsp (20 ml) butter

1. Core apples. Peel a thin strip from top of each apple. Place in 8-inch (2-l) microproof dish or 4 individual microproof dishes.
2. Combine syrup, raisins, and walnuts in a small bowl. Spoon into core of each apple. Dot each with a teaspoon (5 ml) butter. Cover with microproof plastic wrap and cook for 5 to 7 minutes at maximum power or until apples are tender.
Serves 4

APPLES BAKED IN RED WINE

These wine-soaked apples are an interesting twist on an old favorite. Serve warm or at room temperature with Port Sabayon (see page 230).

4 large apples   ¼ cup (50 ml) white sugar
4 3-inch (7.5-cm) cinnamon sticks   ½ cup (125 ml) dry red wine
                                        ½ tsp (2 ml) grated lemon peel

1. Partially core apples, but do not peel. Place a cinnamon stick in cored apple. Stand apples close to each other in a small buttered casserole or individual ovenproof dishes.
2. Mix sugar, wine and lemon peel until sugar dissolves. Pour over the apples. Bake at 300°F (150°C) for 45 minutes, or until apples are tender but not mushy. Baste several times during baking with syrup.
Serves 4

WHOLE POACHED APPLES WITH HOT CARAMEL SAUCE

A simple but elegant dessert. Have the apples chilled and the sauce hot.

6 apples with stems	**Caramel Sauce**
2 tbsp (25 ml) fresh lemon juice	1 cup (250 ml) whipping cream
4 to 5 cups (1 to 1.4 l) water	1 cup (250 ml) white sugar
	2 tbsp (25 ml) water
	1 tsp (5 ml) vanilla
	¼ cup (50 ml) toasted sliced almonds

1. Core apples from the bottom. Peel apples without removing stems. Rub with lemon juice to prevent discoloration.
2. Bring water to a boil in a large deep skillet, saucepan, or Dutch oven. Place apples in skillet. Lower heat and simmer uncovered, turning occasionally, until tender but still firm. This will take about 10 minutes. Transfer apples and cooking liquid to a deep bowl. Make sure apples are completely submerged. Cool, cover with plastic wrap, and chill until serving time.
3. To prepare caramel sauce, heat cream in a small saucepan until bubbles form around edge. (Do not boil.)
4. Heat sugar and water in a large saucepan over high heat, stirring constantly. When sugar begins to turn golden, reduce heat and continue to stir until a deep golden brown. Remove from heat and slowly add the hot cream, stirring constantly, until sauce is smooth. If syrup hardens, continue stirring and cooking until dissolved. Stir in vanilla.
5. To serve, drain apples. Place on individual serving plates. Spoon hot sauce over apples and sprinkle with toasted almonds.
Serves 6

APPLE PORCUPINES

Toasted slivered almonds stud these whole poached apples.

4 large apples
2 cups (500 ml) water
1 cup (250 ml) white sugar

2 tbsp (25 ml) fresh lemon juice
1 3-inch (7.5-cm) strip of lemon rind
1 cup (250 ml) slivered almonds

1. Peel and core apples. Combine water, sugar, lemon juice, and lemon rind in a large saucepan, (one just big enough to fit the apples into). Boil syrup for 5 minutes.
2. Add the apples; reduce heat and simmer for 20 to 25 minutes until the apples are tender. Baste frequently with syrup. Do not let syrup boil or apples will be mushy.
3. Carefully transfer apples to serving dishes. Boil syrup until reduced to about ¾ cup.
4. Toast almonds in a small skillet over low heat stirring until golden, or in a 350°F (180°C) oven for 5 to 8 minutes.
5. Stick almond slivers all over apples. Glaze apples with syrup. Chill. Serve with whipped cream if desired.
Serves 4

POACHED APPLES AND PEARS

An old-fashioned dessert. Crème Fraîche (see page 231) or a custard sauce makes it special.

3 apples
3 pears
1 tbsp (15 ml) fresh lemon juice

1 cup (250 ml) fresh orange juice
1½ tsp (7 ml) grated orange rind
⅓ cup (75 ml) white sugar

1. Peel, quarter, and core apples and pears.
2. Combine lemon juice, orange juice, orange rind, and sugar in a large saucepan or skillet. Add fruit and heat to boiling point. Partially cover saucepan or skillet; reduce heat and simmer until fruit is just tender, about 10 minutes.
3. Serve warm or chilled.
Serves 6

APPLES WITH MACAROON-WALNUT FILLING

Apple halves are lightly poached and filled with a delectable mixture of macaroons and walnuts. Save the poaching liquid for mixing with drinks. Serve with whipped cream or a custard sauce.

3 cups (750 ml) water
⅓ cup (75 ml) white sugar
3 tbsp (45 ml) fresh lemon juice
6 large apples

Macaroon-Walnut Filling
6 macaroons
½ cup (125 ml) walnuts
3 tbsp (45 ml) whipping cream

2 tbsp (25 ml) white sugar
1 tbsp (15 ml) melted butter
1 tbsp (15 ml) brandy or orange
   juice
1 egg yolk
½ tsp (2 ml) vanilla
¼ tsp (1 ml) cinnamon
⅛ tsp (½ ml) nutmeg

1. Heat water, sugar, and lemon juice in a skillet or large saucepan. Stir until sugar dissolves.
2. Peel, halve, and core apples. A melon baller makes this job easy. Remove blossom ends.
3. Place apples in skillet or saucepan. Reduce heat and simmer uncovered until tender, about 10 minutes. Turn once during cooking. Remove from heat and let cool in poaching liquid for 20 minutes. Remove apples from liquid and drain on a wire rack.
4. To make filling, process macaroons and walnuts in a blender or food processor until finely ground. Add remaining ingredients and process briefly until well mixed.
5. Arrange apples in a buttered baking dish, core sides up. Fill each apple half with about 1 tbsp (15 ml) filling. Bake at 375°F (190°C) until filling is golden, about 20 minutes.
Serves 6

APPLE-MACAROON BAKE

Sliced apples are sweetened with apricot jam and Amaretto liqueur and are topped with toasted macaroon crumbs.

6 large apples
2 cups (500 ml) macaroon crumbs
¼ cup (50 ml) fresh orange juice

¼ cup (50 ml) apricot jam
¼ cup (50 ml) Amaretto liqueur
1 tbsp (15 ml) grated orange peel
3 tbsp (45 ml) butter

1. Peel, quarter, and core apples. Cut apple quarters into ½-inch (1-cm) wedges. Toast macaroon crumbs at 300°F (150°C) for 15 minutes.
2. Combine orange juice, apricot jam, liqueur, and orange peel.
3. Layer apple slices in a buttered 9 × 13-inch (3.5-l) baking dish or use individual ovenproof dishes. Sprinkle macaroon crumbs over apple slices. Dot with butter. Pour orange juice mixture over apples.
4. Bake at 375°F (190°C) for 25 minutes or until top is golden brown and apples are tender. Cover with foil if macaroon crumbs are browning too quickly.
Serves 6

POACHED APPLES WITH GINGER CREAM

Ginger poached apples are topped with a spoonful of tangy yogurt-ginger cream.

4 large apples
½ cup (125 ml) white sugar
¼ cup (50 ml) water
¼ tsp (1 ml) ground ginger

Ginger Cream
1 cup (250 ml) plain yogurt
2 tbsp (25 ml) finely chopped
   candied ginger
½ cup (125 ml) whipping cream

1. Peel, quarter, and core apples. Slice apple quarters in half lengthwise.

2. Combine sugar, water, and ginger in a medium saucepan and boil until sugar has dissolved. Add apple wedges and stir carefully, spooning syrup over apples. Poach apples until barely tender, about 5 minutes. Remove from heat, cover, and let cool in syrup. Cover and chill. Divide apple wedges among four dessert dishes.

3. Prepare ginger cream just before serving. Combine yogurt and candied ginger in a small bowl. Whip cream and fold into yogurt. Spoon over each serving.

Serves 4

ROSY BAKED APPLE WEDGES

Cinnamon candies flavor and tint the apples.

¾ cup (175 ml) white sugar	1 cup (250 ml) water
4 tbsp (60 ml) red cinnamon candies	2 tsp (10 ml) fresh lemon juice
	6 to 8 large apples

1. Combine sugar, cinnamon candies, water, and lemon juice in a small saucepan. Bring to a boil and stir until sugar dissolves. Reduce heat and simmer for 10 minutes or until candies dissolve. Remove from heat.

2. Peel, quarter, and core apples. Slice apples into ½-inch (1-cm) wedges. Arrange in a buttered 9 × 13-inch (3.5-l) baking dish.

3. Pour syrup evenly over apples. Bake at 350°F (180°C) for 20 minutes or until apples are tender. Baste several times with syrup.

Serves 6

APPLES WITH SHERRY ORANGE SAUCE

Crisp diced apples are served in wine or sherbet glasses with a luscious tangy sauce and topped with sour cream and a sprinkling of brown sugar.

½ cup (125 ml) white sugar
1 tbsp (15 ml) cornstarch
1 tbsp (15 ml) grated orange rind
½ cup (125 ml) fresh orange juice

½ cup (125 ml) dry sherry
1 tbsp (15 ml) fresh lemon juice
4 large apples
6 tbsp (90 ml) sour cream
6 tsp (30 ml) brown sugar

1. Blend sugar and cornstarch in a small saucepan. Stir in orange rind, orange juice, sherry, and lemon juice. Cook over medium heat, stirring constantly, until sauce is thickened and clear. Cool sauce to room temperature.
2. Quarter and core apples. Dice into wine or sherbet glasses.
3. Pour sauce over apples. Top with a dollop of sour cream and sprinkle each with a teaspoon (5 ml) brown sugar. Serve immediately.
Serves 6

BAKED WINTER COMPOTE

Serve warm with sour cream or Crème Fraîche (see page 231).

1 orange
1 cup (250 ml) pineapple chunks
    (fresh or drained canned)
½ cup (125 ml) chopped dried
    apples
½ cup (125 ml) chopped dried
    apricots

½ cup (125 ml) apple juice
¼ cup (50 ml) brown sugar
2 tsp (10 ml) quick-cooking tapioca
¼ tsp (1 ml) cinnamon
¼ tsp (1 ml) nutmeg

1. Grate rind from orange and set aside. Cut off and discard white pith. Slice orange.
2. Place orange rind, orange slices, pineapple, and dried fruit in a 1-quart (1-l) casserole.
3. Mix apple juice, sugar, tapioca, cinnamon, and nutmeg. Pour over fruit and mix. Cover and bake at 350°F (180°C) for 30 minutes. Stir once or twice. Remove from oven and let cool for 10 minutes before serving.
Serves 5 to 6

HONEYED DRIED FRUIT COMPOTE

Apples, peaches, and apricots in a honey brandy syrup.

3 cups (750 ml) water	½ orange, sliced
½ cup (125 ml) honey	4 oz (115 g) dried apple slices
2 whole allspice	4 oz (115 g) dried peaches
1 3-inch (7.5-cm) cinnamon stick	4 oz (115 g) dried apricots
½ lemon, sliced	¼ cup (50 ml) brandy

1. Place water in a large saucepan and bring to a boil. Add honey and stir until dissolved.
2. Add the spices, lemon and orange slices, and dried fruit. Reduce heat; cover and simmer for 10 minutes. Remove from heat and discard spices.
3. Stir in brandy. Cover and allow fruit to sit overnight.
Serves 8

FRUIT RUM COMPOTE

Take your friends a bottle of rum-plumped winter fruit.

2 cups (500 ml) dried prunes
2 cups (500 ml) dried apricots
½ cup (125 ml) raisins
6 to 7 cups (1.5 l to 1.75 l)
    apple juice
1 2-inch (5-cm) cinnamon stick

2 oranges
2 apples
1 lemon
1 grapefruit
½ to ¾ cups (125 to 175 ml)
    white rum

1. Place prunes, apricots, and raisins in a very large bowl.
2. Bring 4 cups (1 l) juice and cinnamon stick to a boil in a large non-metallic saucepan. Pour over fruit. Set aside until cool.
3. Meanwhile prepare citrus fruit and apples. Cut into interesting shapes. Peel, section, and remove membranes from one orange and the grapefruit. Slice other orange, including peel, into thin rounds (discard seeds). Cut lemon, including peel, into small wedges. To prepare apples, leave peel intact and cut out balls with a melon baller, or slice into wedges with a knife.
4. Add citrus fruit, apples, and rum to bowl. Blend and pour into small bottles. Top with apple juice. Seal and refrigerate overnight. The flavor improves with age. Serve plain or with ice cream.
Yields 3 quarts (3 l)

GINGERSNAP APPLE CRUMBLE

A spicy variation on traditional apple crumble.

5 cups (1.25 l) sliced, cored, peeled apples	½ cup (125 ml) brown sugar
1 tsp (5 ml) minced preserved ginger	1 tsp (5 ml) cinnamon
1½ cups (375 ml) crushed gingersnap cookies	¼ cup (50 ml) butter

1. Mix ginger and apple slices in an 8-inch (2-l) square baking dish.
2. Combine gingersnap crumbs, brown sugar, and cinnamon in a medium bowl. Cut in butter until mixture resembles breadcrumbs.
3. Spread evenly over apple slices and bake at 375°F (190°C) for 30 minutes or until apples are tender. Cover with foil if topping is browning too quickly.
Serves 4 to 6

PEANUT BUTTER APPLE CRUMBLE

This crumble tastes like a wholesome cookie.

1 cup (250 ml) quick-cooking rolled oats	½ cup (125 ml) peanut butter
⅓ cup (75 ml) all-purpose flour	5 cups (1.25 l) sliced, cored, peeled apples
½ cup (125 ml) brown sugar	2 tbsp (25 ml) fresh orange juice
	3 tbsp (45 ml) water

1. Mix oats, flour, and sugar in a medium bowl. Cut in peanut butter until mixture resembles coarse crumbs.
2. Place apples in a buttered 8-inch (2-l) baking dish. Sprinkle with orange juice. Sprinkle crumb mixture evenly over top. Sprinkle crumb mixture with water. Cover with a sheet of foil, but do not seal.
3. Bake at 350°F (180°C) for 30 minutes or until apples are tender.
Serves 9

MICROWAVE APPLE CRISP

Try combining apples with other fruit, such as plums, pears, and rhubarb.

6   cups (1.5 l) sliced, cored, peeled
     apples
½ cup (125 ml) brown sugar

Topping
½ cup (125 ml) all-purpose flour
½ tsp (2 ml) cinnamon
⅓ cup (75 ml) brown sugar
⅓ cup (75 ml) quick-cooking rolled
     oats
¼ cup (50 ml) butter

1. Mix apples and brown sugar in a buttered microproof 8-inch (2-l) square dish.
2. Mix flour, cinnamon, brown sugar, and rolled oats in a medium bowl. Cut in butter until mixture resembles coarse crumbs. Sprinkle over apples.
3. Cook at maximum power for 9 to 12 minutes. Rotate dish ½ turn after 5 minutes. Let stand for 5 minutes before serving.
Serves 6

CARAMEL APPLE CRISP

Apples are coated with a creamy caramel sauce and topped with buttery crisp crumbs.

6   to 8 apples

Caramel Sauce
1   cup (250 ml) brown sugar
¼ cup (50 ml) all-purpose flour
¾ cup (175 ml) water
1   tbsp (15 ml) cider vinegar or
     lemon juice
2   tbsp (25 ml) butter
1   tsp (5 ml) vanilla

Crumb Topping
1¼ cups (300 ml) all-purpose
     flour
½ cup (125 ml) brown sugar
½ cup (125 ml) butter

1. Peel, quarter, and core apples. Slice apples into a 2-quart (2-l) ovenproof casserole.
2. Mix brown sugar, flour, water, and vinegar in a small saucepan. Cook over medium heat until thick, stirring constantly. Remove from heat. Stir in butter and vanilla. Cool, then pour over apples.
3. To make topping, mix sugar and flour in a small bowl. Cut in butter until mixture resembles coarse meal. Sprinkle over apples.
4. Bake at 375°F (190°C) for 35 minutes or until topping is browned and apples are tender.
Serves 8

APPLE CHEESE CRISP

Brown sugar and cheddar cheese are added to the traditional crumb topping for apple crisp.

4 *large apples*	½ *tsp (2 ml) cinnamon*
1 *tbsp (15 ml) fresh lemon juice*	1 *cup (250 ml) all-purpose flour*
1 *cup (250 ml) brown sugar*	1 *cup (250 ml) grated medium cheddar cheese*
	½ *cup (125 ml) melted butter*

1. Peel, quarter, and core apples. Slice thinly into a buttered 9-inch (2.5-l) baking dish. Sprinkle with lemon juice.
2. Combine brown sugar, cinnamon, flour, and grated cheese in a medium bowl. Drizzle melted butter over flour mixture and mix with a fork until evenly moistened.
3. Crumble mixture evenly over apples. Bake at 325°F (160°C) for 40 minutes or until apples are tender and topping is golden brown. Serve warm or at room temperature either plain, with cream, or with ice cream.
Serves 4 to 6

APPLE OAT CRISP

Serve hot or cold, with cream or ice cream.

1   cup (250 ml) all-purpose flour   1   tsp (5 ml) cinnamon
1   cup (250 ml) rolled oats   ½ cup (125 ml) butter
1   cup (250 ml) brown sugar   6   cups (1.5 l) sliced, cored, peeled
                                             apples

1. Mix flour, oats, brown sugar, and cinnamon in a large bowl. Cut
in butter until mixture is crumbly.
2. Place apples in a 9-inch (2.5-l) baking dish. Mix about ¼ of the
crumb mixture with the apples. Spread remaining crumbs evenly
over apples and pat down slightly.
3. Bake at 350°F (180°C) for 35 to 40 minutes or until topping is
browned and apples are tender.
Serves 6 to 8

MAPLE APPLE CRISP

Apple crisp with a maple twist.

6   cups (1.5 l) sliced peeled apples   ½ cup (125 ml) all-purpose flour
½ to ⅔ cup (125 to 150 ml) maple   ½ cup (125 ml) rolled oats
    syrup   ½ cup (125 ml) brown sugar
                                         ½ cup (125 ml) butter

1. Place apples in a buttered 9-inch (2.5-l) square baking dish. Drizzle
maple syrup over apples.
2. Combine flour, rolled oats, and brown sugar in a medium bowl.
Cut in butter until mixture resembles coarse breadcrumbs. Sprinkle topping over apples.
3. Bake at 350°F (180°C) for 30 to 35 minutes or until topping is
golden brown and apples are tender.
Serves 6 to 8

ALMOND CREAM CREPE DESSERT

The crepe recipe is generous enough to allow for mistakes. Toasted macaroon crumbs could be substituted for the almonds—just reduce sugar to ⅓ cup (75 ml) in Almond Cream.

Crepes
¾ cup (175 ml) water
¾ cup (175 ml) milk
2 large eggs
1 tbsp (15 ml) white sugar
¼ tsp (1 ml) salt
1⅓ cups (325 ml) all-purpose
    flour
1 tbsp (15 ml) vegetable oil

Almond Cream
1 cup (250 ml) whole blanched
    almonds
⅔ cup (150 ml) white sugar
½ cup (125 ml) unsalted butter
2 large eggs
¼ cup (50 ml) Amaretto or 3 tbsp
    (45 ml) dark rum + ½ tsp
    (2 ml) almond extract
½ tsp (2 ml) vanilla

Apple Layer
10 large apples
¼ cup (50 ml) fresh lemon juice
2 tbsp (25 ml) melted butter
¼ cup (50 ml) white sugar

1. To make the crepes, process all crepe ingredients in a blender or food processor until smooth. Heat an 8-inch (20-cm) crepe pan over medium-high heat. Brush with a little vegetable oil. Add a scant ¼ cup (50 ml) batter and swirl to cover bottom of pan. Cook for 30 seconds or until brown on one side. Turn and lightly brown other side. Transfer to a wire rack and cool. When cooled, place on a plate and cover with a slightly damp towel. Any extra crepes can be wrapped and frozen.

2. Toast almonds in a glass pie plate at 350°F (180°C) for 15 to 20 minutes or until toasted and light brown. Stir several times during toasting. Process in a blender or food processor with sugar until finely ground. Add butter, eggs, Amaretto or rum and almond extract, and vanilla. Process until light and fluffy.

3. Peel, quarter, and core apples. Slice into thin wedges and sprinkle with lemon juice. Pour melted butter into a rimmed cookie sheet

or large casserole. Add apples in a single layer and sprinkle with sugar. Bake at 375°F (190°C) for 15 to 20 minutes or until apples are tender. Toss several times during cooking.

4. To assemble dessert, place one crepe in a buttered 10-inch (25-cm) pie plate. Arrange one layer of apple slices on crepe. Spread about ¼ cup (50 ml) almond cream over apples. Top with another crepe and continue in same manner using all the almond cream and ending with a layer of apples.

5. Drizzle any baking juices from apples over top layer. Bake at 375°F (190°C) until hot and apple topping is lightly browned, about 30 minutes. Serve hot or warm.

Serves 6 to 8

APPLE CREPE DESSERT

This assembly of crepes and layers of lemon and apple fillings, is shaped like a small cake and is cut in wedges. It makes a dramatic ending to a dinner party and leftovers are equally delicious the next morning for breakfast.

Crepes

3   *eggs*
2   *cups (500 ml) milk*
1   *cup (250 ml) all-purpose flour*
½ *tsp (2 ml) salt*
3   *tbsp (45 ml) white sugar*
1   *tsp (5 ml) vanilla*
3   *tbsp (45 ml) melted butter*
    Vegetable oil

Lemon Filling

⅓ *cup (75 ml) butter, at room*
    temperature
⅔ *cup (150 ml) icing sugar*
½ *tsp (2 ml) cinnamon*
1   *tbsp (15 ml) fresh lemon juice*
1   *tsp (5 ml) grated lemon rind*
1   *egg*

Apple Filling

1   *tbsp (15 ml) butter*
¼ *cup (50 ml) apple juice*
8   *cups (2 l) coarsely chopped*
    peeled apples
    Cinnamon

1. To make crepes, process eggs, milk, flour, salt, sugar, vanilla, and melted butter in a blender or food processor until smooth.

2. Heat an 8-inch (20-cm) crepe pan over medium-high heat and brush lightly with vegetable oil. Oil pan as needed. To make crepes, pour about ¼ cup (50 ml) batter into the hot pan, tipping it to distribute evenly. Cook for about 30 seconds, until the crepe has separated from side of pan and bottom is slightly browned. Turn crepe and cook for 10 seconds on other side. Continue in this manner until all the batter has been used. Cover crepes with a damp tea towel to prevent drying out.

3. To make lemon filling, cream together butter, icing sugar and cinnamon. Add lemon rind, lemon juice, and egg. Blend well.

4. To make apple filling, heat 1 tbsp (15 ml) butter and apple juice in a large saucepan. Add apples and simmer, stirring gently, until tender but not mushy.

5. To assemble, place a crepe on a large ovenproof plate. Spread with a thin layer of lemon filling, and a layer of apple filling. Continue in this manner making last layer an apple and lemon layer. Dust with cinnamon.

6. Bake for 30 to 45 minutes at 375°F (190°C) or until edges are crisp and crepes are heated through.

Serves 8

DESSERT OMELET

Stiffly beaten egg whites make this sweet apple omelet light and puffy.

2 *large apples*	4 *separated eggs*
2 *tbsp (25 ml) unsalted butter*	2 *tbsp (25 ml) white sugar*
2 *tbsp (25 ml) Calvados or Apple Cordial (see page 131) or apple juice*	1 *tsp (5 ml) vanilla*
	1 *tbsp (15 ml) icing sugar*

1. Peel, quarter, and core apples. Coarsely chop apples. Melt 1 tbsp (15 ml) butter in medium saucepan. Add apples and Calvados or Apple Cordial or apple juice. Partially cover and simmer for 5 minutes. Set aside.

2. Preheat broiler. Beat egg yolks, sugar, and vanilla extract until thick. In a separate bowl, beat egg whites until stiff but not dry. Fold into yolk mixture.

3. Heat remaining butter in a 10-inch (25-cm) omelet pan or cast iron skillet over medium-high heat. When butter foams, pour egg mixture into skillet and cook for 1 or 2 minutes until golden on bottom. Top should still be soft. Place under broiler for about 20 seconds or until dry on top. Pour apple sauce over half of omelet. Fold omelet over and slide onto a serving plate.
4. Dust with icing sugar and serve immediately.
Serves 4

SPUN SUGAR APPLES

This dessert originated in Peking. Apple fritters are covered with hot caramel. When the fritters are pulled from the serving dish, the caramelized sugar spins threads. Dipped quickly into ice water, the sugar hardens into a brittle glaze.

Batter	Caramel
3 *tbsp (45 ml) all-purpose flour*	*Ice water*
3 *tbsp (45 ml) cornstarch*	½ *cup (125 ml) white sugar*
1 *large egg*	1 *tbsp (15 ml) water*
1 *tbsp (15 ml) water*	*Thermometer for deep frying*
2 *large firm apples*	
2 *cups (500 ml) peanut oil*	

1. Select a medium glass, porcelain, or earthenware serving dish. Oil dish so caramel will not stick.
2. Combine flour and cornstarch in a medium bowl. Beat egg in a cup with 1 tbsp (15 ml) water until thoroughly mixed. Gradually add beaten egg to flour mixture, stirring until batter is smooth.
3. Peel, quarter, and core apples. Slice each quarter in half. Add apple wedges to batter and turn to coat.
4. Heat oil in a large saucepan over high heat to 350°F (180°C). Reduce heat to medium-high and add half the apple wedges. Cook for about 1 minute on each side or until lightly browned. Remove to a platter lined with paper towels. Fry remaining apple wedges. This step can be done several hours in advance. Keep apples at room temperature. Pour oil through a fine sieve into a 2-cup (500-ml) measure. Wipe out saucepan.

5. Fill a deep dish with ice water and set on dining table. Set table with chopsticks or two forks for each serving.

6. Combine sugar and water in a heavy skillet, and heat over high heat until mixture spins a thread. Reduce heat to low and continue cooking until sugar begins to caramelize. The idea is to have the caramel ready when fritters have finished frying the second time, so slow this step down by removing skillet from heat if it seems to be progressing too fast. Burnt caramel is bitter and unusable.

7. Meanwhile return oil to saucepan and heat over high heat to 375°F (190°C). Refry apples until brown, while caramel is cooking. Drain the apples on platter with paper towels.

8. When all apple wedges are cooked and caramel is a rich golden brown, add the apples to the caramel. With a spatula, turn apples in the caramel until coated. Immediately turn into the oiled serving dish.

9. Serve immediately. Let each guest, using chopsticks or forks, pull as many wedges as they wish and dip quickly into the ice water. Separate all the wedges while still hot or they will stick together.

Serves 3 to 4

QUESO DE MANZANA (Apple Cheese)

We've adapted this Venezuelan dessert to include apple juice instead of pineapple juice. It is rich, unusual, and delicious.

2 cups (500 ml) apple juice concentrate	2 cups (500 ml) white sugar
	8 eggs
	1 tsp (5 ml) vanilla

1. Combine apple juice concentrate and sugar in a medium bowl. Stir until sugar has dissolved.

2. Crack eggs into a large bowl and with a whisk, stir, do not beat, for 30 minutes. (Yes, 30 minutes!)

3. Slowly stir in apple syrup and continue stirring for another 30 minutes or until completely blended.

4. Pour mixture into 8 small, lightly buttered custard cups. Place on folded paper towels in a Dutch oven. Add 1 inch (2.5 cm) boiling

water. Place over low heat and simmer, uncovered, for 1 hour or until firm. Replenish boiling water when necessary.

5. Remove from Dutch oven and cool. Chill several hours. Serve with unsweetened crackers or whipped cream.

Serves 8

DANISH DESSERT

This "top of the stove" dessert can be made using hazelnuts or walnuts instead of almonds.

8 cups (2 l) thickly sliced, cored, peeled apples	½ cup (125 ml) brown sugar
1 tbsp (15 ml) fresh lemon juice	½ cup (125 ml) chopped blanched almonds
⅓ cup (75 ml) butter	1 tsp (5 ml) cinnamon
2 tbsp (25 ml) white sugar	1 cup (250 ml) whipping cream
1 cup (250 ml) graham cracker crumbs	1 tbsp (15 ml) icing sugar
	2 tsp (10 ml) rum, brandy, or vanilla

1. Place apple slices in a large bowl and sprinkle with lemon juice. Toss lightly.

2. Melt 2 tbsp (25 ml) butter in a large skillet. Add apples and sprinkle with white sugar. Cook uncovered over low heat for 10 to 15 minutes, stirring often, until apples are tender. Do not brown. Remove from heat.

3. Melt remaining butter in a medium saucepan or skillet. Stir in graham cracker crumbs, brown sugar, almonds, and cinnamon. Cook over low heat, stirring often, for 10 minutes.

4. Spread half of crumb mixture in the bottom of a 7-inch (17.5-cm) round serving dish. Spread apple slices over crumbs and top with remaining crumbs. Let cool to room temperature.

5. Just before serving, whip cream with icing sugar until soft peaks form. Beat in rum, brandy, or vanilla. Serve a spoonful on each serving, if desired.

Serves 6 to 8

APPLE PANDOWDY

Drop biscuits cook atop a sweet apple sauce. Serve plain or with ice cream.

1 cup (250 ml) brown sugar
¼ cup (50 ml) all-purpose flour
½ tsp (2 ml) cinnamon
¼ tsp (1 ml) nutmeg
 Dash of salt
1 cup (250 ml) water
2 tbsp (25 ml) butter
1 tsp (5 ml) vanilla
1 tsp (5 ml) fresh lemon juice
6 cups (1.5 l) sliced, cored, peeled
 apples

Biscuit Dough

1¼ cups (300 ml)
 all-purpose flour
¼ cup (50 ml) white sugar
1 tbsp (15 ml) baking powder
¼ tsp (1 ml) salt
⅓ cup (75 ml) shortening
1 beaten egg
½ cup (125 ml) milk

1. Blend brown sugar, flour, cinnamon, nutmeg, and salt in a medium saucepan. Stir in water and cook over medium heat, stirring constantly until mixture comes to a boil and has thickened slightly.
2. Stir in butter, vanilla, and lemon juice. Spread apple slices in a buttered 9-inch (2.5-l) square baking pan, at least 2 inches (5 cm) deep. Pour hot sauce over apples.
3. Blend flour, sugar, baking powder, and salt in a medium bowl. Cut in shortening until mixture resembles fine crumbs. Mix egg and milk in a cup and add to flour mixture. Stir with a fork until mixture is evenly moistened. Drop spoonfuls of batter over apple mixture. Do not stir.
4. Bake at 375°F (190°C) for 35 to 45 minutes.
Serves 6 to 8

FINNISH APPLE DESSERT

A golden meringue tops a pie plate of juicy apples.

2 tbsp (25 ml) butter	5 cups (1.25 l) sliced peeled apples
½ cup (125 ml) brown sugar	3 egg whites
2 tsp (10 ml) cinnamon	¼ tsp (1 ml) salt
	½ cup (125 ml) white sugar

1. Melt butter and pour into a 9-inch (22.5-cm) glass pie plate. Mix brown sugar and cinnamon in a cup. Sprinkle half cinnamon sugar over butter.
2. Arrange apple slices evenly in plate. Sprinkle with remaining cinnamon sugar.
3. Beat egg whites until foamy. Add salt and gradually beat in white sugar. Beat until whites stand in stiff peaks. Swirl meringue over apples.
4. Bake at 325°F (160°C) for 30 to 40 minutes or until meringue is golden. Serve warm.
Serves 6 to 8

APPLE SHORTCAKE

The surprise is diced apples folded into the biscuit. Top with Cinnamon Apple Sauce, or one of the other luscious apple toppings on pages 226-232, and whipped cream.

2 cups (500 ml) all-purpose flour	⅓ cup (75 ml) butter
2 tbsp (25 ml) white sugar	1 cup (250 ml) finely diced, peeled apples
4 tsp (20 ml) baking powder	
½ tsp (2 ml) salt	½ cup (125 ml) sour cream
¼ tsp (1 ml) baking soda	⅓ cup (75 ml) milk
2 tsp (10 ml) grated orange or lemon rind	Cinnamon Apple Sauce (see page 230)
	Whipped cream

1. Mix flour, sugar, baking powder, salt, baking soda, and orange rind in a large mixing bowl. Cut in butter until mixture resembles coarse crumbs. Fold in diced apples.

2. Mix together sour cream and milk. Add to flour mixture and blend with a fork to make a soft dough.

3. Turn dough onto a lightly floured surface and knead gently for 4 turns or until dough holds together. Roll or pat dough to a ½-inch (1-cm) thickness. Using a floured 3-inch (7.5-cm) cutter, cut out the biscuits.

4. Arrange on a greased cookie sheet. Bake at 425°F (220°C) for 12 to 15 minutes or until golden brown.

5. Let cool and split in half. Spoon Cinnamon Apple Sauce over bottom. Replace top and garnish with whipped cream and more sauce.

Yields 12 shortcakes

UPSIDE-DOWN APPLE GINGERBREAD

A spicy fragrant gingerbread topped with caramel apple slices.

Gingerbread
½ cup (125 ml) melted butter
½ cup (125 ml) molasses
½ cup (125 ml) white sugar
1 egg
2 cups (500 ml) all-purpose flour
1 tsp (5 ml) ginger
1 tsp (5 ml) cinnamon
½ tsp (2 ml) ground cloves

¼ tsp (1 ml) nutmeg
½ tsp (2 ml) salt
1 tsp (5 ml) baking soda
¾ cup + 2 tbsp (25 ml) hot tea
  or water

Apple Layer
3 tbsp (45 ml) melted butter
⅓ cup (75 ml) brown sugar
3 apples

1. Combine butter, molasses, sugar, and egg in a large mixing bowl and beat until well mixed.

2. Sift flour, ginger, cinnamon, cloves, nutmeg, and salt into a medium bowl. Stir into butter mixture and mix well.

3. Dissolve baking soda in hot tea or water and add to batter. Mix well.

4. Pour melted butter into a 9-inch (2.5-l) square baking pan. Sprinkle evenly with brown sugar. Peel, quarter, core and slice apples. Spread apple slices evenly in pan. Pour batter over apples.
5. Bake at 350°F (180°C) for 35 to 40 minutes or until a cake tester comes out clean. Invert onto a plate. Serve warm with ice cream or whipped cream.
Serves 9

APPLE STRUDEL WITH PHYLLO

Phyllo can be purchased fresh or frozen. Work quickly with the phyllo because it becomes brittle as it dries.

4 cups (1 l) finely diced apples	¼ cup (50 ml) ground walnuts or
¼ cup (50 ml) fresh breadcrumbs	almonds (optional)
¼ tsp (1 ml) grated lemon peel	¼ cup (50 ml) melted butter
¼ cup (50 ml) white sugar	8 sheets phyllo
¼ tsp (1 ml) cinnamon	1 tsp (5 ml) icing sugar

1. In a large bowl, mix together apples, breadcrumbs, lemon peel, sugar, cinnamon, and nuts.
2. Place one sheet of phyllo on a flat surface. Sprinkle with butter and top with another sheet. Repeat until all sheets are used.
3. Place apple mixture along one edge. Roll up. Carefully transfer to a buttered cookie sheet. Sprinkle with remaining melted butter.
4. Bake at 375°F (180°C) until crisp and golden brown. Remove from oven and dust with icing sugar. Serve right out of the oven, or at room temperature. Slice diagonally.
Serves 10

APPLE ENVELOPES WITH CARDAMOM SAUCE

Pastry-wrapped apple slices are baked until golden and drenched in sweet sauce.

Pastry for 9-inch (22.5-cm)
    two-crust pie (see page 94)
3 apples
¼ cup (50 ml) white sugar
3 tbsp (45 ml) butter

Cardamom Sauce
⅔ cup (150 ml) brown sugar
1 tbsp (15 ml) cornstarch
⅔ cup (150 ml) cold water
1 tbsp (15 ml) fresh lemon juice
1 tbsp (15 ml) butter
½ tsp (1 ml) cardamom

1. Preheat oven to 425°F (220°C). Prepare pastry and divide in half. Roll each half on a lightly floured surface into an 8 × 16-inch (20 × 41-cm) rectangle. Cut each rectangle crosswise into four 4 × 8-inch (10 × 20-cm) strips.
2. Quarter and core the apples. Slice each quarter into four wedges. Place 6 apple slices on half of each strip. Sprinkle with 1 heaping teaspoon (6 ml) sugar, and dot with butter. Moisten edges of pastry and fold pastry over apple slices. Press edges with a fork to seal.
3. Place on an ungreased cookie sheet. Bake for 15 to 20 minutes or until pastry is golden brown.
4. Meanwhile, prepare Cardamom Sauce. Mix brown sugar and cornstarch in a medium saucepan. Add water and heat to boiling, stirring constantly. Boil and stir 1 minute. Add remaining ingredients and stir until blended.
5. Serve apple squares warm with Cardamom Sauce.
Serves 8

CINNAMON APPLE DUMPLINGS

Use Cinnamon Pastry (see page 94) or pastry for a double crust
8- or 9-inch (20 to 22.5-cm) pie.

4 medium apples	3 tbsp (45 ml) butter
½ cup (125 ml) brown sugar	½ tsp (2 ml) cinnamon
	¼ tsp (1 ml) grated lemon rind

1. Prepare pastry and chill. Peel and core apples.
2. Combine brown sugar, butter, cinnamon, and lemon rind in a
medium bowl.
3. Divide pastry into four equal pieces. Roll each piece out on a
lightly floured surface. Trim to a square large enough to enclose
each whole apple entirely. Place apples in center of pastry squares.
Fill cores with sugar mixture and spread remainder over fruit.
4. Bring up four corners to cover apple. Press edges together, using
a little water if necessary to make them stick. It is important to have
a good seal or else the pastry will fall apart as it cooks. Decorate
tops with pastry cut in shape of leaves if you wish. Prick top of each
dumpling in several places with a toothpick. Place on an ungreased
cookie sheet or in a 9 × 13-inch (3-l) baking pan.
5. Bake at 375°F (190°C) for about 30 minutes or until apples are
tender when pierced with a cake tester or toothpick.
6. Serve warm, plain, or with cream or a sauce.
Serves 4

VARIATION: APPLE DUMPLINGS COOKED IN CINNAMON SAUCE
1. Proceed as above except save apple cores and peelings. Simmer cores and peelings in 1½ cups (375 ml) water for 15 minutes. Drain and measure 1 cup (250 ml)
into a small saucepan.
2. Add ½ cup (125 ml) white sugar, 2 tbsp (25 ml) butter, and ½ tsp (2 ml) cinnamon.
Bring to a boil and cook for 5 minutes. Pour boiling hot over the dumplings after
they have cooked for 25 minutes or begin to brown. Serve with sauce.

APPLE VERENEKAS (DUMPLINGS)

Verenekas may be refrigerated and reheated later in an oven or a buttered frying pan. Serve with yogurt or sour cream as a main course or dessert.

¼ cup (50 ml) butter
2 cups (500 ml) all-purpose flour
1 tsp (5 ml) salt
1 egg

⅔ cup (150 ml) water
4 to 6 large apples
2 to 3 tbsp (25 to 45 ml) white sugar
¼ tsp (1 ml) cinnamon

1. Melt butter and spread evenly in a 9 × 13-inch (3 l) glass baking dish. Set aside.
2. Sift flour and salt into a medium bowl. Mix egg and water in a small bowl and stir into flour mixture. Knead dough until smooth and shiny. Form into two balls. Cover with a damp tea towel and allow dough to rest for 15 minutes.
3. Peel and core apples. Cut apples into cubes approximately 1-inch (2.5-cm) square.
4. Stir cinnamon into sugar.
5. Place a large pot of water on high heat to boil.
6. Roll out one ball of dough on a lightly floured surface to a thickness of ⅛ inch (3 mm) or less (the thinner, the better). Do not overwork dough or re-roll odd pieces. They make good free-form noodles for soup.
7. Trim dough to a 15-inch (37.5-cm) square. Cut dough into 3-inch (7.5-cm) squares.
8. Pat apple cubes dry and place one in the middle of each square. Sprinkle with ¼ tsp (1 ml) cinnamon-sugar. Stretch, fold over, and pinch edges of dough to form a triangle. Keep moisture from edges or they will not seal. Roll and fill all squares in same manner.
9. Reduce heat under water to simmer. Carefully lower verenekas into water, a few at a time. Do not crowd. Cook for a few minutes until they rise to the surface and look plumped out. With a slotted spoon, remove to a colander and drain. Place immediately in buttered dish, turning to butter both sides.
10. Bake at 350°F (180°C) for 5 to 10 minutes until plumped and slightly crisp on bottom.

Yields 48 dumplings

FAVORITE APPLE PUDDING

Serve with Sweet Cider Sauce (see page 228) or Calvados Hard
Sauce I or II (see pages 231-232).

4 cups (1 l) sliced peeled apples	**Cake**
½ cup (125 ml) white sugar	¼ cup (50 ml) vegetable shortening
½ tsp (2 ml) cinnamon	½ cup (125 ml) white sugar
½ cup (125 ml) melted butter	1½ cups (375 ml) all-purpose flour
	2 tsp (10 ml) baking powder
	¼ tsp (1 ml) salt
	1 cup (250 ml) milk
	1 tsp (5 ml) vanilla

1. Place apples in a buttered 2-quart (2-l) baking dish. Mix sugar
and cinnamon in a cup and sprinkle over apple slices. Drizzle with
melted butter.
2. Cream shortening and sugar in a medium bowl. Sift together the
flour, baking powder, and salt in a small bowl. Mix milk and vanilla.
Add flour mixture to creamed mixture alternately with milk, beating well after each addition. Spread batter over apple slices.
3. Bake at 350°F (180°C) for 50 to 60 minutes or until top is golden
brown and cake tester comes out clean.
Serves 4 to 6

BAKED APPLE-RAISIN PUDDING

Grated apples make this pudding moist. Serve hot with Sweet Butter
Sauce (see page 231).

¼ cup (50 ml) butter	1 cup (250 ml) all-purpose flour
1 cup (250 ml) white sugar	1 tsp (5 ml) baking soda
1 egg	1 tsp (5 ml) cinnamon
3 cups (750 ml) grated unpeeled apples	½ tsp (2 ml) nutmeg
	¼ tsp (1 ml) ground cloves
	½ cup (125 ml) raisins

1. Cream butter, sugar, and egg until light and fluffy in a medium bowl. Stir in grated apples.

2. Sift flour, baking soda, and spices into a small bowl. Add to creamed mixture and stir until combined. Fold in raisins.

3. Pour batter into a buttered 8-inch (20-cm) square cake pan. Bake at 350°F (180°C) for 25 to 30 minutes or until cake tester comes out clean.

Serves 8

MOLDED APPLE-RICE PUDDING

Use an apple that doesn't turn brown quickly. Short grain rice will be more tender than long grain rice.

1 *cup (250 ml) cooked short-grain white rice*	1 *envelope unflavored gelatin*
	¼ *cup (50 ml) water*
2 *cups (500 ml) light cream or milk*	1 *tsp (5 ml) vanilla*
⅓ *cup (75 ml) white sugar*	1 *cup (250 ml) sour cream*
Pinch of salt	1 *cup (250 ml) diced unpeeled apples*
1 *3-inch (7.5-cm) cinnamon stick*	

1. Combine rice, cream or milk, sugar, salt, and cinnamon stick in a medium saucepan. Bring to a boil; reduce heat and simmer for 15 minutes. Remove cinnamon stick.

2. Soften gelatin in water for 5 minutes. Stir over low heat until gelatin dissolves. Add to rice and stir until blended.

3. Chill mixture until partially set, about 30 minutes. Fold in vanilla, sour cream, and apples. Spoon into individual ½-cup (125-ml) molds or a 4-cup (1-l) mold.

4. Cover with plastic wrap and chill until firm. To serve, unmold on a serving plate and garnish with fresh apple wedges, if desired.

Serves 4 *to* 6

APPLESAUCE ANGEL PUDDING

Chunks of angel food cake are layered with thick applesauce and whipped cream.

1 7-inch (17.5-cm)–diameter angel food cake	½ tsp (2 ml) vanilla
	½ tsp (2 ml) cinnamon
1 cup (250 ml) whipping cream	2 cups (500 ml) cold applesauce
1 tbsp (15 ml) icing sugar	¼ cup (50 ml) chopped walnuts or grated semisweet chocolate

1. Tear angel food cake into chunks.
2. Whip cream with icing sugar and vanilla in a medium bowl until stiff.
3. Blend cinnamon with applesauce in a small bowl.
4. Layer cake, whipped cream, and applesauce in a 6-cup (1.5-l) serving dish. End with whipped cream and sprinkle with nuts or grated chocolate.
5. Chill for 30 minutes before serving.
Serves 6 to 8

APPLE BRANDY ZABAGLIONE

Serve with ladyfingers and you have an elegant dessert or use as a sauce over fruit.

4 egg yolks	4 tbsp (60 ml) apple brandy
2 tbsp (25 ml) white sugar	1 cup (250 ml) whipping cream

1. Mix egg yolks, sugar, and apple brandy in top of a double boiler. Place over simmering water.
2. Using a wire whisk, stir briskly until thick and foamy. Remove from heat and cool. Cover and chill.
3. Whip cream in a small deep bowl. Fold chilled custard into cream and serve immediately.
Serves 4 to 6

APPLE TRIFLE

Poached apple wedges are nestled between layers of sponge cake, custard sauce, and whipped cream.

Sponge Cake
4 separated eggs
   Pinch of salt
⅓ cup (75 ml) white sugar
1 tsp (5 ml) vanilla
¼ cup (50 ml) sifted cornstarch
¼ cup (50 ml) all-purpose flour

Poached Apples
8 apples
4 cups (1 l) water
1 cup (250 ml) white sugar
2 tbsp (25 ml) fresh lemon juice

Custard Sauce
4 egg yolks
⅓ cup (75 ml) white sugar
1 cup (250 ml) whipping cream
1 cup (250 ml) milk
1 tsp (5 ml) vanilla
4 tbsp (60 ml) apple brandy,
   sherry, or apple juice
½ cup (125 ml) apricot jam
1 cup (250 ml) whipping cream
1 tbsp (15 ml) icing sugar
1 tsp (5 ml) apple brandy

1. Butter a 9 × 13-inch (3-l) baking pan. Line with waxed paper and butter paper. Dust with flour.
2. In a large bowl, beat egg whites and salt until soft peaks form. Gradually beat in sugar until very stiff but not dry.
3. In a small bowl, beat egg yolks and vanilla until thick and lemon colored. Fold into beaten egg whites.
4. Mix cornstarch and flour in a small bowl. Sift ingredients over egg mixture and fold until thoroughly blended.
5. Pour into prepared pan and bake at 400°F (200°C) until cake is lightly browned, 12 to 15 minutes. Invert onto a wire rack and cool for 10 minutes. Remove waxed paper. Let stand uncovered for 2 to 3 hours or until slightly dried out.
6. Peel, quarter, and core apples. Slice into ¼-inch (½-cm) wedges. Bring water, sugar, and lemon juice to a boil in a Dutch oven or large saucepan. Add the apple wedges and simmer for 10 to 15 minutes until tender. Do not overcook or apples will be mushy. Remove from syrup; drain and cool. Reserve syrup for poaching fruit or mixing in drinks.

7. To make custard, beat egg yolks and sugar until thick and lemon colored. Scald cream and milk in top of double boiler over simmering water. Gradually stir hot cream mixture into egg yolk mixture. Return to saucepan and cook, stirring, until mixture thickens. Cool and stir in vanilla.

8. To assemble trifle, cut cake in half. Place half in a 2-quart (2-l) serving dish. Sprinkle with 2 tbsp (25 ml) apple brandy, sherry, or apple juice. Trim cake to fit dish if necessary. Spread with half the apricot jam. Arrange drained apple wedges on top of jam. Cover with other half of cake. Sprinkle with remaining apple brandy and spread with apricot jam.

9. Pour custard sauce over top and sides of cake. Cover and chill for several hours or overnight.

10. Just before serving, whip cream with icing sugar; stir in apple brandy. Pipe or spoon cream over trifle.

Serves 8

APPLESAUCE BRÛLÉE

Broiled brown sugar crust is made in advance and placed on top of dessert just before serving. Only homemade applesauce does justice to this dessert.

2 *tsp (10 ml) butter*
½ *cup (125 ml) brown sugar*

2 *cups (500 ml) thick sweetened cold*
   applesauce
1¼ *cups (300 ml) sour cream*

1. Line a cookie sheet with aluminum foil. Butter four circles the diameter of the dessert dishes on the foil. Sprinkle brown sugar in a lacy pattern, ¼-inch (6 mm) thick, on the buttered circles. Pat sugar firmly.

2. Place sugar-covered foil under a broiler until sugar is glazed. It does not melt completely. Remove from oven and cool. Remove crust with a spatula and place on each serving. This step can be completed several hours in advance.

3. Divide applesauce among four small dessert dishes. Spread a layer of sour cream over each serving. Place a sugar crust on each serving. Serve immediately.

Serves 4

APPLE-RHUBARB-STRAWBERRY SORBET

Make this rose-colored sorbet for your Valentine.

1½ cups (375 ml) chopped,
   cored, peeled apples
1½ cups (375 ml) sliced fresh
   or frozen rhubarb
1 cup (250 ml) white sugar

1½ cups (375 ml) water
1 cup (250 ml) mashed fresh or
   frozen strawberries
1 tbsp (15 ml) fresh lemon juice
3 tbsp (45 ml) whipping cream

1. Place apples and rhubarb in a medium saucepan. Add sugar and ½ cup (125 ml) water. Simmer, covered, until apples and rhubarb are tender, about 15 minutes. Cool.
2. Process all fruit in a blender or food processor with lemon juice, whipping cream, and remaining water. Taste and add a little more sugar or lemon juice if necessary.
3. Pour into a bowl, cover with plastic wrap, and freeze until slushy. Beat with electric beater for 1 minute. Freeze until solid. If you have an ice cream maker, follow manufacturer's instructions.
Yields 1 quart (1 l)

ICY FRUIT YOGURT

Frozen yogurt is low in fat but still satisfying and refreshing.

2 apples
2 bananas
¼ cup (50 ml) fresh lemon juice

1 cup (250 ml) plain yogurt
1 tsp (5 ml) grated lemon rind
2 egg whites
⅓ cup (75 ml) white sugar

1. Peel and chop apples and bananas.
2. Process apples, bananas, lemon juice, yogurt, and lemon rind in a blender or food processor until smooth.
3. In a medium bowl, beat the egg whites until soft peaks form. Beat in the sugar until stiff peaks form.
4. Fold fruit mixture into the egg whites until thoroughly mixed. Cover bowl with plastic wrap and freeze until slushy. Beat until smooth and freeze mixture until solid. Remove from freezer 10 minutes before serving.
Serves 4 to 6

APPLESAUCE FOOL

For a special dinner, layer pink applesauce and cream sauce in glass parfait dishes. Assemble dessert just before serving.

6 cups (1.5 l) diced red-skinned apples
¼ cup (50 ml) water or cranberry juice
1 3-inch (7.5-cm) cinnamon stick
½ cup (125 ml) white sugar

1 4-oz (250-g) pkg cream cheese, at room temperature
1 tsp (5 ml) vanilla
¼ cup (50 ml) icing sugar
1 cup (250 ml) whipping cream

1. Place apples, water or cranberry juice, and cinnamon stick in a large saucepan. Cover and cook over low heat until the apples are soft, about 20 minutes. Remove cinnamon stick and rub apples through a sieve or food mill. Add sugar and stir to dissolve. Cool. Cover and chill applesauce.
2. Just before serving, beat cream cheese, vanilla, and icing sugar until smooth. Gradually add the cream and beat until fluffy.
3. To serve, alternate layers of applesauce and cream into small serving dishes or wine goblets.
Serves 6

BUTTERMILK PRESERVE ICE CREAM

Simple to make; just blend ingredients and freeze.

2 cups (500 ml) buttermilk
2 cups (500 ml) apple preserves
¾ cup (175 ml) whipping cream

1. Process buttermilk and preserves in a blender or food processor until smooth. Add whipping cream and process again until thoroughly combined.
2. Pour into a medium bowl, cover with plastic wrap, and freeze until slushy, about 2 hours. Beat with an electric beater until smooth. Freeze until firm. If you have an ice cream maker, freeze according to manufacturer's instructions.
Makes about 5 cups (1.2 l)

APPLE SNOW

Garnish this delicate dessert with a twist of red apple peeling just before serving.

1 cup (250 ml) cold thick applesauce	2 egg whites
⅛ tsp (½ ml) cinnamon	Pinch of cream of tartar
2 tbsp (25 ml) liquid honey	2 tbsp (25 ml) white sugar
	½ cup (125 ml) whipping cream

1. Combine applesauce, cinnamon, and honey in a large bowl.
2. Beat egg whites and cream of tartar in a medium bowl with an electric mixer until stiff peaks form. Sprinkle with sugar and beat until combined.
3. Fold egg whites into applesauce just until mixed. Spoon into dessert dishes and chill for 30 minutes.
4. Whip cream until stiff and spoon over each portion. Cover and freeze for 45 minutes before serving.
Serves 4

FRESH APPLE SHERBET

The color of this sherbet will remind you of autumn.

1 cup (250 ml) white sugar	6 medium apples
½ cup (125 ml) water	⅓ cup (75 ml) apple brandy, cider, or apple juice

1. Combine sugar and water in a small saucepan. Stir over medium heat until sugar has dissolved.
2. Peel, quarter, and core apples. Place apples in a food processor or blender container. Pour in sugar syrup and apple brandy, cider, or apple juice. Process until smooth.
3. Pour into a bowl. Cover and freeze until partially frozen. Beat until smooth and freeze until firm.
Serves 4 to 6

APPLE-GINGER ICE

Top off a heavy meal with this light refreshing slush.

2 cups (500 ml) water	2 tsp (10 ml) grated lemon rind
1 cup + 2 tbsp (250 + 25 ml) white sugar	¼ cup (50 ml) fresh lemon juice
	¼ cup (50 ml) brandy (optional)
1 cup (250 ml) firmly packed, grated, peeled apples	¼ cup (50 ml) minced crystallized ginger

1. Combine water and sugar in a medium saucepan and bring to a boil, stirring to dissolve sugar. Boil for 2 minutes. Remove from heat and stir in grated apples, lemon juice, and lemon rind.
2. Pour into a bowl and freeze until mixture is slushy. Beat mixture until smooth and freeze again until slushy. Add brandy and ginger, and beat again. Divide ice among 6 dessert glasses. Cover and freeze for 4 hours or until serving time.
Serves 6

Sweet Sauces

AMARETTO APPLES

Serve over ice cream or in sherbet glasses topped with a dollop of whipped cream. If you are adventurous, try different liqueurs, such as Anisette. Do not use a cream liqueur, however, because it will curdle.

4 large apples   ¼ cup (50 ml) white sugar
½ cup (125 ml) Amaretto liqueur   Juice and rind of 1 orange

1. Peel, quarter, and core apples. Slice apple quarters into thin wedges.
2. Combine all ingredients in a skillet or large saucepan. Simmer uncovered until apples are tender and most of the liquid has evaporated. Stir occasionally.
3. Chill and serve.
Serves 4

MICROWAVE BUTTERSCOTCH APPLES

A rich topping for shortcake.

½ cup (125 ml) brown sugar   2 tbsp (25 ml) butter
¼ cup (50 ml) rum   4 apples

1. Stir brown sugar and rum in a 6-cup (1.5-l) microproof casserole. Add butter. Cover and cook at maximum power for 4 to 5 minutes, stirring after 2 minutes, until sugar is dissolved.
2. Peel, quarter, and core apples. Add apple quarters to syrup, stirring to coat each piece. Cook at maximum power for 1 to 2 minutes, until hot.
Serves 4

GINGER APPLE SAUCE

A spicy dessert or garnish.

2 cups (500 ml) sweetened applesauce
1 tsp (5 ml) grated orange rind
1 tbsp (15 ml) finely minced preserved ginger

1. Mix all ingredients in a medium saucepan. Simmer for 10 minutes, stirring often. Serve warm or cold.
Yields 2 cups (500 ml)

APPLE SYRUP

A light fruit syrup for pancakes or waffles.

4 cups (1 l) apple juice or cider

1. Place apple juice or cider in a large saucepan. Bring to a boil, regulating heat so that mixture is boiling but not boiling over. Boil until reduced to 1 cup (250 ml). Cool, then store in refrigerator.
Yields 1 cup (250 ml)

CHUNKY CINNAMON SAUCE

Make this to serve over cooked cereal or pancakes.

1 cup (250 ml) brown sugar   ¼ cup (50 ml) butter
¾ cup (175 ml) apple juice   1 cup (250 ml) finely chopped
1 tsp (5 ml) cinnamon   unpeeled apples

1. Combine brown sugar, apple juice, and cinnamon in a medium saucepan. Boil for 5 minutes or until it forms a thick syrup.
2. Stir in butter and apples. Serve immediately.
Yields 1½ cups (375 ml)

MICROWAVE SPICY APPLE CHUNKS

A delicious topping for ice cream, pancakes, or waffles.

4 medium apples	½ tsp (2 ml) cinnamon
⅓ cup (75 ml) brown sugar	2 tbsp (25 ml) butter

1. Peel, quarter, and core apples. Place in a 1-quart (1-l) microproof casserole.
2. Combine brown sugar and cinnamon in a small bowl. Sprinkle over apples and dot with butter. Cover with lid or with microproof plastic wrap.
3. Cook for 7 to 8 minutes on maximum power, stirring after 4 minutes. Serve warm.
Serves 4

BROWN SUGAR APPLE TOPPING

Use this sauce as a topping for ice cream, crepes, or a simple cake.

½ cup (125 ml) brown sugar	2 cups (500 ml) coarsely chopped
2 tsp (10 ml) cornstarch	peeled apples
½ cup (125 ml) water	2 tbsp (25 ml) rum or brandy
Dash salt	2 tbsp (25 ml) butter (only if using as a topping for a hot dessert)

1. Combine sugar, cornstarch, water, and salt in a medium saucepan. Bring to a boil, stirring constantly.
2. Add apples; reduce heat and simmer for 10 minutes or until apples are tender.
3. Remove from heat and stir in rum or brandy and butter. Serve warm or at room temperature.
Yields 2 cups (500 ml)

CIDER SAUCE

Cider may vary in sweetness, so sugar may not be needed in this recipe.

1 tbsp (15 ml) butter	1 ½ cups (375 ml) cider
2 ½ tsp (12 ml) all-purpose flour	White sugar to taste
	½ tsp (2 ml) cinnamon

1. Melt butter over low heat; blend in flour. Stir for 1 minute.
2. Add the cider and stir until mixture is thick and smooth. Sweeten to taste.
3. Stir in cinnamon. Serve hot or cold.
Yields 1 ½ cups (375 ml)

SWEET CIDER SAUCE

A lightly spiced sauce to serve over waffles or gingerbread.

2 tbsp (25 ml) cornstarch	1 2-inch (5-cm) cinnamon stick
2 cups (500 ml) sweet apple cider	Pinch of salt
	Freshly grated nutmeg

1. Stir cornstarch and cider until smooth in a small saucepan. Add cinnamon stick, salt, and nutmeg. Cook over medium heat, stirring constantly, until sauce thickens and is translucent. Serve hot.
Yields 2 cups (500 ml)

APPLE MERINGUE SAUCE

This just might become your favorite topping for gingerbread. It does not keep long, so serve immediately.

2 egg whites   1½ cups (375 ml) grated,
    Dash of salt   cored, unpeeled apples
½ cup (125 ml) white sugar   2 tsp (10 ml) fresh lemon juice

1. Beat egg whites and salt in a medium bowl until whites form soft peaks. Gradually beat in sugar until mixture is stiff and glossy.
2. Mix grated apples with lemon juice in a small bowl. Fold apples into meringue and serve immediately.
Serves 4 to 6

CRANBERRY APPLE SAUCE WITH PORT

Make at least a day before serving to allow flavors to mellow.

2 cups (500 ml) fresh or frozen   ¼ cup (50 ml) port
    cranberries   ¼ cup (50 ml) water
1¼ cups (300 ml) finely   1 tbsp (15 ml) lemon or orange
    chopped peeled apples   juice
¼ cup (50 ml) raisins   4 whole cloves
¾ cup (175 ml) white sugar   4 allspice berries

1. Combine cranberries, apples, raisins, sugar, port, water, and lemon or orange juice in a medium saucepan. Tie spices in a small piece of cheesecloth. Add to saucepan.
2. Bring mixture to a boil, stirring occasionally. Reduce heat and simmer, uncovered, until cranberries pop and sauce is thick. This will take about 15 minutes. Remove from heat.
3. Let cool, then remove spice bag and ladle into a glass jar or serving dish. Cover and chill.
Yields 2 cups (500 ml)

CINNAMON APPLE SAUCE

Enjoy this buttery brown sauce on shortcake, cottage pudding, or pancakes.

1 cup (250 ml) brown sugar   1 cup (250 ml) finely chopped peeled
1 cup (250 ml) apple juice or cider   apples
½ tsp (2 ml) cinnamon   ¼ cup (50 ml) unsalted butter

1. Combine sugar, apple juice, and cinnamon in a medium saucepan. Bring to a boil and cook for 10 minutes or until it forms a heavy syrup.
2. Stir in apples and butter. Heat for 3 to 4 minutes and serve immediately.
Yields 1½ cups (375 ml)

PORT SABAYON

A light foamy custard sauce that is also delicious served over wine poached apples or diced fresh apples in sherbet glasses.

3 egg yolks   ⅔ cup (150 ml) port
½ cup (125 ml) white sugar   ¼ tsp (1 ml) finely grated lemon rind

1. Whisk egg yolks, sugar, port, and lemon rind together in top of double boiler. Cook, whisking constantly, over simmering water until thick and creamy. Continue to whisk until mixture is almost triple in volume. This will take about 8 minutes.
2. Serve immediately or place in a large bowl of ice water and whisk until cold. Will keep for 2 days in refrigerator.
Serves 6

CRÈME FRAÎCHE

This version of Crème Fraîche uses yogurt instead of buttermilk to thicken the cream. You can halve or double this recipe.

1 cup (250 ml) plain yogurt
1 cup (250 ml) whipping cream

1. Stir yogurt and cream together in a small non-metallic bowl. Cover and let sit at room temperature overnight until thick.
2. When ready it will be the consistency of sour cream. Chill and serve.
Yields 2 cups (500 ml)

SWEET BUTTER SAUCE

Serve this rich, sweet sauce over hot baked or steamed puddings. It will keep in the refrigerator for several days.

½ cup (125 ml) butter
½ cup (125 ml) light cream

1 cup (250 ml) white or brown sugar
½ tsp (2 ml) vanilla

1. Combine all ingredients in a small saucepan and heat to boiling point. Reduce heat and simmer, stirring occasionally, for 20 minutes or until slightly thickened.
2. Serve hot.
Yields about 1¼ cups (300 ml)

CALVADOS HARD SAUCE I

Use this on steamed puddings or hot desserts.

½ cup (125 ml) unsalted butter
⅓ cup (75 ml) white sugar
3 tbsp (45 ml) Calvados or Apple Cordial (see page 131)

1. Cream butter and sugar until light and fluffy. Gradually add Apple Cordial or Calvados while beating continuously. Cover and chill. *Yields ¾ cup (175 ml)*

CALVADOS HARD SAUCE II

This is a fluffy hard sauce. It keeps for weeks in the refrigerator.

⅓ cup (75 ml) unsalted butter
1 cup (250 ml) icing sugar

1 tbsp (15 ml) Calvados or Apple Cordial (see page 131)
3 tbsp (45 ml) whipping cream

1. Cream butter and sugar until light and fluffy. Gradually add Apple Cordial or Calvados while beating continuously. Beat in whipping cream. It may be necessary to add a little more icing sugar. Cover and chill.
Yields ¾ cup (175 ml)

MICROWAVE RAISIN APPLE BRANDY SAUCE

Serve this sauce warm with ham, squash, gingerbread, or baked apples.

½ cup (125 ml) raisins
¼ cup (50 ml) apple brandy or cider
3 tbsp (45 ml) brown sugar
1 tbsp (15 ml) cornstarch

1 cup (250 ml) apple cider or juice
2 tbsp (25 ml) fresh lemon juice
⅛ tsp (½ ml) ground cloves
⅛ tsp (½ ml) nutmeg

1. Heat raisins and brandy or cider in a small microproof bowl for 1 minute on maximum power. Remove from oven and set aside.
2. Mix sugar and cornstarch in a medium microproof bowl. Stir in cider or juice and lemon juice until smooth. Cook for 2 to 3 minutes on maximum power, stirring every minute, until thick and clear.
3. Stir in spices and brandy raisin mixture. Cook for 1 to 2 minutes on maximum power.
4. Let stand for 5 minutes then serve warm.
Yields 1½ cups (375 ml)

CHAPTER SEVEN

Apples for Keeps

JARS AND SEALS

The best containers for preserving are vacuum-sealed jelly jars. Any small jar can be sealed with paraffin, but paraffin seals sometimes loosen and are not recommended for long periods of storage.

If preserves are to be used quickly, put them in whatever jars you have on hand and store in the refrigerator.

Before using vacuum-sealed jelly jars, make sure the rims are free from nicks that might prevent a good seal. Use new lids each time. Wash the jars, lids, and bands in hot soapy water. Rinse well.

Place jars, ladle, and preserving funnel in a large pot of water to cover, and bring to a boil. Boil for 20 minutes. Boil lids and bands for 5 minutes just before filling jars. Keep jars, ladle, preserving funnel, lids, and bands in hot water until ready to fill and seal jars.

Be sure preserves are boiling when ladling into jars. Fill to within ¼ inch of the top. With a clean damp cloth, wipe the rim of the jar. Place lid on jar and screw the band on evenly. As jars cool, you should hear a pop and the lid will have a slight depression.

Some recipes call for a boiling water bath. Place jars on a rack in a preserving kettle. Cover to a depth of 1 inch (2.5 cm) with boiling water. Time the boiling water bath from the time the water returns to a boil.

After the jars have cooled completely, store in a cool, dark, dry place.

EQUIPMENT FOR PRESERVING, PICKLING, AND CANNING

You probably have most of the necessary utensils in your kitchen, but it may be wise to invest in a few extras.

Large heavy enamelled or stainless steel preserving kettle
Ladle
Preserving funnel
Accurate measuring cups and spoons

Large colander or strainer
Containers: commercial canning jars, in cup (250 ml), pint (500 ml)
    and quart (liter) sizes
Seals for jars: metal lids and screw bands
Labels
Candy or jelly thermometer
Large wooden spoons
Cheesecloth or jelly bag
Blender, food mill, grinder, or food processor
Clock with second hand

HOW TO TEST FOR JELL POINT

There are three ways to determine if jam or jelly has been cooked
long enough. The temperature and freezer tests are used for jelly,
jam and preserves; the spoon or sheet test is for jelly.

Temperature Test
Check the temperature of boiling water with a candy or jelly thermometer. The temperature at which water boils differs at different
altitudes. For jam and preserves, cook mixture to a temperature 9°F
(5°C) above the boiling point of water. For jelly cook the mixture
to a temperature 8°F (4°C) above the boiling point of water.

Freezer Test
Remove the jam or jelly from heat. Spoon a small amount of the
mixture onto a cold plate. Put the plate in the freezer for 3 minutes.
For jelly, the mixture is ready if it jells. For jam, only a small amount
of liquid will surround the mound.

Spoon or Sheet Test
Dip a cold metal spoon in the boiling jelly mixture. Lift the spoon
so that the jelly runs off the side. When the drops run together and
fall off the spoon in a sheet, the jelly is done.

Jellies, Condiments, and Preserves

BASIC APPLE JELLY

3   lb (1.4 kg) tart apples
3   cups (750 ml) water
    White sugar

1. Remove stem and blossom ends of apples. Cut into small chunks; do not peel or core. Place in a large, heavy bottomed saucepan or Dutch oven. Add water to just below the top layer of apples. Cover and cook over low heat until apples are soft, about 30 minutes.
2. Pour apples into a damp jelly bag or into a colander lined with several layers of damp cheesecloth. Let drip into a large bowl for several hours or overnight. For the clearest jelly, do not squeeze or press the jelly bag.
3. Measure juice. (You should have 4 cups [1 l].) Pour into a Dutch oven. Add ¾ cup (175 ml) white sugar for each cup (250 ml) of juice. Bring to a boil and cook until the mixture jells. This will take from 10 to 30 minutes.
4. Skim off the foam and pour jelly into hot sterilized jars. Seal and cool. Store in a cool, dark place.
Yields about 3 cups (750 ml)

CRANBERRY-APPLE JELLY

Fresh or frozen cranberries can be used to make this tart, ruby-colored jelly.

8   cups (2 l) cranberries   6   cups (1.5 l) water
6   large tart apples   White sugar

1. Coarsely chop the apples. Do not peel or core. Combine with cranberries in a Dutch oven. Pour water over fruit and bring to a boil. Reduce heat, cover, and simmer for 20 minutes or until apples are tender and cranberries have popped.

2. Line a large sieve with damp cheesecloth or use a jelly bag if you have one. Ladle fruit into sieve or jelly bag and let drip over a bowl for 4 hours or overnight. Discard fruit pulp.

3. Boil juice for 3 minutes. Measure, and for each cup (250 ml) of juice, add 1 cup (250 ml) sugar. Bring to a boil, stirring constantly. Boil for 5 to 6 minutes until mixture reaches the jelling point.

4. Remove from heat; skim foam from surface. Pour jelly into hot sterilized jars to within ½ inch (1 cm) of top. Seal.

Yields 6 cups (1.5 l)

CRABAPPLE JELLY

Be sure the crabapples are firm, tart, and not overripe.

5 *lb (2 kg) red crabapples*
8 *cups (2 l) water*
   White sugar

1. Wash crabapples. Remove stems and blossom ends. Cut in half but do not core or peel.

2. Place crabapples in a preserving kettle with water. Cover and cook over medium-high heat for 20 minutes or until fruit is soft.

3. Pour mixture into a wet jelly bag or a colander lined with several layers of damp cheesecloth. Allow to drip overnight. Do not squeeze or force juice through bag or juice will be cloudy.

4. Next day, measure juice into a preserving kettle. There should be about 7 cups (1.75 l). Add ¾ cup (175 ml) sugar for every cup of juice. Bring to a full rolling boil, and boil rapidly until jell stage is reached, about 15 minutes.

5. Remove from heat and skim off foam. Pour into hot sterilized jars. Seal.

Yields 2 pints (1 l)

BRAMBLE JELLY

A traditional English combination of crabapple and blackberry juices yields a firm dark jelly.

6   cups (1.5 l) blackberries
2   cups (500 ml) crabapple juice (see page 237)
3   cups (750 ml) white sugar

1. Follow steps 1, 2 and 3 in preceding recipe to extract crabapple juice.
2. Crush blackberries in a large saucepan and cook over low heat until juice separates from pulp. Pour into a damp jelly bag or colander lined with several layers of damp cheesecloth. Let drip over a bowl for 4 hours or overnight. Measure juice; there should be 2 cups (500 ml).
3. Pour blackberry and crabapple juices into a Dutch oven or preserving kettle. Add sugar and stir until dissolved. Bring to a boil and cook for about 10 minutes or until mixture reaches jell point.
4. Ladle into hot sterilized jars. Seal. Cool and store in a cool, dark place.
Yields 2 pints (1 l)

SUGARLESS FRESH CIDER JELLY

Jelly consistency is achieved by boiling until cider is reduced to one-eighth of original volume.

8   cups (2 l) fresh apple cider

1. Place cider in a large saucepan (the larger the diameter of the pan, the quicker it will be reduced in volume). Bring to a boil; regulate heat so that mixture is boiling but not boiling over. Boil until reduced to 1 cup (250 ml).
2. Remove from heat; pour into sterilized container. Cool then chill. Keep refrigerated.
Yields 1 cup (250 ml)

APPLE HERB JELLY

Make this jelly as strong as you like by increasing the amount of chopped herbs.

10 cups (2.5 l) coarsely chopped
   unpeeled apples (include cores)
4 cups (1 l) water

¼ cup (50 ml) chopped fresh herbs
   (sage, thyme, marjoram, oregano,
   or summer savory)
   White sugar
5 herb sprigs, washed and dried

1. Combine apples and water in a large saucepan or Dutch oven. Bring to a boil; reduce heat and simmer partially covered until mushy, about 30 minutes. Crush apples during cooking period with a potato masher.

2. Ladle apple sauce into a dampened jelly bag or colander lined with several layers of damp cheesecloth. Let drip into a bowl for 6 hours or overnight. Do not squeeze or press, or jelly will be cloudy.

3. Combine apple juice and chopped herbs in a large saucepan. Bring to a boil; remove from heat and cover for 30 minutes. Strain through a fine sieve, pressing to extract all the juice.

4. Measure juice and combine in a Dutch oven or preserving kettle with an equal amount of sugar. Stir and bring to a rolling boil. Boil until mixture jells when a little is placed on a cold plate. This should only take 10 minutes.

5. Remove from heat. Skim off foam and pour into hot sterilized jars. Place 1 herb sprig in each jar. Seal. Cool completely before storing in a cool, dark place.

Yields 4 to 5 cups (1 to 1.4 l)

MINT CIDER VINEGAR JELLY

A sweet-sour mint jelly that is perfect with lamb.

1½ cups (375 ml) finely
   chopped fresh
   mint leaves
1½ cups (375 ml) water
¾ cup (175 ml) cider vinegar

2 tbsp (25 ml) strained fresh lemon
   juice
3½ cups (875 ml) white sugar
½ bottle liquid pectin

1. Combine mint, water, and vinegar in a medium saucepan. Crush mint with a potato masher as it is heating. Cover and bring to a boil. Reduce heat to very low and steep for 30 minutes. Strain through a fine sieve and press to extract all juices.

2. Combine strained liquid, lemon juice, and sugar in a large saucepan. Stir to mix, and bring to a rolling boil. Pour in liquid pectin and when mixture returns to a rolling boil, boil for 1 minute. Remove from heat and skim off foam.

3. Pour jelly into prepared jars, leaving ½ inch (1 cm) headspace. Seal and cool completely before storing in a cool, dark place.
Yields 3 to 4 cups (750 ml to 1 l)

APPLE PEELING JELLY

Save the peelings and cores from apple pies to make this jelly. Occasionally if your apples are too ripe, it will not jell, but then you have a wonderful pancake syrup.

8 cups (2 l) or more apple peelings and cores
   Water
   White sugar

1. Place at least 8 cups (2 l) packed apple peelings and cores in a large saucepan. Add water to half the depth of the peelings in the saucepan.

2. Cover and cook over medium heat for 30 minutes or until the peelings are tender. Pour peelings and juice into a damp jelly bag or

a colander lined with several layers of damp cheesecloth. Let drip into a bowl for 4 hours or overnight. For the clearest jelly do not squeeze jelly bag.

3. To make jelly, measure juice. For each cup of juice, add ¾ cup (175 ml) sugar. Only cook 4 to 6 cups (1 to 1.5 l) of juice at a time.

4. Place juice and sugar in a Dutch oven or preserving kettle. Stir until sugar dissolves. Bring to a rolling boil and boil until the jell point has been reached.

5. Skim off foam. Ladle hot jelly into hot sterilized jars. Seal. Store in a cool, dark place.

Yields about 1½ cups (375 ml)

AUTUMN JELLY

An unusual combination of apples, tomatoes, and grapes.

6 *large apples*	2 *lb (1 kg) underripe blue grapes*
6 *medium ripe tomatoes*	*Water*
	White sugar

1. Slice apples, but do not peel or core. Slice tomatoes. Place apples and tomatoes in a Dutch oven. Place over medium heat and cook until juice begins to flow from fruit.

2. Stem grapes and add to Dutch oven. Add water to within ½ inch (1 cm) of top of fruit. As fruit gets hot, mash with a potato masher. Increase heat to bring mixture to a boil. Cook for 15 to 20 minutes or until grapes are soft.

3. Pour fruit into a damp jelly bag or a colander lined with several thicknesses of cheesecloth. Let drip over a bowl for 6 hours or overnight.

4. Measure juice. Pour into a Dutch oven or preserving kettle. Add 1 cup (250 ml) sugar for each cup (250 ml) juice. Bring to a boil, stirring frequently. Boil rapidly for 10 minutes or until mixture reaches jell point.

5. Skim jelly and pour into hot sterilized jars. Cool before storing in a cool, dark place.

Yields about 6 cups (1.25 l)

Apple Butters, Dried Apples

APPLE BUTTER: Spiced apple jam made from applesauce, which is cooked down very slowly to a thick, smooth paste. Usual additions include apple cider or juice, sugar and spices. It can be cooked in a large heavy bottomed pot or in a slow warm oven. It was developed as a means of preservation.

APPLE BUTTER

4 lb (2.2 kg) tart apples	2 tsp (10 ml) cinnamon
2 cups (500 ml) sweet cider	½ tsp (2 ml) cloves
White sugar	½ tsp (2 ml) allspice
Dash of salt	Juice and rind of 1 lemon

1. Coarsely chop apples without peeling or coring. Place apples and cider in a preserving kettle or heavy bottomed pot. Cover and cook over medium heat until soft (about 30 minutes).
2. Press through a food mill, large sieve, or applesauce cone. Measure. Return to kettle adding ½ cup (125 ml) sugar for each cup of applesauce. Stir in salt, spices, lemon juice and rind.
3. Cook over low heat until sugar dissolves.
FAST METHOD: Increase heat to medium. Cook, stirring often to prevent scorching, for 45 minutes.
SLOW METHOD: Continue to simmer over low heat, stirring every 20 minutes, for about 1½ hours.
OVEN METHOD: Place in an uncovered enamelled roasting pan or bean crock. Bake in a 300°F (150°C) oven for about 2-3 hours
4. Apple butter is ready when sauce is reduced by half to a thick, smooth butter. Spoon into hot, sterilized jars. Seal.
Yields 3 pints (1.5 l)

HONEY APPLE BUTTER

Honey and orange juice and rind give this butter a special flavor.

10 apples
¼ cup (50 ml) water
½ tsp (2 ml) grated orange rind
¼ cup (50 ml) fresh orange juice

2 cups (500 ml) white sugar
½ cup (125 ml) mild liquid honey
¼ tsp (1 ml) freshly grated nutmeg
(optional)

1. Remove stem and blossom ends from apples. Chop coarsely and place in a Dutch oven with water. Cover and cook, stirring to prevent scorching for 30 minutes or until very soft. Press through a sieve or a food mill. There should be 5 cups (1.25 l) applesauce.
2. Return applesauce to Dutch oven, and add orange rind, orange juice, sugar, and honey. Stir to combine. Cook over low heat, stirring frequently, until sauce is reduced by half to a thick butter. This may take as long as 2 hours.
3. Stir in nutmeg and spoon into hot sterilized jars. Seal.
Yields 2 pints (1 l)

APPLE LEATHER

1 cup (250 ml) unsweetened applesauce
1 tbsp (15 ml) corn syrup
Plastic wrap

1. Process applesauce and corn syrup in a blender or food processor for 1 minute or until very smooth.
2. Stretch a piece of plastic wrap tightly over a dinner plate. Pour applesauce over plastic wrap and shake plate vigorously to spread applesauce in a thin smooth sheet. Place in a warm location (e.g. on top of refrigerator, in a sunny, breezy spot, in front of a fan). Do not place in oven. Let dry until it feels leathery to touch. This may take as long as two days, depending on humidity and temperature.
3. Lift an edge of leather from plastic wrap and pull to remove. Place between sheets of plastic wrap and roll loosely to store. Better yet, enjoy right away.
Yields two 9-inch (22.5-cm) rounds of leather

CHRISTMAS APPLE CONSERVE

A marvelous mixture of apples, raisins, preserved ginger, oranges, and walnuts. Share a bottle with your friends.

8 large apples	¾ cup (175 ml) fresh orange juice
1 cup (250 ml) golden raisins	1 tsp (5 ml) cinnamon
3 cups sugar	½ tsp (2 ml) ginger
½ cup (125 ml) finely chopped preserved ginger	½ tsp (2 ml) nutmeg
⅓ cup (75 ml) candied orange peel	½ cup (125 ml) coarsely chopped walnuts or blanched almonds

1. Peel, quarter, and core apples. Finely dice apples. Combine all ingredients except walnuts in a Dutch oven or preserving kettle.
2. Cook over medium heat, stirring often, until thickened. Add walnuts and cook 5 minutes longer.
3. Pour into hot sterilized jars. Seal.
Yields 2 pints (1 l)

HONEY-APPLE CONSERVE

Use a mild honey. This recipe can be varied by combining apples, pears, peaches, or plums. Just keep the proportion of ½ cup (125 ml) honey to 1 cup (250 ml) prepared fruit.

4 cups (1 l) finely diced, cored, peeled apples
2 cups (500 ml) mild honey
2 tbsp (25 ml) fresh lemon juice

1. Combine apples, honey, and lemon juice in a large saucepan. Simmer, stirring continuously, until thick, approximately 20 minutes.
2. Ladle into hot sterilized jars. Seal.
Yields 2 pints (1 l)

APPLE PRESERVES

For an elegant touch, try adding 2 tbsp (25 ml) apple brandy, or almond or orange liqueur to preserves after they are cooked. These preserves make nice gifts.

2   cups (500 ml) white sugar
1   cup (250 ml) boiling water
6   cups (1.5 l) sliced, cored, peeled, tart apples

1. Combine sugar and water in a large saucepan. Bring to a boil, stirring to dissolve sugar. Boil, stirring occasionally, until syrup forms a hard ball when a little is dropped in cold water (250°F [120°C] on a candy thermometer).
2. Add apple slices and stir to cover with syrup. Reduce heat and simmer until slices are transparent and mixture is thick. Stir often because mixture can scorch easily.
3. Add liqueur if desired, and ladle into hot sterilized jars. Seal.
Yields 3 cups (750 ml)

CRABAPPLE RELISH

Fragrant with cinnamon and cloves, serve this relish with cheese and crackers, ham, or pork roast.

2   lb (1 kg) crabapples   ¼ tsp (1 ml) salt
⅔ cup (150 ml) white vinegar   ½ tsp (2 ml) ground cloves
2⅓ cups (575 ml) white sugar   1   tsp (5 ml) cinnamon

1. Remove stem and blossom ends from crabapples. Quarter and core crabapples, then grind in a food grinder or food processor.
2. Heat vinegar and sugar in a stainless steel or enameled Dutch oven or preserving kettle. Add ground crabapples, salt, cloves, and cinnamon. Stir to combine.
3. Simmer over low heat for 45 minutes, stirring frequently, until thick.
4. Ladle into hot sterilized jars. Seal.
Yields 2½ pints (1.25 l)

APPLE MARMALADE

Firm tart apples, which are high in pectin, are necessary for this recipe. You can easily make half a batch.

1 large orange	8 cups (2 l) thinly sliced, peeled
1 lemon	apples
Water	5 cups (1.25 l) white sugar

1. Peel orange and lemon. Slice peel very thinly (scissors make this job easy). Place peel in a small saucepan and cover with cold water. Simmer for ½ hour or until peel is tender. Drain.
2. Section orange and lemon and chop pulp. Place pulp in a preserving kettle or Dutch oven with 1¼ cups (300 ml) water, apples, sugar, and peel.
3. Bring to a boil, stirring often, and cook over medium-high heat until thickened. This will take about 20 minutes. Remove from heat.
4. Skim, and ladle into hot sterilized jars. Seal.
Yields 6 to 7 cups (1.5 to 1.75 l)

RHUBARB DRIED APPLE CHUTNEY

A rich dark chutney to serve with meat or cheese.

5 cups (1.4 l) coarsely chopped rhubarb	1 tbsp (15 ml) finely chopped crystallized ginger
1¼ cups (300 ml) chopped onions	1 tsp (5 ml) curry powder
1 cup (250 ml) cider vinegar	½ tsp (2 ml) salt
1 cup (250 ml) brown sugar	1 crushed garlic clove
1 cup (250 ml) chopped dried apples	¼ tsp (1 ml) cinnamon
⅓ cup (75 ml) currants	Pinch allspice
¼ cup (50 ml) raisins	Pinch cayenne pepper

1. Combine all ingredients in a Dutch oven or preserving kettle. Slowly bring to a boil, stirring frequently. Reduce heat and simmer until chutney is thick. Stir frequently.
2. Ladle into hot sterilized jars. Process in boiling water bath for 10 minutes. Store in a cool, dark place.
Yields 5 cups (1.25 l)

PUNGENT APPLE CHUTNEY

Hot red peppers and lots of garlic!

1 sweet red pepper, seeded	1 tbsp (15 ml) pickling salt
2 fresh hot red peppers, or 1 tsp	1⅓ cups (325 ml) cider vinegar
(5 ml) dried red pepper flakes	1 tbsp (15 ml) ground ginger
10 cloves garlic	1 cup (250 ml) raisins
2 cups (500 ml) brown sugar	10 medium apples

1. Finely chop the sweet red pepper. Process the hot red peppers or dried red pepper flakes and garlic in a blender or food processor until puréed.
2. Combine sweet red pepper, hot pepper-garlic purée, brown sugar, salt, vinegar, ginger, and raisins in a Dutch oven or preserving kettle.
3. Peel, core, and chop apples. Add apples to pepper mixture and stir to combine.
4. Cook over medium heat until mixture is thick and apples are transparent, about 40 minutes.
5. Ladle into hot sterilized jars. Seal. Process in boiling water bath for 15 minutes.
Yields 3 pints (1.5 l)

INDIA RELISH

Sour apples are best for this basic chutney.

6 large apples	2½ cups (625 ml) white or
6 medium green tomatoes	brown sugar
1 large onion	1 tsp (5 ml) hot red pepper flakes
2½ cups (625 ml) cider vinegar	or to taste
	1½ tsp (7 ml) ginger
	½ tsp (2 ml) turmeric
	½ tsp (2 ml) salt

1. Peel, quarter, and core apples. Cut out stem end of tomatoes. Put through a food grinder, or food processor, or chop until very fine.
2. Combine all ingredients in a preserving kettle. Stir and bring to a boil. Reduce heat and simmer for 30 minutes.
3. Pack relish into hot sterilized jars. Seal. Process in boiling water bath for 15 minutes.

Yields 3 to 4 pints (1.5 to 2 l)

TOMATO FRUIT CHILI SAUCE

A wonderful way of dealing with your fall bounty. Serve this fruity sauce with meat loaf or a cheese tray.

8 apples, peeled, cored, and chopped	2 sweet red peppers, seeded and chopped
4 pears, peeled, cored, and chopped	
4 peaches, peeled, pitted, and chopped	1 fresh hot red pepper, chopped
30 medium ripe tomatoes, peeled and chopped	1 bunch celery, chopped
	4 cups (1 l) white sugar
6 medium onions, chopped	2 tbsp (25 ml) pickling salt
3 sweet green peppers, seeded and chopped	2 cups (500 ml) cider or white vinegar

1. Place fruit and vegetables in a preserving kettle. Slowly bring to a boil. Reduce heat and cook, uncovered, stirring frequently, until mixture begins to thicken, about 1 hour.
2. Tie pickling spice in a piece of cheesecloth. Add to sauce along with sugar, salt and vinegar. Continue cooking until mixture is thickened to desired consistency. The sauce will thicken as it cools. Taste and add more sugar or salt if desired.
3. Ladle into hot sterilized jars to within ½ inch (1 cm) of top. Seal. Process in a boiling water bath for 5 minutes.

Yields 7 to 8 pints (3.5 to 4 l)

APPLE KETCHUP

A thick, spicy sauce to serve with meat or poultry.

12 tart apples	2 grated onions
2 cups (500 ml) water	1 tsp (5 ml) dry mustard
1 cup (250 ml) sugar	1 tsp (5 ml) ground cloves
2 cups (500 ml) cider vinegar	2 tsp (10 ml) cinnamon
	1 tbsp (15 ml) pickling salt

1. Cut apples into small pieces and place in a Dutch oven or preserving kettle. Add water; cover and simmer until apples are very soft. Rub apples through a large sieve or put through a food mill.
2. Place applesauce in a Dutch oven. Add the sugar, vinegar, onions, mustard, cloves, cinnamon, and salt.
3. Bring the ketchup to a boil; reduce heat and simmer for 1 hour or until thick.
4. Ladle into hot sterilized jars and seal.
Yields 2 pints (1 l)

SPICY PICKLED CRABAPPLES

Be careful not to overcook the crabapples or the skins will split.

15 crabapples	2 cups (500 ml) white sugar
1 cup (250 ml) white vinegar	2 tsp (10 ml) whole cloves
	1 3-inch (7.5-cm) cinnamon stick

1. Remove blossom ends of crabapples. Do not remove stems. Prick each crabapple in several places with a darning needle or skewer.
2. Bring vinegar and sugar to a boil in a large saucepan. Tie cloves in a small piece of cheesecloth. Add cloves and cinnamon stick to saucepan. Reduce heat and add crabapples. Simmer for 2 to 3 minutes.
3. Pack crabapples in hot sterilized pint jars. Remove spice bag and cinnamon stick. Pour hot syrup over crabapples. Seal.
Yields 2 pints (1 l)

END-OF-SUMMER MINCEMEAT

Green tomatoes and apples are blended with molasses and rum to make this vegetarian pie filling.

12 medium apples	½ tsp (2 ml) salt
15 large green tomatoes	1 lb (454 g) seedless dark raisins
1 cup (250 ml) molasses	1 tsp (5 ml) cinnamon
½ cup (125 ml) dark rum	1 tsp (5 ml) allspice
3 cups (750 ml) dark brown sugar	½ tsp (2 ml) ginger
	1 cup (250 ml) cider vinegar

1. Remove stems and blossom ends of apples. Quarter and core, but do not peel. Remove stem end of tomatoes. Put apples and tomatoes through the coarse blade of a food processor or grinder.
2. Combine all ingredients in a preserving kettle. Stir over medium heat until sugar has dissolved, then increase heat and boil until mixture is thick. Stir constantly while cooking.
3. Immediately ladle into hot sterilized jars and seal.
Yields about 4 qt (3.75 l)

MICROWAVE DRIED APPLES

This method is ideal for making small quantities of dried apples.

2   apples
2   tsp (10 ml) fresh lemon juice

1. Peel, quarter, and core apples. Slice into ¼-inch (½-cm) thick wedges. Place in a small bowl and sprinkle with lemon juice. Toss lightly to coat.
2. Arrange slices in a single layer on a double thickness of paper towels on a plate, glass tray, or microwave roasting rack. Cook on 30 percent power for 15 minutes. Remove from oven and arrange on a dry piece of paper towel. Return to oven and cook on 30 percent power for 10 minutes longer or until limp and slightly moist.
3. Remove warm apple slices from oven and place on wire rack. Let dry overnight before using.
Yields ½ cup (125 ml)

DRIED APPLES

Use a dehydrator if you have one, but an oven or a breezy spot indoors or out will also work.

5 lb (2 kg) apples	½ cup (125 ml) fresh lemon juice or
1 gallon (4 l) cold water	ascorbic acid (use according to
1 tbsp (15 ml) salt	package directions)

1. Mix water, salt, and lemon juice or ascorbic acid in a large non-metallic container.
2. Peel and core apples. Cut into ¼-inch (½-cm) slices or rings. Place in water and let soak for 10 minutes. Drain for 30 minutes in a colander.
3. To dry outdoors, spread apple slices in a single layer on wire racks covered with cheesecloth. Cover with cheesecloth if drying outdoors. Place in a warm breezy place. It will take 1 to 2 days to dry the slices, depending on warmth and humidity. Bring indoors at night.
4. If using a dehydrator, follow manufacturer's instructions.
5. To dry using an oven, set oven to 120°F (49°C). Place apple slices on wire cooling racks (cheesecloth is not necessary) in oven. Leave door slightly ajar to allow moisture to escape. Dry for 5 to 7 hours, interchanging racks occasionally.
6. Apples are ready when they are dry to the touch but still slightly moist inside. Store in a cool, dry place.
Yields approximately 6 cups (1.5 l)

Cider Vinegars

GARLIC AND WINE VINEGAR

A basic component of salad dressings, this vinegar can also be used in mayonnaise.

1   cup (250 ml) red wine
2   cups (500 ml) cider vinegar
2   peeled and crushed cloves garlic

1. Combine ingredients in top of double boiler and place over boiling water. Heat for 10 minutes. Remove from heat and cool to room temperature.
2. Strain vinegar through a fine sieve or coffee filter. Pour into clean bottles and seal. Store in refrigerator.
Yields a scant 3 cups (725 ml)

HOT CHILI VINEGAR

A dash of this vinegar will perk up a pot of chili, a stew, or salad.

8   fresh hot red peppers
    Cider vinegar

1. Chop hot peppers (wear rubber gloves for this job) and place in a 1-quart (1-l) mason jar.
2. Fill jar with vinegar. Seal and refrigerate.
3. Shake the jar every day for 2 weeks. Strain vinegar into a clean bottle and seal. Keep in refrigerator.
Yields about 4 cups (1 l)

RED RASPBERRY VINEGAR

This vinegar can serve as a base for a raspberry vinaigrette or a marvelous summer drink. The recipe can be halved.

4 quarts (4 l) ripe red raspberries
4 cups (1 l) cider vinegar
   White sugar

1. Rinse and drain raspberries in a large colander. Place raspberries in a large enamel or non-metallic bowl. Cover with vinegar and crush lightly to submerge berries.
2. Cover and let sit in a cool place for 48 hours. Strain and measure the vinegar into an enamel or stainless steel pan. Add an equal amount of sugar.
3. Bring to a boil, stirring to dissolve sugar. Reduce heat and simmer 10 minutes. Skim and cool.
4. Pour into sterilized jars and seal.
Yields about 2 qt (2 l)

GINGER VINEGAR

Use this vinegar in a curry or marinade.

1 cup (250 ml) cider vinegar
4 1-inch (2.5-cm) pieces dried ginger root
2 tbsp (25 ml) white sugar

1. Place all ingredients in a small jar and seal. Shake to dissolve sugar. Let sit for 1 week or longer and then strain into a clean jar.
Yields a scant cup (225 ml)

HERB VINEGAR

If you grow your own herbs, harvest in the early morning for best color and flavor. Vary the herbs to suit your taste or use a mixture.

4 *sprigs fresh tarragon, thyme, marjoram, or chervil*
4 *cups (1 l) cider vinegar*

1. Rinse herbs and pat dry with paper towels. Place in clean jars.
2. Heat vinegar in a saucepan until very hot but not boiling. Pour into jars. Seal. Age for 2 weeks before using. Remove herbs. Keep in a cool, dark place for up to 1 year.
Yields 1 qt (1 l)

Canning and Freezing Apples

CANNING APPLES

Canning Apple Slices in Syrup or Apple Juice

For each quart jar, you will need approximately 3 apples and 2 cups (500 ml) of syrup or juice.
1. Prepare syrup according to your taste. (We prefer a thin syrup or unsweetened apple juice.) See syrup chart, page 256.
2. Peel, core, and slice apples. To avoid discoloration, place slices in 2 quarts (2 l) of cold water containing 1 tbsp (15 ml) lemon juice or ¼ tsp (1 ml) powdered or crystalline ascorbic acid.
3. Drain apples and fill sterile hot jars. Cover with boiling hot syrup or juice leaving a ½-inch (1-cm) headspace. Remove air bubbles. Wipe jar rim and seal.
4. Process in a boiling water bath: 15 minutes for pints (500 ml), 20 minutes for quarts (liters). Alternative: Process in a pressure canner at 5 lb pressure for 8 minutes (for both sizes).

Canning Applesauce

1. Prepare your favorite applesauce. Reheat it to boiling.
2. Pack in hot sterile jars leaving a ½-inch (1-cm) headspace. Remove air bubbles. Wipe jar rim and seal.
3. Process small and medium jars in a boiling water bath for 25 minutes, or process in a pressure canner at 5 lb pressure for 8

Canning Apple Pie Filling

NOTE: 1 quart (liter) of filling is enough to fill a 9- to 10-inch (22.5 cm to 25-cm) pie.
1. Prepare multiples of your favorite apple pie filling including apples, sugar, lemon juice, and spices. (You may wish to dip apples in water and lemon juice or ascorbic acid before draining and adding other ingredients.)
2. Cook filling on top of the stove over medium heat, stirring often, until sugar is dissolved.

3. Pour hot filling into hot sterile jars. Remove air bubbles. Wipe jar rim and seal.
4. Process in boiling water bath for 25 minutes, or process in a pressure canner at 5 lb pressure for 8 minutes.

When you are ready to bake a pie, roll out 2 pie crusts. Line pie plate with one and sprinkle with 1 tbsp (15 ml) cornstarch. Pour in canned filling. Sprinkle filling with 1 tbsp (15 ml) cornstarch. Top with pastry. Trim and cut steam vents. Bake at 450°F (230°C) for 10 minutes. Reduce heat to 350°F (180°C) and bake 30 to 40 minutes until browned.

Canning Baked Apples

1. Prepare apples according to your favorite recipe. Bake only half the normal time.
2. Pack hot in hot sterile jars. Cover with boiling hot thin sugar syrup. Wipe jar rim and seal.
3. Process in a boiling water bath for 20 minutes (any size jar).

Canning Apple Cider

1. Strain if you prefer. Pour into hot sterile jars, leaving a ¼-inch (½-cm) headspace. Wipe jar rim and seal.
2. Process in a boiling water bath for 30 minutes (any size jar).

Syrup Chart

Use this syrup chart when preparing apples for both canning and freezing in syrup.

Type of Syrup	Sugar	Water	Final Yield
Light	1 cup (250 ml)	2 cups (500 ml)	2½ cups (650 ml)
Medium	1 cup (250 ml)	1 cup (250 ml)	1½ cups (375 ml)
Heavy	1 cup (250 ml)	¾ cup + 2 tbsp (200 ml)	1⅓ cups (325 ml)

To make syrup
Combine sugar and water in a saucepan. Slowly bring to a boil, stirring to dissolve sugar. Cook over medium heat for 5 minutes. Up to ¼ of the sugar may be replaced with honey or light corn syrup. Allow ¾ to 1 cup (175 to 250 ml) of syrup for each 2-cup (500-ml) container. You can add ¼ tsp (1 ml) powdered or crystalline ascorbic acid (vitamin C) or 800 mg in tablet form, dissolved in 1 tbsp (15 ml) water to each quart (liter) of cold syrup.

FREEZING APPLES

Frozen apples are sold at the grocery store or you may wish to freeze the fall crop yourself. Because fresh apples contain large amounts of water, their texture and flavor are altered considerably when frozen. Processed apple products like sauce and juice, however, do not taste very different from the unfrozen products.

Freezing Apple Slices

Select ripe, high-quality fruit. Do not use underripe, overripe, bruised, or partially spoiled apples.
Frozen apple slices may be stored for one year at 0°F (− 18°C).

Dry Pack Method:
Apple slices are frozen with a little sugar.
1. Peel, core, and slice apples.
2. To avoid discoloration, use lemon juice or ascorbic acid.
Lemon juice. For every quart (liter) of apple slices use 2 quarts (2 l) cold water and 1 tbsp (15 ml) lemon juice mixed together. Immediately after slicing, drop apple slices into water and lemon juice for 5 minutes. Drain well. Sprinkle with 4 tbsp (60 ml) white sugar for every quart (liter) of apples.
Ascorbic acid. For every quart (liter) of apple slices, dissolve ¼ tsp (1 ml) powdered or crystalline ascorbic acid (Vitamin C) in 4 tbsp (60 ml) cold water. Sprinkle liquid and 4 tbsp (60 ml) white sugar for every quart (liter) of fruit over apples. Blend well.

3. Pack into freezer bags and seal.

To thaw. To use dry pack slices in a recipe, thaw them only enough to break them into separate pieces. Proceed as with fresh fruit.

Steam-Blanch Method:

Apple slices are blanched with steam or boiling water and dry packed with or without sugar. Blanch small quantities to ensure every piece is properly processed.

1. Peel, core, and slice apples.

2. Bring water to a boil in a large pot with a steamer rack. Place apple pieces on rack over boiling water for 1½ minutes. (*Alternative:* Bring water to a boil in a large pot. Plunge apple pieces into boiling water for 1 minute.)

3. Drain, cool, and place in single layers on cookie sheets. Freeze solid.

4. Remove apple slices. If desired, sprinkle with 4 tbsp (60 ml) white sugar for every quart (liter) of apple slices.

5. Pack in freezer bags, remove air, and seal.

Syrup Method:

Apple slices are placed in rigid containers, covered with syrup, and frozen.

1. Peel, core, and slice apples.

2. Make a light, medium, or heavy syrup to suit your sweet tooth and the tartness of the apples.

3. Place sliced apples directly in freezer containers or, to avoid discoloration, you may wish to dip them in lemon juice and water and drain them first.

4. Cover with syrup, leaving ½ inch (1 cm) headspace for expansion.

To thaw. For 2 cups (500 ml) apples frozen in syrup, allow 6 to 8 hours in the refrigerator, or 3 hours at room temperature, or 1 hour if container is placed in a pan under cold running water, or approximately 15 minutes on "Defrost" in a microwave.

Freezing Applesauce

1. Fill plastic bags with cold (sweetened or unsweetened) applesauce.

2. Remove air, and seal. If using rigid containers, leave ½ inch (1 cm) headspace for expansion.

Freezing Apple Pie Fillings

1. Prepare your favorite apple pie fillings including apples, sugar, spices, with an extra teaspoon (5 ml) of cornstarch. Mound in metal or aluminum pie plates lined with plastic wrap.
2. Place in plastic bags, seal, and freeze. After they have frozen solid, slip them out of the plates, rewrap, and put them back in the freezer.
3. When you want to make a pie, roll out a double pie crust, and place frozen apple filling in bottom crust. Cover with top crust. Bake at 400°F (200°C) for about an hour or until crust is nicely browned and filling is bubbly and fork tender.

Freezing Whole Unbaked Apple Pies

Disposable aluminum pie plates are handy when you want to put down a number of pies in the freezer.
1. Roll out and fill your favorite apple pies with an extra teaspoon (5 ml) of cornstarch in the filling. Do not cut steam vents in top crust.
2. Carefully place pie(s) in freezer and freeze solid.
3. Remove from freezer and seal pies, removing air in plastic bags. (Place extra aluminum pie plates over top crust and you can save space by stacking a number of pies.)
4. To bake: Cut steam vents in top crust and place frozen pie in a 400°F (200°C) oven for 1 to 1½ hours, until crust is nicely browned and filling is bubbly and fork tender.

Freezing Apple Cider or Juice

Pour into rigid containers. Leave 1 inch (2.5 cm) headspace for expansion. Cider retains its almost fresh taste for 7 to 8 months.

CHAPTER EIGHT

Fun with Apples

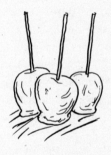

Candy

MARZIPAN APPLES

Marzipan is the modeling clay of the confectionery world. These
apples are easy and fun to make.

1 cup (250 ml) almond paste
2 small egg whites
3 cups (750 ml) unsifted icing sugar
¼ tsp (1 ml) almond flavoring

Red and green food coloring
Vodka or white rum
1 2-inch (5-cm) cinnamon stick
Small clean paint brush

1. Place almond paste in a medium bowl. Add egg whites and knead
until thoroughly mixed. Add icing sugar a little at a time until marzipan reaches a firm consistency. Knead in almond flavoring. Wrap
in plastic and chill overnight. Mixture will keep for a long time.
2. To make apples and leaves, divide marzipan into small balls and
mold into apple and leaf shapes. Place on waxed paper and chill
until firm.
3. Dilute food coloring with vodka or white rum until desired shade
of color is obtained. When painting apples and leaves, don't load
brush with too much paint. Blot brush on paper towel. Let apples
dry. Cover and keep in refrigerator until serving time. Before serving, break apart cinnamon stick into slivers to use for stems.
Yields 1 lb (500 g) marzipan (number of apples varies according to size)

RED CANDY APPLES

Duplicate those fairground candies at home. It is best to make these
on a cool, dry day.

4 to 5 apples
2 cups (500 ml) white sugar
⅔ cup (150 ml) light corn syrup
1 cup (250 ml) water
1 3-inch (7.5 cm) cinnamon stick

Red vegetable food coloring
Wooden skewers
½ cup (125 ml) finely chopped
walnuts, pecans, or peanuts
(optional)

1. Wash apples and dry with a soft cloth.

2. Mix sugar, corn syrup, water, and cinnamon stick in top of double boiler. Bring to a boil and cook, covered, for 3 to 4 minutes. Uncover and cook, without stirring, nearly to the hard crack stage (290°F or 130°C). Remove cinnamon stick. Add red food coloring until mixture is as red as you desire. Keep candy hot over boiling water.

3. Insert skewers into stem end of apples. Quickly dip apples into candy, then into chopped nuts. Place stick side up on a buttered piece of foil to cool and harden.

Serves 4 to 5

AMBER ALMOND CANDY

These tasty apple candies have a lemon tang and crunch of almonds. Serve them the same day you make them. Do not refrigerate.

1 cup (250 ml) white sugar
¼ cup (50 ml) water
1 cup (250 ml) finely chopped peeled apples

1 cup (250 ml) finely chopped blanched almonds
Juice and grated rind of 1 lemon
1 cup (250 ml) icing sugar or ground almonds

1. Combine sugar and water in a medium saucepan. Stir over medium heat until sugar has dissolved. Increase heat to medium-high and cook without stirring until syrup reaches soft-ball stage (240°F or 116°C).

2. Reduce heat to very low and add apples. Cook uncovered for 10 minutes, stirring occasionally.

3. Stir in chopped almonds, lemon juice, and grated lemon rind. Cook for another 15 minutes or until mixture is golden and thick.

4. Spoon mixture onto a platter coated with ½ cup (125 ml) icing sugar or ground almonds. Let cool until lukewarm.

5. Form into small balls and roll lightly in remaining icing sugar or ground almonds. Place in fluted paper candy cups if you have them.

Yields 2 dozen candies

MICROWAVE CARAMEL APPLES

Great birthday party treats!

4 *apples*	1 *tbsp (15 ml) water*
30 *soft caramel candies*	*Wooden skewers*

1. Wash apples and dry with a soft cloth.
2. Unwrap caramels and place in a small bowl, just large enough to dip apples. Add water. Cover with waxed paper and cook at maximum power for 2 to 3 minutes, or until mixture is smooth when stirred. Remove from oven.
3. Insert skewers into stem ends of apples. Dip apples, one at a time, into caramel coating. Place apples on buttered wax paper, stick side up, until cool.
Serves 4

BACKPACK SNACK

Package in small plastic bags, and they're all set for lunch boxes.

2 *cups (500 ml) dried apples*	1 *cup (250 ml) sunflower or*
2 *cups (500 ml) raisins*	*pumpkin seeds*
1 *cup (250 ml) salted peanuts*	1 *cup (250 ml) large-flake coconut*

1. Mix all ingredients in a large bowl. Package and seal in small bags.
Yields 7 cups (1.75 l)

ROASTED APPLES

This is a leisurely way to enjoy apples around a campfire or an open hearth.

4 apples	½ tsp (2 ml) cinnamon
1 cup (250 ml) white sugar	¼ tsp (1 ml) nutmeg

1. Have each person place an apple on the sharpened end of a green stick.
2. Place close to a bed of coals until the skin of the apple is scorched.
3. Peel skin off the apple. It will be easy to remove.
4. Mix sugar, cinnamon, and nutmeg in a shallow dish or aluminum pie plate. Roll apple in sugar mixture.
5. Hold apple near coals, rotating slowly until melting sugar forms a glaze. Slice and eat the glazed portions. Repeat glazing until you reach core.
Serves 4

DRIED APPLE-COCONUT CANDY

Serve these not-too-sweet little goodies in paper candy cups. The kids can help make them because there's no cooking required.

1½ cups (375 ml) dried apples	¾ cup (175 ml) sweetened condensed
2½ cups (625 ml) flaked	milk
coconut	1 cup (250 ml) finely chopped nuts
	(any kind)

1. Pick over dried apples and remove any pieces of peel or core. Process apples and coconut in a blender or food processor until very finely chopped.
2. Mix apples, coconut, and condensed milk in a bowl. Shape into small firm balls. Roll in finely chopped nuts.
3. Let stand at room temperature for 2 hours.
Yields 3 dozen candies

DRIED APPLE-MAPLE CANDY

A toffee-apple confection that is crisp the first day and soft the next.
Crumble over yogurt for a quick dessert.

½ cup (125 ml) butter
1 cup (250 ml) brown sugar
½ cup (125 ml) maple syrup

⅔ cup (150 ml) chopped dried apples
1 tsp (5 ml) vanilla
1 tsp (5 ml) baking soda
2 cups (500 ml) rolled oats

1. Place butter, brown sugar, maple syrup, and apples in a medium
saucepan. Bring to a boil and cook for 3 minutes, stirring frequently.
2. Remove from heat and stir in vanilla, baking soda, and rolled
oats.
3. Pour into a buttered 9 × 9-inch (2.5-l) baking pan. Bake at 325°F
(160°C) for 8 to 10 minutes or until puffed and golden brown. Cut
when cool.
Yields 18 squares

DRIED APPLE CANDY

These chewy nuggets of dried fruit and almonds make a fine addition to a Christmas cookie platter.

2 cups (500 ml) dried apples
1 cup (250 ml) raisins

1 cup (250 ml) blanched almonds
1 tbsp (15 ml) liquid honey
⅓ cup (75 ml) icing sugar

1. Pick over apples and remove any pieces of core or peel. Put apples,
raisins, and almonds through a food mill using a coarse disk or process
in a blender until mixture resembles coarse meal. Place in a medium
bowl.
2. Add the honey and knead until thoroughly mixed. Shape into
small balls and roll in the icing sugar. Store in an airtight container.
Yields 2 dozen candies

Crafts

APPLE CANDLE HOLDERS

These candle holders will brighten your table almost any month of the year. Place them on your Thanksgiving table, surrounded by sprays of colored autumn leaves or flowers.
For this project you will need:

> *Large perfect apples*
> 4- to 8-inch (10 to 20 cm) candles, one for each apple. Green candles
> are especially pretty.

Make certain apples are stable when placed on a flat surface. Measure diameter of candles and cut core of apple to fit. Fit candle in hole and place apple on a flat surface to test stability before lighting.

APPLE FEATHER GARNISHES

Make these to garnish cheese trays and desserts.

> 1   *apple*
> *Lemon juice or ascorbic acid powder (Fruit Fresh)*

1. Wash apple and polish with a soft cloth. Cut apple in half. Using a long, straight, sharp knife, make four cuts on one side, ¼-inch (½ cm) apart, and at a 45 degree angle to the center line of the apple half. Repeat on the opposite side, so that the first cut on the right side meets first cut on left side.
2. You will have four layered v-shaped or chevron-shaped pieces. Gently push pieces forward to form a feather shape.
3. Brush with lemon juice or dip in ascorbic acid solution.
4. Smaller garnishes can be made by cutting apple into quarters before "feathering."

APPLE FEATHER GARNISHES

Apple Quarter
Back View

Apple Quarter
Front View opened into feather

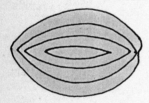

Apple Quarter – cut but not
opened
front view

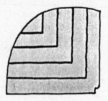

Apple Quarter – cut but not
opened
side view

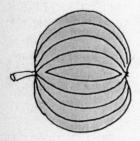

Apple Half
cut but not opened

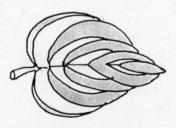

Apple Half
opened into feather

FORCING APPLE BLOSSOMS

There is nothing quite like fresh flowers to banish the winter blues. On a sunny day in late winter or early spring, select a branch being careful to pick one with "fat" buds not vegetative buds. Vegetative buds will only yield green leaves and not blossoms. Cut a 2- to 3-foot (¾- to 1-meter) branch. Hammer the bottom 3 inches (7.5 cm) until the wood and bark are split. Place branch in a vase of lukewarm water in a sunny spot. In about three weeks there will be light green leaves and pale pink blossoms. Change water once a week.

APPLE POMANDERS

These old-fashioned pomanders make welcome gifts. They impart a spicy scent to clothing and linen closets.

Select four small, firm apples. For each apple you will need about ¼ cup (50 ml) whole cloves.

Pierce the skin of each apple with the cloves, studding the entire surface except for a small space at the top and bottom, through which you will thread a ribbon. The cloves should not touch each other. The apple will shrink as it dries.

Mix any or all of the following ground spices in a small bowl, to make 1 tbsp (15 ml): cinnamon, nutmeg, allspice, mace, ground cloves. Dust each pomander with the spice mixture.

With a long darning needle, thread a piece of string through each pomander from top to bottom (through the spaces where you did not put any cloves), and tie a knot. Hang the pomanders in a cool, dry place for 3 weeks. After they have dried completely, tie a 12-inch (30-cm) length of narrow ribbon to the end of the string. Pull the ribbon through each apple. Remove the string and knot the ribbon at bottom of pomander. Instead of threading pomanders with ribbon, they can be individually enclosed in squares of lightweight printed fabric and tied with narrow ribbon.

APPLE IN A BOTTLE

1 large, narrow-mouthed bottle, such as a large plastic pop bottle
   Weatherproof tape

In the spring, select a thin, blossoming branch of an apple tree that
has blossoms at or near the end so that the bottle will fit over the
blossoms. Wait a few days so that you can be certain the blossoms
have been pollinated. The petals will drop off and a tiny apple will
begin to form. Insert branch tip carefully into bottle and secure
with tape. Now be patient and wait until the apple is fully formed
and colored before undoing tape. Either pull the branch out, leaving
the apple behind, or cut the branch off flush with bottle, leaving it
inside the bottle.

APPLE DOLLS

These instructions were kindly given to us by Mrs. Alice White of
Liverpool, Nova Scotia.
You will need the following supplies to make an apple doll:

Several large very firm apples (Mrs. White uses Granny Smith)
Lemon juice to prevent excessive darkening
Needle and thread to sew on hair and back of head
Heavy gauge (as thick as lead in a pencil) copper wire to use as basis for
body, arms, and legs
Clean pantyhose or nylon stockings to wrap around wire to form body
Small quantity of quilt batting or cotton balls for stuffing head and hair
Large scraps of small print and plain material for clothing
Scraps of narrow ribbon and lace
Scraps of black suede or felt for boots
White and black oil or acrylic paint or beads for eyes
Lipstick
Fine brush

1. First peel several apples. That way you can pick the best face for
your doll. Dip into lemon juice.

2. Using a small sharp knife cut out a ¼-inch (5 mm) deep by ⅛-inch (2 mm) wide slit for each eye. For the mouth cut a ¼-inch (5 mm) deep by ⅛-inch (2 mm) wide, half-moon shape. For the nose cut a ¼-inch (5 mm) deep by ⅛-inch (2 mm) wide trench in a slightly triangular shape. Dip apple in lemon juice several times.

3. Pass a needle and knotted thread through center of apple and leave enough thread to hang apple to dry. Heat oven to lowest temperature and hang apple from rack in oven to dry for a few hours. Remove from oven and hang in a dry warm place to finish drying process. Do not place apple directly on a surface or it will rot before it dries.

4. As apple dries and becomes soft and leathery, pinch nose and other features into desired shape. After apple has dried (this will take several days to a week or more), split back of "head" with a sharp knife and carefully remove core. You will be left with a shell.

5. Stuff shell with a firm ball of quilt batting or cotton. Carefully sew the back of head, being careful not to pull thread too tight or apple will rip. There will still be a hole in the top, but both the seam and hole will be covered with "hair." Paint eyes or glue beads in place and apply a bit of lipstick to give a bit of blush to cheeks and lips, if you wish.

6. Cut the wire for body several inches longer than double the desired height of the doll. Carefully work the wire up through the stuffing in the head, fold it in half, and work the wire back down through head.

7. Cut another piece of wire to form the hands and arms. Wrap this piece around body wire and twist tightly to secure. Twist wire to form a tiny thumb and hand, and twist to form a bit of foot. The doll at this point will look somewhat like this.

8. Cut pantyhose or nylons into strips and wrap around body, arms and legs. Crisscross strips in front to form bodice and shoulders. Using patterns below, cut out clothes for the doll. Sew seams and hem pantaloons. Stitch a bit of lace over hem. Put pantaloons on doll and gather around waist. Stitch pantaloons to body.

9. Cut dress on fold. Hem neck, sleeves, bottom, and back edge. Stitch ribbon or lace around neck and sleeves. Dress doll and stitch back of dress to body to secure. Tie a ribbon around waist and spread gathers evenly.

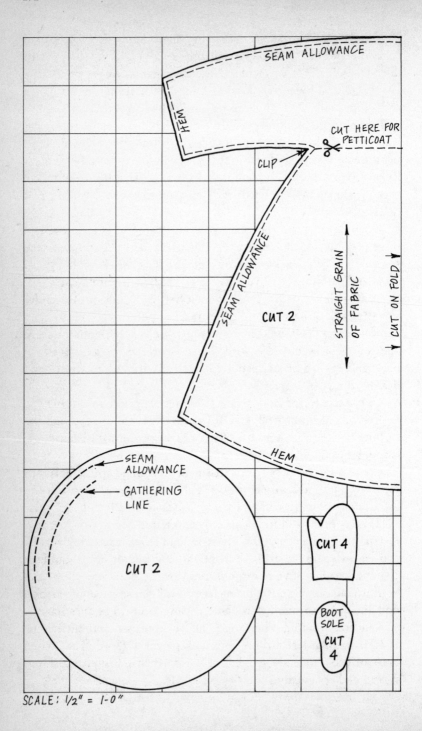

SEAM ALLOWANCE

HEM

CUT HERE FOR
PETTICOAT

CLIP

SEAM ALLOWANCE

CUT 2

STRAIGHT GRAIN
OF FABRIC

CUT ON FOLD

HEM

SEAM
ALLOWANCE

GATHERING
LINE

CUT 2

CUT 4

BOOT
SOLE
CUT
4

SCALE: 1/2" = 1-0"

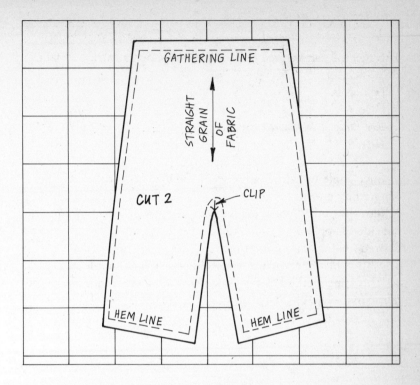

10. Cut out sole of boot. Cut a strip of suede or felt about ¾ inch (15 mm) wide, the length of the perimeter of boot. Stitch top of boot to sole and sew up the back of boot. Stuff toe of boot with a little quilt batting or cotton. Fit boot on doll and gather around ankle and stitch to leg.

11. To make the bonnet, sew the two pieces together wrong side out, leaving a small space to turn right side out. Stitch the opening closed. Run a gathering stitch ½ inch (10 mm) from edge all around bonnet. Leave thread and needle attached to allow for adjustment once the hair has been sewn in place.

12. Pull quilt batting or cotton apart to fluff. Arrange on top, back, and sides of head. Stitch in place, being careful not to pull too tightly. Place bonnet on head and pull gathering stitch to fit. Stitch in place to secure.

13. Now you can bend the doll to sit in a doll's chair and add finishing touches such as knitting needles, spectacles, books, garden tools—let your imagination be your guide.

APPLE PRINTS

This method can be used to decorate notepaper, giftwrap, or fabric.

1 *firm apple*
   Paper towels
   Red ink pad or tempera paint
   Paper

1. Slice apple in half lengthwise. Remove seeds if they have been exposed by cutting.
2. Blot the cut side of apple with a paper towel. Firmly stamp the cut side of apple onto the ink pad and press onto paper. Repeat as desired, inking apple each time.
3. With a black ink pen, draw seeds and stem on apple print.
4. This same method can be used to print on fabric, using a special fabric dye available at art stores.

Appendices

APPENDIX 1

Measuring Apples

NOTE: The larger the apple, the less the waste.

Applesauce

Servings: Allow 2 apples per person.

To make	You will need
⅓ cup (75 ml)	1 small apple
½ cup (125 ml)	1 medium apple
¾ cup (175 ml)	1 large apple
1 cup (250 ml)	2 medium apples
1½ cups (375 ml)	1 lb (500 g) apples
500 g = 350 ml	3 medium apples
1 quart	2½ to 3½ lb apples
16 to 20 quarts (American)	1 bushel apples

Apple Pie

One 9-inch (22-cm) pie can be made from:
8 to 9 small apples
6 to 8 medium apples
4 to 5 large apples
2 to 2.5 lb (1 kg) apples

Dried Apples

3½ to 4 lb (1½ to 2 kg) raw apples will make 1 lb (450 g) dried apples
1 lb (450 g) reconstituted (plumped in water or juice) = 2⅔ cups (650 ml)
1 lb (450 g) cooked and puréed = 2⅓ cups (575 ml)

Apple Cider and Juice

1 bushel apples will make 3 gallons (10 to 12 qts or liters) of cider or juice.

Finely Chopped, Diced Apples

If the recipe calls for	You will need
½ cup (125 ml)	1 small apple or (½ medium)
¾ cup (175 ml)	1 medium apple
1 cup (250 ml)	1 medium apple or (2 small or ½ large)
1½ cups (375 ml)	1 large apple or (1 medium + 1 small) or (3 small)

Coarsely Chopped, Cubed, Sliced, Apples

If the recipe calls for	You will need
½ cup (125 ml)	1 small apple or (½ medium)
¾ cup (175 ml)	1 medium
1 cup (250 ml)	1 medium apple or (2 small) or (½ large)
2 cups (500 ml)	1 large or (2 medium) or (4 small)
4.5 l basket (2300 g) = 2.9 l chopped apples	

Grated Raw Apples with Juice

If the recipe calls for	You will need
½ cup (125 ml)	1 small apple or (½ large)
¾ cup (175 ml)	1 medium apple
1 cup (250 ml)	1 large apple or (2 small)

Canned Apple Pieces

Amount of raw, whole apples	Will fill
3 medium apples	1 quart (liter) jar
1 lb (450 g)	1 quart (liter) jar
1 bushel (42 to 48 lb) (19 to 22 kg)	approximately 28 quart (liter) jars

(The bushel is a volume measurement, so the weight varies according to the size and density of the apples)

Apple Weights

5 oz (150 g)	= 1 medium apple
1 lb (450 g)	= 4 small or 3 medium or 2 large apples
	= 3 to 4 cups (750 ml to 1 l) pared, diced or sliced apples
2.2 lb (1 kg)	= 6 large apples
3 lb (1.4 kg)	= 12 small or 9 medium or 6 large apples
5 lb (2.3 kg)	= 20 small or 15 medium or 10 large apples
	= 4 quart (liter) basket
7 lb (3.2 kg)	= 28 small or 21 medium or 14 large apples
	= 6 quart (liter) basket
1 bushel apples	= 42 to 48 lb (19 to 22 kg)

APPENDIX 2

Grading Apples

Standards are set by provincial, state, and federal governments and the apple industry (producers and packers) to regulate the quality of fruit sold. Federal grades are necessary for interprovincial and interstate trade and export. Although they are helpful from a consumer's point of view, don't forget that apples labelled "Extra Fancy" when packaged may have deteriorated considerably by the time you buy them. Also, apples which do not make a high grade because they are wobbly-shaped, or greenish may be far superior in flavor and texture to perfectly formed, solid red apples. Different grades of apples comply with these standards to varying degrees. Top grade apples must be:

- *Mature*, having reached a point of development at which completion of the ripening process is ensured;
- *Handpicked*, showing no evidence of rough handling or having been on the ground;
- *Clean*, having an appearance free of dirt, dust, spray residue or other foreign material;
- *Smooth*, with an absence of russeting beyond the stem cavity, where it is uncharacteristic of the variety;
- *Well formed*, that is, at least half the apple is the shape characteristic of the variety, and the other half deviates only slightly;
- *Sound*, meaning free from insects and insect injury, and free from damage including bruises, hail injury (broken skin, discoloration), soft spots, drought spots, sprayburn, sunscald, storage scald, freezing;
- *Colored*, having a percentage of redness which varies according to the variety. For example, an Extra Fancy Winesap is expected to be 66 percent (U.S.) or 65 percent (Canada) red, whereas an Extra Fancy McIntosh may be 50 percent (U.S.) or 55 percent (Canada) red. A lower grade of Winesap is expected to be only

25 percent (U.S.) or 15 percent (Canada) red. Different expect-
ations are set for red-cheeked and blushed varieties (Cox's Orange
Pippin, Melba) and the yellow, green, and russet varieties;
- *Sized*, with minimum 2¼ inch (5.7 cm) and maximum 3 inch (7.6
  cm and up) diameters (the greatest distance at right angles to the
  longitudinal axis of the apple), and sold in a package in which the
  diameters of the apples do not vary from each other more than
  ¼ to 5/16 inch (6.3 mm), depending on the size of the package;
- *Properly packaged*, that is, not packed slackly, overpressed, or
  in any condition that is likely to result in damage from handling
  transit; and
- *Sold as one variety*.

Canadian apple grades are: Canada Extra Fancy, Canada Fancy,
Canada Commercial (Canada "C" or Canada Cee), Canada Com-
mercial Cookers, Canada Hailed, Canada No. 1 (Peelers), and Canada
No. 2 (Peelers).

U.S. grades are: U.S. Extra Fancy, U.S. Fancy, U.S. No. 1, Utility.
Combination or Mixed Grades are also sold. Local apples may be
graded and marketed as Grade A, Grade B, and Grade C.

Grading Apple Juice

Apple juice by legal definition is prepared:
- from the unfermented liquid obtained from the first pressing of
  properly prepared, sound, clean, mature, fresh apples;
- without concentration or dilution;
- without the addition of sweetening ingredients;
- with or without the addition of anti-oxidants to prevent discoloration;
- with or without the addition of natural apple esters;
- with or without ascorbic acid to increase the vitamin C content,
  but if added, must contain a certain amount (not less than 35 mg
  ascorbic acid per 100 ml of juice) and be labelled "vitamin C
  added"; and
- in 3 styles: 1) Clear or clarified;
  - 2) Unclarified, cloudy, or opalescent—not or par-
       tially clarified but not containing visible particles
       of apple pulp;
  - 3) Crushed: containing suspended visible particles
       of apple pulp.

Apple juice is graded according to:

- *Flavor*: Possessing a fine, distinct flavor with a fruity odor of well-ripened apples without any trace of objectionable flavors from scorching, green fruit, excessive oxidation, or over-processing;
- *Color*;
- *Percentage of soluble solids*;
- *Percentage of malic acid*; and
- *Freedom from defects* such as sediment and residues.

Canadian grades for apple juice are Canada Fancy and Canada Choice.

U.S. grades for apple juice are U.S. Grade A, U.S. Grade B, and Substandard.

Grading Canned Applesauce

Applesauce is graded according to:

- *Color* (uniform bright color);
- *Aroma*;
- *Consistency*: granular (even particles in which liquid does not separate from solids), or chunky; and
- *Freedom from defects* such as seed specks, pieces of skin and core, bruised portions.

Canadian grades for applesauce are Canada Fancy and Canada Choice.

U.S. grades for applesauce are U.S. Grade A, U.S. Grade B, and Substandard.

APPENDIX 3
Apple Nutrition

	Apple (raw, 6 per kg, 6 cm diameter)	Apple Juice (canned, vitaminized)	Applesauce (canned, sweetened)
Measure	1	250 ml/1 cup	250 ml/1 cup
Weight (g)	150	262	269
Moisture (% water)	85	88	76
Food Energy (kcal) (calories)	70	130	240
Protein (g)	tr.	tr.	1
Carbohydrates (g)	18	32	64
Fat (g)	tr.	tr.	tr.
Cholesterol (mg)	0	0	0
Calcium (mg)	8	16	11
Iron (mg)	0.4	1.6	1.3
Sodium (mg)	2	3	5
Potassium (mg)	165	265	175
Vitamin A (RE)	5	—	11
Thiamin (mg) (vitamin B_1)	0.04	0.02	0.05
Riboflavin (mg) (vitamin B_2)	0.02	0.04	0.03
Niacin (NE)	0.2	0.3	0.2
Folate (mcg)	9	1	9
Vitamin C (mg)	3	93	3
Dietary Fiber (g)	2.2	N/A	—

g = gram   mg = milligram   mcg = microgram   tr = trace

RE = Retinol Equivalent   NE = Niacin Equivalent

Adapted From: *Nutrient Value of Some Common Foods*, Health and Welfare Canada and *Composition of Foods*, Agriculture Handbook No. 8-9, United States Department of Agriculture Human Nutrition Information Service

Applesauce (canned, unsweetened)	Two-crust Apple pie (1/6 of pie)	Crabapples	Oranges
250 ml/1 cup	1/6-23 cm pie	3½ oz	1-6½" DA
257	160	100G	180
88	48	81.1	86
110	410	68	165
1	3	0.4	1
27	61	17.8	16
tr.	18	tr.	tr.
0	0	0	0
11	1	6	54
1.2	0.5	0.3	0.5
5	482	1	2
200	128	110	360
11	5	2	26
0.05	0.03	0.03	0.13
0.02	0.03	0.02	0.05
0.2	1.4	0.1	0.9
9	10	—	43
2	2	8	66
—	—	—	3.6

Leading Commercial Varieties

CANADIAN APPLE PRODUCTION (%)

McIntosh	34
Red and Golden Delicious	33
Northern Spy	9
Spartan	7
Cortland	2
Gravenstein	1
Idared	.8
Newton Pippin	.7
Melba	.7
Lobo	.7
Winesap	.6
Rome	.2
Mixed Varieties	10

U.S. APPLE PRODUCTION (%)

Red Delicious	37
Golden Delicious	17
McIntosh	9
Rome	7
Jonathan	5
York	4
Stayman	3
Cortland	2
Rhode Island Greening	2
Newtown Pippin	2
Winesap	2
Idared	2
Northern Spy	2
Granny Smith	2
Gravenstein	1
Mixed Varieties	6

NOTE: These percentages have been rounded off, therefore the sum adds up to less than 100 percent.

LEADING APPLE VARIETIES BY PROVINCE

Listed in order of volume produced.

Nova Scotia: McIntosh, Red and Golden Delicious, Cortland, Northern Spy, Gravenstein, Idared, King, Mixed Varieties (28 percent)
New Brunswick: McIntosh, Cortland, Mixed Varieties (19 percent)
Quebec: McIntosh, Melba, Lobo, Cortland, Red and Golden Delicious, Mixed Varieties (10 percent)
Ontario: McIntosh, Spy, Red and Golden Delicious, Idared, Rhode Island Greening, Wealthy, Mixed Varieties (17 percent)
British Columbia: Red and Golden Delicious, McIntosh, Spartan, Newton Pippin, Winesap, Rome Beauty, Tydeman, Mixed Varieties (0.3 percent)

NOTE: Mixed Varieties includes popular local varieties.

LEADING STORED WINTER VARIETIES GROWN IN THE UNITED STATES

These are listed in order of amount grown by each state. Mixed varieties include popular local varieties.

Northeast

Maine: McIntosh, Red Delicious, Cortland, Golden Delicious, Mixed Varieties, Northern Spy, Empire.
New Hampshire: McIntosh, Red Delicious, Cortland, Mixed Varieties, Golden Delicious.
Vermont: McIntosh, Red Delicious, Golden Delicious, Cortland, Empire, Northern Spy, Mixed Varieties, Idared, Rome.
Massachusetts: McIntosh, Red Delicious, Cortland, Mixed Varieties, Golden Delicious, Northern Spy, Rome.
Rhode Island: Red Delicious, McIntosh, Mixed Varieties, Cortland, Golden Delicious, Empire, Winesap, Rome.
Connecticut: Red Delicious, McIntosh, Cortland, Idared, Mixed Varieties, Golden Delicious, Empire, Rome, Stayman, Northern Spy, Jonathan, Winesap, Granny Smith.

Eastern New York: McIntosh, Red Delicious, Rome, Golden Delicious, Cortland, Empire, Mixed Varieties, Idared, Stayman, Northern Spy, Jonathan, Winesap, Granny Smith.

Western New York: Mixed Varieties, Rome, Idared, McIntosh, Red Delicious, Golden Delicious, Northern Spy, Cortland, Empire, Jonathan, York, Winesap, Stayman.

New Jersey: Red Delicious, Rome, Stayman, Golden Delicious, Winesap, Jonathan, McIntosh, Mixed Varieties, Idared, York, Empire, Cortland, Northern Spy, Granny Smith.

Delaware: Red Delicious, Rome, Winesap, Golden Delicious, Stayman, McIntosh, Jonathan, Empire.

Maryland: Red Delicious, Golden Delicious, Rome, York, Stayman, Jonathan, Winesap, Mixed Varieties, Idared, McIntosh.

Pennsylvania: York, Golden Delicious, Red Delicious, Rome, Stayman, Mixed Varieties, Jonathan, Idared, Winesap, McIntosh, Granny Smith, Empire, Cortland, Northern Spy.

South

West Virginia: York, Red Delicious, Golden Delicious, Rome, Stayman, Idared, Mixed Varieties, Winesap, Jonathan, McIntosh, Empire, Granny Smith.

Virginia: York, Golden Delicious, Red Delicious, Rome, Mixed Varieties, Stayman, Winesap, Idared, Jonathan, McIntosh, Empire, Granny Smith.

North Carolina: Rome, Golden Delicious, Red Delicious, Stayman, Mixed Varieties, Jonathan, Idared, Cortland, McIntosh, Granny Smith, Winesap.

South Carolina: Red Delicious, Rome, Winesap, Golden Delicious.

Kentucky: Red Delicious, Golden Delicious, Winesap, Jonathan.

Midwest

Ohio: Red Delicious, Rome, Golden Delicious, Mixed Varieties, Jonathan, Stayman, Winesap, Idared, McIntosh, Cortland, Empire, York, Northern Spy, Granny Smith.

Michigan: Red Delicious, Jonathan, Rome, Golden Delicious, Idared, Northern Spy, McIntosh, Mixed Varieties, Winesap, Empire, Cortland.

Wisconsin: McIntosh, Red Delicious, Cortland, Mixed Varieties, Golden Delicious, Jonathan, Rome, Empire, Winesap, Northern Spy.
Indiana: Rome, Red Delicious, Golden Delicious, Jonathan, Winesap, Idared, Stayman, Mixed Varieties, Empire, Cortland, McIntosh, Granny Smith, York.
Illinois: Jonathan, Red Delicious, Golden Delicious, Rome, Mixed Varieties, Winesap, Idared, Stayman, Cortland, McIntosh.
Missouri: Red Delicious, Jonathan, Golden Delicious, Rome, Winesap, Mixed Varieties, Granny Smith.
Minnesota: Mixed Varieties, Red Delicious, McIntosh, Jonathan, Golden Delicious, Cortland.
Kansas: Jonathan, Red Delicious, Mixed Varieties, Winesap, Golden Delicious, York, Rome.
Iowa: Red Delicious, Stayman, Jonathan, Golden Delicious, Winesap, Mixed Varieties.
Oklahoma: Jonathan, Red Delicious, Golden Delicious, Winesap, Rome, Mixed Varieties.
Nebraska: Red Delicious, Winesap, Golden Delicious, Stayman, Mixed Varieties, Jonathan.
Arkansas: Jonathan, Golden Delicious, Red Delicious, Winesap, Rome, Empire, Mixed Varieties, York.

West

Idaho: Red Delicious, Rome, Golden Delicious, Jonathan, Granny Smith, Mixed Varieties.
Colorado: Red Delicious, Golden Delicious, Rome, Jonathan, Winesap.
New Mexico: Red Delicious, Golden Delicious, Rome, McIntosh, Jonathan, Winesap, Mixed Varieties.
Utah: Red Delicious, Golden Delicious, Rome, Jonathan, Granny Smith, McIntosh, Mixed Varieties.
California: Newtown Pippin, Granny Smith, Red Delicious, Rome, Golden Delicious, Mixed Varieties, McIntosh, Jonathan, Winesap.
Oregon: Red Delicious, Newtown Pippin, Golden Delicious, Rome, Mixed Varieties, Granny Smith, Jonathan.
Washington: Red Delicious, Golden Delicious, Granny Smith, Winesap, Rome, Newtown Pippin, Mixed Varieties.

APPENDIX 5

Some Excellent Books About Apples

Beach, S.A., N.O. Booth, and O.M. Taylor. *The Apples of New York; Report of the New York Agricultural Experiment Station for the Year 1903.* Albany: J.B. Lyon Company, 1905.

Bultitude, John. *Apples: A Guide to the Identification of International Varieties.* London and Basingstoke: The Macmillan Press Ltd. (Macmillan Reference Books), 1983.

Carlson, R.F., and others. *North American Apples: Varieties, Rootstocks, Outlook.* East Lansing: Michigan State University Press, 1970.

Lape, Fred. *Apples and Man.* New York: Van Nostrand Reinhold Company, 1979.

Martin, Alice A. *All About Apples.* Boston: Houghton Mifflin Company, 1976.

Proulx, Annie, and Lew Nichols. *Sweet and Hard Cider: Making It, Using It, and Enjoying It.* Pownal, Vermont: Garden Way, Inc., 1980.

Taylor, H.V. *The Apples of England.* London: Crosby Lockwood and Son Ltd., 1936.

General Index

Recipe Index